BUZZARDS & BANANAS

Fragments from my Journals Across South America
- Peru, the Amazon, Chile and Bolivia 1977-78

GEORGE L. AYERS

918
AYE

◆ FriesenPress

Suite 300 - 990 Fort St
Victoria, BC, Canada, V8V 3K2
www.friesenpress.com

ISBN
978-1-4602-7911-3 (Hardcover)
978-1-4602-7912-0 (Paperback)
978-1-4602-7913-7 (eBook)

1. Travel, South America

Distributed to the trade by The Ingram Book Company

CONTENTS

Time it was

And what a time it was

It was

A time of innocence

A time of confidences

Long ago, it must be

I have a photograph

Preserve your memories

They're all that's left you.

—Paul Simon, "Bookends"

"A vivid well written journey into places and culture most of us only dream of experiencing. Buzzards and Bananas is an incredibly enjoyable and engrossing read".

—*Frances Pruin (Alliston Ontario)*
—*book critic and owner of The Next Chapter bookstore.*

"For both seasoned world wanderers and armchair explorers alike, Buzzards and Bananas offers a fascinating traveler´s tale. Ayers, punctuates the story with lively detail".

—*Deirdre Cleary (Querétaro México)*
—*professor at Tecnológico de Monterrey teaching International Communication and Advanced Writing.*

"Buzzards and Bananas is a witty and engaging narrative, interwoven with informative historical and political anecdotes. Ayers' personable writing style issues an invitation to a daring time and a frankly personal journey."

—*Karen Reczuch (Acton Ontario) - illustrator and writer, co-winner of the TD Norma Fleck award for non-fiction.*

"Riveting—a pure pleasure to read. Ayers' hard-edged description of the economic and political realities under military repression is unique for an English-written narrative. Buzzards and Bananas is a well-informed contribution to contemporary travel literature".

—*Charles R. Harper (Saint- Hilaire d'Ozilhan, France) —honored by both the Chilean (2010) and Argentinian (2014) governments for his emblematic legacy of international mobilization for human rights.*

PROLOGUE

Machu Picchu, October 1977

> *"Alone, Mary and I strode the last couple hundred yards from the veranda of the tourist hotel to the gates of Machu Picchu, under the archway, and then up the long, stone steps to the summit. Before us lay the summer home of Pachacuti, ninth emperor of the Incan dynasty.*

> *It wasn't the thin, high mountain air that took our breath away. Those stone steps led us up to a place unlike any other on earth. We were overcome by the vision spreading out before us; a purely mystical embodiment of space, time, setting, and silence. Up here the noise of our fellow travelers was strangely absent, muffled beneath a cloak of quiet that permeated the mountain-top city. No one was immune. In that first view, in that first moment, every visitor absorbed the essence of Machu Picchu in reverent stillness."*

It was the early days of October 1977 when my wife Mary and I explored Machu Picchu. We sat together in the Sacred Plaza surrounded by the stillness of the long abandoned Incan city, recounting the spidery threads that had brought us here and the inertia that was propelling us forward to new adventures.

I'm not sure exactly when the urge to travel to South America took root. Every midwinter since our marriage in 1971, as the Minnesota mercury dropped into the mind-numbing, finger-freezing below zeros, Mary and I traveled down to Mexico. It was an exhausting 2,000-mile road trip as we stuffed ourselves into our underpowered, noisy Volkswagen Westfalia camper van. Tentatively at first, we vacationed in the Pacific Coast tourist towns of Puerto Vallarta and Manzanillo. The route from the Texas border to the coast took us through small pueblos and cities. We began to enjoy the culture of the town square, the friendliness of the Mexican people, the frenetic pace of the open-air markets, and the colorful adobe architecture. Gradually, over the next few years, we moved off the main roads and explored deeper south and east, into the states of Oaxaca, Campeche, Quintana Roo, and Yucatán. As Mexico opened up to us, so did our interest in the Mayan and Aztec cultures. We collected books, maps, guides, and sometimes artifacts of the Mayan civilization. Our trips began to coalesce around the ancient ruins of Palenque, Chichen Itza, Yaxchilan, Tulum, Bonampak, Edzna, and Uxmal. We photographed them in detail and sought out ways to learn more.

In those early days the sites were not well protected. It was a time of intense excavation and reconstruction by the Mexican government and international universities, each vying to unearth and document the story of those early peoples. There were guards at most sites, but we were free to wander along with the workers everywhere we pleased. All the archeological sites were open to us, and we climbed through new excavations and overgrown unearthed mounds, entering into and exploring hidden passages, rooms, and antechambers. The ancient cultures intrigued us, and slowly, without being openly expressed, a longing for more travel began to emerge.

We knew to do justice to our journey it would take us longer than any vacation time our employer—the Minnesota Mining and Manufacturing Company, 3M—could offer. We knew we had to quit. That revelation changed everything. Our goal was to save fifteen thousand dollars and then make the announcement. But unsurprisingly, life got in the way, and after a year, the money we saved got spent on furniture, a piano, new tires, and just plain living. We feared we might never reach a financial trigger point that would launch us into the journeys we dreamed of. We realized that if we really wanted to travel, we needed to set a firm departure date, and not just a monetary goal. So we picked one. Regardless of the amount of money saved by April 30, 1976, we would announce our plans to 3M and the world. Whatever money we had by then would fund our trip.

On May 3, we visited 3M's Personnel Department in Saint Paul, Minnesota, and dropped the bomb. We fidgeted quietly, our butts parked in aseptic office chairs as we waited for the personnel director. She stared at us across the desk, her face knotted into a kind of perplexed bewilderment as she reacted to the news that we had tendered our resignations from great jobs, and that (heresy upon heresy) we were dumping our 3M stocks. She was not amused and let out a long, huffy expulsion of air through pursed lips. She cajoled and implored us to reconsider throwing our careers away so frivolously.

"Why go chasing a dream with all its uncertainty," she puzzled, "when you've got so much invested right here?" Perhaps the only tactic she didn't use was to wag her finger in our faces and tsk-tsk us. It's true; we did have remarkable careers ahead of us. I was a process engineer in Dyanacolor, a division of 3M's emerging photographic department. Mary was in records management, a fast-growing and vital segment of data processing. Our jobs were challenging, interesting, and well paying, and with a rock-solid company like 3M, life-long employment was virtually guaranteed. As we departed and she shook our hands, she also shook her head. *What the heck were these two kids doing?*

We probably didn't understand all the ramifications of what we were about to do, either. Ray Bradbury, author of *Fahrenheit 451*, once said that sometimes "you have to jump off a cliff and build your wings on the way down." Our decision to do what others thought irresponsible—or at best, questionable—wasn't necessarily all that well thought out on our part. We took a leap of faith. During the course of our two years of travel, we learned inner secrets about ourselves, our spirits, and our relationship with each other; we became intimate not only with what moved and inspired us, but what challenged us.

We also learned how naive we were about the world around us. We had been sheltered all our lives, protected from the excess of government control and the cruelty of dictatorships. Back in the 1970s, America's "world" ended pretty much at its northern and southern borders and the edges of the two oceans, east and west. The daily news generally ended there, too. Maybe people living in the border states had inklings of what went on in the two adjacent countries, but few outside those narrow boundaries had any knowledge—or, for that matter, any *interest*—in events that didn't directly affect them. This was America before the twenty-four-hour news cycle. Similar to Roman times, when sailors believed the oceans ended at the horizon off the rocky coast of Finisterre, the vast majority of Americans truly believed nothing of any consequence existed beyond the sightlines of their shores. The seventies were the time of bell-bottoms, disco, sticky notes, protest songs, Kent State, Nixon, and Watergate. The only broadcast news from overseas of any relevance was the Vietnam War and the oil embargo. The Vietnam War lay on the social consciousness not because of the chaos and the almost two million Vietnamese, Laotian, and Cambodian casualties, but because of the constant TV reminders of flag-covered metal coffins returning with the American dead. The OPEC oil embargo was newsworthy, not because of the of the US foreign policy in the Middle East, but rather because of the long gas lines, oil shortages, and inconvenience that tested the patience of the American public.

When it came to South America, there was limited contemporary information available to us. It just wasn't on the mainstream news' radar screen. Maybe there was a word here and a comment there about a coup in Chile or a dictator in Brazil, but nothing, it seemed, of any real relevance to our plans. Our information came not from the Internet or Google searches (they were still a long way off in the future), but rather from old, rarely used, and sadly outdated books in our local library. Our best and most current political information came from the 1976 *South American Handbook* we purchased. It rattled off, country-by-country, what we might expect as we ventured southward: Argentina was in a "highly complex political situation after the death of Juan Peron, of which a high level of violence is a regrettable feature," and in Bolivia, "the constitution is, at present, suspended." In Brazil, "Military leaders [had overthrown] the left-leaning government," and in Chile, "a new junta now rules the country." In short, the citizens of South America labored under the rule of dictatorships or mock democracies.

Just as the handbook forewarned us, as we traveled southward we moved through countries whose citizens were beaten down and driven to despair and fear by the very forces that had promised to protect them. Secret police in Argentina, Chile, Bolivia, Paraguay, and Brazil banded together, rounding up, murdering, or disappearing over sixty thousand people. Sometimes we noticed this helplessness, sometimes small gestures gave us clues to those underlying anxieties, but often we simply traveled naively, outside the local politics and those appalling social and political problems. On rare occasions, we were drawn by circumstance into the middle of it all, and in those fleeting moments we felt and understood the hopelessness and fear of those around us.

In June of 1976 we began our journey in a camper, motoring across Canada and then down to Mexico and Central America. For the first year we ventured westward with the comforts of home, across the prairies then north through the Yukon to Alaska, retreating when the winter weather forced us southwards. We stopped a while in Mexico and studied Spanish for several weeks before moving south again, into the new cultures of Central America. From Guatemala southward we'd park the camper for long stretches and explore the country using public transportation, buses, collectivos, trains, and the beds of passing trucks. We discovered that traveling felt more gratifying as we moved and lived unencumbered, carrying only a backpack and a map. It brought us closer to the land and to the people, their daily lives, and cultures. Our decision to backpack intensified as we traveled south through El Salvador, Honduras, Nicaragua, and Costa Rica. By the time we reached Panama's Darién Gap we were determined to sell the camper and head as free spirits to South America. That story was told in *Chasing the Dream*, my first book.

The South American adventure began August 11, 1977. Over the course of the next year we traveled twenty-six thousand miles, sat in over 110 long-distance buses, sailed on twenty-one boats and barges, took sixteen trains, flew on fourteen planes, rode in nine long-haul collectivos, and hitched rides in the beds of various trucks. And of course, we walked hundreds of miles along trails, dusty roads, and city streets.

Both Mary and I kept journals. The diaries recorded the exciting times, the mundane day-to-day experiences such as where we visited, slept, and what we did, and sometimes those genuine moments of happiness, despair, anger, and love. They were written as our trip unfolded, occasionally in shorthand, but mostly in truncated sentences, shortened to make them easier to express. We wrote letters and postcards to friends and family back in the States and Canada. Those who received letters kept them and returned them to us when we finished our travels. These letters provided another glimpse at who we were and how we communicated our travels and travails to those outside our immediate relationship. Sometimes we found it easier to confide in a friend and put to words some deep feeling that could be expressed, dropped in a letterbox, and banished from the mind. It's funny and strange how difficult it can be to unburden your soul to someone you love.

Like most journals, there were gaps when writing didn't suit the circumstances, or when we were perhaps feeling lazy. In those situations, I tried to backfill missing information using the letters home, reminiscing with Mary, letting pictures stir up recollections, and simply exploring the lingering memories of an aging mind.

Buzzards and Bananas chronicles our story of South America through Peru, the Amazon, Chile, and Bolivia. It describes our adventures, the companions we met along the way, and the social, economic, and political turbulence through which we traveled.

Of course, there are more stories still untold, still waiting to awaken from the journals—Venezuela, Brazil, Paraguay, Argentina, and Ecuador all have tales to tell. Maybe someday; in the meantime, this journey has become an enduring foundation to my day-to-day life.

I'm delighted to be able to share my experiences with you and hope that my own journey inspires you to travel the long road and never stop dreaming.

BUZZARDS & BANANAS

GEORGE L. AYERS

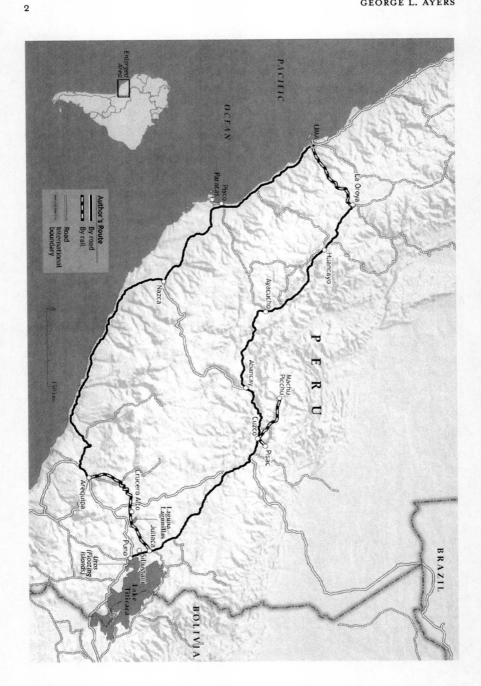

PERU

Tuesday, September 13, 1977: Lima, Day One

Arriving from Caracas, we formulated a few irrefutable truisms about Lima in the short six-mile bus route that took us from our first steps off the tarmac of the Jorge Chavez airport to Plaza San Martin in the city's center.

The first thing we noticed was the dirt. Lima was a city where it never rained. It was a temperate, rainless desert metropolis. In fact, Lima's climate was pretty boring. This time of the year there was neither wind nor sun, the temperature was neither hot nor cold. It was simply dull and humid. Outside the city core, few roads were paved, plants and trees were scarce, and the tons of dust and dirt that swept down from the surrounding hills every day aggravated our noses and settled on every stationary object in the city. How could you miss it—it was everywhere. Nothing escaped that taupe-brown coating of grit.

Climate was Lima's counterbalance to its traffic. It was intense, congested, and noisy. Drivers didn't stop honking their horns until they turned the engines off. In the Latino culture, horns seemed to be the most important feature of the car, much more relevant, for example, than the brakes. Horns were used continuously, the brakes rarely at all. Traffic was a free-for-all with crowded chaotic roadways, laws unenforced, roundabouts from hell, and pedestrians streaking through the maze of cars, trucks, scooters, and combi-buses that clogged the roads. Our combi wove in and out of traffic, the driver concentrating on speed, while the *cobrador*—his sidekick, the guy who took the money—dealt with tardy passengers too slow in his view to get on or get off. "*Bajan, bajan, bajan*," he yelled at every stop, banging his palm on the combi roof and berating hesitant passengers to "Get off, get off, get off!" At every red light we stopped at—those few our driver didn't simply gun it through—we were surrounded by newspaper sellers and street entertainers who timed their act with well-practiced precision, ending with outstretched hands moments before the chaos began again. Intersections were always jammed full of crisscrossing traffic with irritated drivers honking and maneuvering into the smallest of spaces that would keep them moving forward. We made it unscathed to Plaza San Martin in the colonial heartland of the city, scrambled off with shouts of "*bajan*" at our backside, shouldered our packs, and headed down the pedestrian street of Jirón Union towards a little hotel we'd chosen by happenstance from our *South American Handbook*.

And finally, there were the street vendors. We saw them everywhere, peddling their goods. It was like walking through a citywide street sale. Two years ago in 1975, Peru's economy took a nosedive and the government transitioned to military rule with an extremely conservative general at the helm. General Bermúdez used harsh measures to manage the crisis. To please the international moneylenders he slashed public spending, devalued the currency, held down worker's wages, and raised food prices. He got the loans, but he also got an impoverished nation. Even before the government action a majority of the nation's workforce was already marginally employed, or simply out of work. Two years later, we witnessed the results of those harsh government actions: the *ambulantes* (the wanderers), a name the government gave to the street vendors who flooded into every corner of the city in search of the meager revenues to sustain themselves. Here in Lima, the "City of Kings," there were tens of thousands of them, unregulated, economically fragile, and for the most part simply tolerated by police and populace. In our short walk down Jirón Union we passed hundreds of vendors. Most sold products or prepared food from tiny mobile carts, but scores simply wandered with their wares. Brushing aside the constant intrusions to buy, we made a quick catalog of what we saw on our three-block walk: towels, shoes, plastic waving hands on spring-loaded suction cups that fastened to car windows, T-shirts adorned with bizarre ironed-on aphorisms, plastic toys, balloons, stockings, ham sandwiches, buns of all shapes, pants, crude paintings of country landscapes, sweaters, handbags, briefcases, jackets, mothballs, fountain pens, toothbrushes, mirrors, combs, magazines, lettuce shredders, and an inexhaustible supply of cheap costume jewelry. As we navigated our way through the *ambulantes*, we sensed the fragility of these people's lives and the urgency for reform.

Hostal Roma was a cozy little place, up a few flights of narrow stairs above the noisy street. The proprietress was busy cleaning up the communal dining area, but she broke away and showed us some of the rooms. We chose one with a little wrought-iron railed balcony overlooking the street with big wooden French doors that guarded a glassless window and let in lots of light and air. The noise we could handle with extra pillows. The beds were comfortable, there was an old armoire tucked in the corner for storage, and the lamps actually had more than twenty-watt bulbs. And the biggest plus of all was a variable-speed ceiling fan that could be controlled by a long cord that dangled above the bed. We explored the common rooms: the bathroom, showers, kitchen, and a communal gathering place with worn furniture and scads of discarded books from past travelers. Back at the office we paid our 190 Peruvian soles per night—the equivalent of two dollars for room and breakfast. It was a perfect little home surrounded by the city center and a view out our balcony over the heart of *ambulante* commerce.

Wednesday to Saturday: Fragments from my journal—Lima

Lima sat on a wide and fertile plain that sloped gently to the sea. The Andes, whose high crest was within ninety miles, sent their foothills almost to the city gates. Lima was once a pure enchantment of colonial buildings. But its population had swelled to over three million, and amongst the beautiful buildings and dwellings soared the many tall skyscrapers that irrevocably changed the old colonial skyline. The city we saw was surrounded by what the government euphemistically called the *Pueblos Jóvenes* (the Young Towns), shantytown settlements of squatters who migrated in from the sierras seeking work. The locals called them *barriadas*: the impoverished neighborhoods of *campesinos* and migrants who were left entirely to their own resources to build their shelters without infrastructure or services. As far as the government was concerned, housing for the poor was only a matter of providing free land. The result was a massive, expansive slum that was encircling the city like a horseshoe.

Over the course of the next few days, as we prepared for our trip through Peru, we walked Lima's central colonial districts.

Walking was our favorite form of transportation around the city. There were hazards, to be sure. Eventually, you'd have to cross a street, and we'd just driven in those same streets so we knew what to expect. I don't know how many pedestrians are killed each day, but I'll bet you couldn't count them on one hand. We literally put our lives in jeopardy at every crossing. Cars simply didn't stop. They might, at the last moment, simply swerve around us, or perhaps the chivalrous ones might honk at us before stepping on the accelerator, but they didn't stop.

As gringos, our clothes, language, mannerisms, character, and especially Mary's long, blond hair were always on display. So when we walked around it meant a whole lot of staring. Intellectually, we knew the extended looks and furtive glances were just curiosity, but it was difficult to get used to, being so obviously different. It also meant that every drunk in the city would be drawn to us intrinsically, like burrs to woolen socks, to latch onto us, engage in some slurred, tanked-up, one-way conversation to the amusement of other passersby.

But walking allowed us to experience the finer nuances of the city, like where to find the best black market money exchange. After some discreet inquiries, it turned out the doorman at the Gran Bolivar Hotel was the guy to see. The official exchange rate in the banks was about eighty soles to the dollar, but not in a closed hotel elevator heading up to the fourth floor. From a pocket he peeled out a wad of bills, we negotiated the new rate, money passed hands, and down we came to the lobby with an instant twenty percent discount on everything.

An hour's walk from our hotel was Peru's *Museo Nacional de Antropología* (National Museum of Anthropology). We, apparently along with Lima's entire school system, toured the museum housed in an old colonial mansion.

Hand in hand, long chains of giggling faces in gray uniforms sped by us snickering and furtively pointing until we were sure we had been lured into the museum as a traveling exhibit on loan from some foreign culture. Not that it mattered; we enjoyed their energy surrounding us too. As teachers futilely tried to corral their little charges, kids bombarded us with questions about who we were and where we came from and then listened intently to our answers, grimacing at our poor Spanish dashing off to catch up with their friends. Later as we circled back, the main outdoor corridor had become a giant easel as hundreds of anspiring Rembrandts sprawled across the floor. Teachers had asked them to recreate the most interesting part of their experience here at the museum. To our dismay our visages were never crayoned or painted, but instead sculpted vases, animals, plants, gold ornaments, and games of almost every aspect of Incan life found their way from the glass museum cases through each child's imagination to the paper in front of them.

Transplanted from the northern town of Trujillo, the privately-owned Raphael Larco Herrera Museum on Avenida Bolivar, not far from the Museum of Anthropology, was unique. The museum showcased ceramics from the Chimú, Chancay, Nazca, and Inca cultures. The exquisitely-decorated portrait vessels from the Moche river valley near Trujillo were intriguing. Faces of rulers, warriors, princes, prisoners, priests, and healers, simply painted or often in raised, three-dimensional ceramic surfaces, were so well preserved they looked modern—not from civilizations a thousand years old.

For an hour we walked through rows of intricate pottery and ceramics and were awed by the intricate gold filigree of ancient artisans, past the parched, pre-Columbian mummies and shreds of ancient cloth. Then we beat it down to the prurient core of the museum—the erotic art section. Let's be frank. Any curator that dedicates a significant portion of a museum display to erotica and penises has to have a lot of balls. We found row upon row of fornication, masturbation, fellatio, and penises of all shapes and amazing sizes, all of which were indelicately molded into pots; there were ceramic handles of giant penises and suggestive drinking cups. Mary's favorite, judging by her expression, was a little drinking cup of a stubby man holding his erect organ in both hands. I suspected she'd never look at a straw in her soda quite the same way again.

The museum held an amazing collection of pre-Columbia art, pottery, and textiles. We were invited to amble through their storage area. Within those plain, back rooms, housed on metal shelves and racks, were more than forty-five thousand pieces of classified archeological artifacts, the overflow from the museum floor.

Since we were literally surrounded by them, one morning we decided a church day was in order. Neither of us was particularly religious so we simply started at the one with the coolest name: *Convento de Los Descalzos* (The Monastery of the Barefooted Brethren). Originally built as a refuge on the edges of town and surrounded by fields and vineyards, Lima just flowed around it. The convent now sits right in the heart of Lima, just across the Rimac River. The masonry was a bit worn, its paint slightly faded and chipping off the plaster walls, but it was still a quaint little sanctuary where we found solitude in the city.

We wound our way back over to Iglesias San Francisco and got another sense of the Catholic Church. Down in the catacombs were the bones of twenty-six thousand souls, originally of priests and nobles from the eighteen century but, over time, until the practice stopped in 1821, even of lay people. The catacombs filled to capacity, and so to keep up with demand, the clergy doused the bodies with quicklime, rapidly reducing them to skeletons. To keep things in order, the Franciscans started a little art project. Bones were categorized in the tombs by body part. Row upon row of skulls, femurs, tibias, and fibulae were carefully organized into rectangular wooden boxes and earthen corrals. Farther down the narrow, bone-filled hallways were their pivotal works: geometric piles of skulls with leg bones that radiated out to larger concentric circles of skulls and leg bones, circles within circles of human skeletal remains. It just felt macabre and tacky. From up above, inside the chancel, strains of organ music and the high-pitched, droning, monotone voice of the priest echoed eerily through small metal grates in the vaulted ceilings.

By the time we returned to the Lima Cathedral in the Plaza de Armas we were approaching the periphery of our religious endurance. The cathedral interior with its faint ecclesiastical smell, was architecturally beautiful. It was a real insight into the spiritual history of the Catholic Church in Peru, with its ornate, delicately-carved stalls, the silver-covered altars, and mosaic-covered walls with Lima's coat of arms and an allegory of the Thirteen Men of Isla de Gallo, those thirteen conquistadors who stood by Pizarro's side during desperate times. In fact, the shriveled remains of Pizarro's four-hundred-year-old body were on display and for the paltry sum of a few céntimos we viewed the great conqueror behind his glass casket.

It was the wealth of the church that inspired the most conversation between the two of us. We were both stunned by the endless gold- and silver-clad carvings, the vastness of these cavernous limestone monuments, the inexhaustible centuries of old art, and tapestries that hung around us or were stored hidden in the catacomb vaults below. A believer might see this great accumulation of wealth and architecture as a celebration of the greatness of God. A skeptic might wonder if these treasures were amassed on the backs of the indigenous poor and oppressed.

Saturday afternoon, back in the Plaza of San Martin, a small but boisterous demonstration of peasants returning from the countryside was marching with placards and slogans, blocking traffic as they spilled out of the plaza and onto the busy streets. Over the noise of car horns and chanting demonstrators, a waiter smiled as he likened the rally to someone selling magic herbs. The herbs turned out to be a socialist Marxist philosophy, an ideology not particularly encouraged by the ruling regime. The agrarian reforms touted by the central military government, those that they had promised would be a blessing to the peasantry, had ended in failure. Without proper financial and managerial support, without educational reform, the large tracts of freed land simply handed to the local rural cooperatives had gone unused and fallow. However, the seeds of insurrection had taken root. Up in the remote highlands on the university campus of Ayacucho, a chubby, young philosophy professor with an idealistic Marxist–Maoist agenda was already encouraging students to take up the cause of radical socialism. Within two years, Abimael Guzmán would transform his radical ideologies into one of the most brutal terrorist groups ever seen. *Sendero Luminoso* (The Shining Path) was about to launch its violent Maoist, anti-capitalist, guerrilla campaign against the government and the *campesinos* of the high-lands. Over the next decade, seventy thousand people would die, trapped between the Maoist insurgency and the brutality of the ruling military response.

Perhaps Peru was good at preserving its cultural past, but it was having difficulties with its cultural present.

Sunday, September 18, 1977: Pisco, Peru

Roggero buses could well have been the original inspiration for demolition derbies. They were big, roaring, aluminum monsters. In low gear the Detroit V6 diesel made a deafening racket that ricocheted off buildings as we navigated the narrow streets out of Lima. Cars and pedestrians swerved out of our way when the air horn blasted our intentions to crash through busy intersections. Ten o'clock found us tearing southward, the undulating coastal desert scarcely visible out the cracked and dirt-streaked windows. Roggero was one of the few trans-Peruvian bus companies. It was such a big-time operation they actually handed us an official receipt when our luggage was stowed in the storage pods below. A closer inspection of the fine print offered an interesting perspective on how different cultures valued property. The company, it confidently stated, was responsible for any and all misdirected or lost baggage during the trip. It would reimburse us immediately. Of course, their limit was twenty soles, or the equivalent of a mere twenty-five cents for each wayward piece of luggage. Finally, we could relax knowing everything was under control.

The route took us out along the coast. We had glimpses and sometimes long expanses of the deep blue Pacific. Everything around us looked gritty and brown. The desert sand twisted the landscape into a dusty drabness. Trees lost their greenness. Grime covered homes, cars, buildings, and streets. Nothing escaped the sun-roasted and windswept desert dust.

What was to be a short three-hour, hundred-and-fifty-mile bus ride south to Pisco took a little longer. Like the vehicle itself, the bus tires had seen better days, and the treads were a mere existential impression on the otherwise smooth, rubber surfaces. Travelers always had to allow for "tire timeouts." In our case, there were two. Flats rarely occurred near civilization, but generally on remote stretches of road. It was more interesting that way. Every passenger disembarked and encircled the driver. As he examined the flat, we all offered unsolicited advice as to how best approach the problem, and then deliberated with him on the selection of a fitting replacement from the assortment of spare tires stashed in the luggage hold. When the real dirty work began we backed away, content to watch the process from a distance. Repairs, especially the messy part, everyone concurred, were strictly company business.

Our bus dropped us off at the Plaza de Armas and we marched diagonally across the street over to Hotel Pisco, a salmon-colored building. The hotel was on the second floor, above a takeout food vendor and a sparsely-stocked grocery store. We spent the rest of the day wandering the streets of Pisco. Back at the plaza we enjoyed the sunshine and sat under the stern, bronzed gaze of a statue of Peru's national hero, San Martin, on his mighty steed while we nibbled on local dumpling treats of pecans and dried fruit. Towards dinner we stopped at an open-air restaurant to sample Pisco Sours; we were, after all, in the hometown namesake of that drink.

Monday: Pisco, Peru

I hate getting swindled. I hate that someone would deliberately scheme to take advantage of us. After the fact, I'm always annoyed at myself for not recognizing the ruse in the first place.

There were a lot of different scams, each usually executed with a remarkable grace of practiced smoothness. We'd already fallen prey to the hotel scam. Late at night, in some strange town, we'd hop off the bus or train into the arms of waiting taxi drivers. We'd ask them to take us to a specific hotel. They'd nod their head affirmatively and throw our backpacks in the trunk. After a long taxi ride we'd be escorted into some nondescript shanty hotel owned by a friend or owner who paid drivers to bring customers there, rather than the place the customers were expecting. There'd be arguments, threats, wringing of hands, but the end result was often the same: it was late, it was dark, and we didn't always know exactly where we were. We had been scammed.

Today's rip-off was a variation of the same theme. Mid-morning, we set off to see *El Candelabro*, the giant, enigmatic, six-hundred-foot ground drawing, cut two feet deep into the slopping soil of the Paracas Peninsula. Its origins and its meaning were shrouded in mystery. It was shaped like a trident. Archeologists believed it was created two thousand years ago, but beyond that all bets were off. Modern society tried to infuse theories with a modern perspective. Wild notions abounded that the hillside marking served as a directional signal for extraterrestrial space-craft or a navigational beacon for marauding eighteenth-century pirates. It seemed more likely that the trident was some pre-Incan ritual object, a representation of the Tree of Life or desert cactus, created by the sun-worshipping priests of Paracas.

We knew the best vantage point to view this amazing, ancient geoglyph was from out on the water, and decided to travel a few kilometers down the road to the small town of Paracas. There, we'd hire a local fisherman to take us out into the bay. We negotiated the first stage easily enough; we hitchhiked. A worker from the local Pesca Peru fish fertilizer factory offered us a ride down to Paracas. Fish fertilizer trucks, as it turns out, weren't the most fragrant form of transportation. But the driver was talkative and friendly and dropped us off downtown, right at the water. As we searched for water transportation, a taxi driver hailed us over.

"*¿Oye, a dónde vas?*" (Where are you off to?) he inquired.

"To find a boat out to the trident at Paracas," we answered.

"I'll help—hop in." Twenty minutes later, the water was a distant memory behind us as he drove further out into the desert. After another twenty minutes he stopped in some godforsaken little one-horse town with the improbable name of Salinas de Tombes. Now he had us by the short hairs. We were in the middle of frigging nowhere. All we saw was desert at every compass point. "Hey," he said with a smile, "if you want to go back, I can take you. Only eight hundred soles and I'll drop you off at the edge of town." In every sense of the word we were pissed—at him for his trickery, and at ourselves for our gullibility. I could sense the machinations in Mary's mind. She was a feisty Minnesota girl and a veteran traveler. Rile her up and you'd face the consequences. I know; I'd done it a few times. She was mentally calculating whether to lay a good whoop-ass on the driver right on the spot or bite her tongue and take the offer for the ride back to civilization. Fortunately for all of us, her cooler nature prevailed and we decided eight hundred soles sounded about right for a return to town. Seven dollars may not seem like a lot to get worked up about. Under normal circumstances, you'd probably be right, but just to put it in perspective, over the last month or so we'd traveled for under twenty dollars a day, period. This additional seven dollars put us over the high end of a day's food, lodging, travel, and living combined. Back safely at the edge of Paracas, we watched as the taxi reversed and disappeared from view. Another experience, another lesson learned.

The real problem here wasn't the cost of our little diversion, but the time it took. Before we left to find the candelabra we'd purchased bus tickets to Nazca. It was mid-afternoon and our bus left at six-thirty that evening. Inquiries in town suggested the trip out on Paracas Bay to see the trident would bring us back near sunset—possibly. The timing was awkward. One small delay and we'd miss our bus. We gathered what self-esteem was left to our day and caught a collectivo back to our hotel. The candelabro would wait.

Dusk brought softness to the desert landscape. The bright colors muted, sharp shadows softened, and the sky took on an indulgent, waxy quality. The new bus we traveled on was Brazilian-made and luxurious. I sprawled across the wide seats, listened to quiet music, and watched through freshly-washed windows as the desert countryside, silhouetted under a crescent half-moon, slipped by.

We arrived in the sleepy, dusty town of Nazca shortly before ten. Our bus dropped us off on Calle Callao at the edge of town and we checked in at the nearby Hotel Monte Carlo, a rambling, two-story stucco hotel that had seen better days. Tomorrow we would explore the lines, the mysterious etchings of the desert.

Tuesday: Lines of Nazca

At noon, out at the airstrip, our little red-and-white Cessna 172 taxied to the end of the dirt runway and turned about into the wind. The pilot nodded over at me assuredly and increased the throttle. The engine revved and the metal skin of our plane vibrated in anticipation. When he released the brake we surged forward and I watched the airspeed indicator. As we reached fifty-five knots, he slowly pulled back on the controls and we lifted off, hung there a few feet above the runway as if breaking gravity, and then climbed skyward. After a slow bank took us out over the rich green farming oasis north of the Nazca River Valley, our pilot trimmed out around two thousand feet. The ride up had been bumpy. Turbulent air over the desert meant a constantly jolting rollercoaster ride. Sitting in the front copilot seat, I at least had the advantage of a broad panorama to help settle my nerves. For Mary strapped in directly behind me, the view was more restricted, and I'm sure the ride more gut-wrenching.

The lines were virtually invisible from the ground. They went unnoticed from the time of the Spanish conquest until the 1930s when an errant pilot overflew the area. The pilot reported big rectangles and lines crisscrossing the pampa floor. Now, below us, stretched a maze of trapezoids and lines, some miles long, crossing and crisscrossing the arid valley. The lines formed angles, triangles, spirals, and rectangles, wavy lines and concentric circles. We circled north out over the Pan-American Highway to a small spur of Andean cordillera that jutted down into the valley. Our pilot banked and pointed. There, cut into the spur on the side of a plateau below us, was a bird perhaps sixty feet across that he identified as a baby condor. Moments later, we approached a figure cut into the side of another spur. "*Astronauta*," he dramatically exclaimed. Sure enough, it was a faint hundred-foot outline of a bug-eyed and bulbous-headed figure with one arm above his head, waving in perpetual greeting. It did look like a giant spaceman, although that was hardly a role found in an ancient, two-thousand-year-old civilization. Modern interpretations sometimes played a little loose with reality.

We banked north again and flew towards the highway. We spotted the *Mirador*, the tall, man-made lookout beside the highway. To one side of the lookout a mysterious set of hands reached out towards us. One was obviously human; the other hand had only three fingers and a thumb. Adjacent to the hands grew a huarango tree, the Tree of Life, with its branches and roots radiating out into the rocky plain. We flew over a raised plateau embraced by two rocky arms of encroaching mountains and glanced down at the Hummingbird, perhaps the most recognizable of all the Nazca etchings. Our pilot dipped the wings and we flew around it. Ironically, even though it represented one of the smallest birds in real life, the desert biomorph below was enormous. From beak tip to tail it was over three hundred feet with a rocky wingspan of over two hundred. As we headed southward we circled around one of the larger creatures on the Nazca plains, the frigate bird with its massive wingspan and fantail. In the distance behind it we easily spotted the Spider with its round hourglass body and eight protruding legs. It seemed ready to scamper to safety along a web of lines traced across the desert. Finally, we soared over the Monkey, its spiral tail and playful demeanor softly outlined in the desert.

A VIEW OF THE HUMMINGBIRD GEOGLYPH AS WE FLEW OVER THE NAZCA DESERT

Woven through this magical and ancient landscape were the lines of modern man: tire tracks. Until the last couple of years this desert was well-studied but poorly preserved. Trucks rumbled across it, looters dug up ancient gravesites, and squatters disturbed acres of land. Even city trucks dumped garbage out on the plains, leaving their tire marks rutted in the soil. It was like a great canvas drawn in disappearing ink, soiled by graffiti and looking tattered around the edges. At times the ancient biomorphs seemed lost amongst tangles of countless tire tracks and careless pathways that crisscrossed the desert. There were over four hundred square miles to protect, and little money or interest in doing so. With fewer than twenty minutes of rain in an entire year and a flat, stony surface that minimized the effects of wind, even small disturbances that broke through the reddish desert crust left gashes of man's intrusion for untold centuries.

Thirty-two years ago, the Peruvian government built the Pan-American Highway across this plain and, without any consideration for cultural preservation, bulldozed a giant etching of a six-hundred-foot lizard in two, obliterating the hind legs in the process. Today, about a fifth of the original etchings have been vandalized or simply destroyed. Perhaps the greatest proponent for this desert landscape was a frail, determined German woman who lived in town across from our hotel. She'd thwarted attempts to hold motorcycle races across the iconic plains, halted military exercises, and stopped local farmers from irrigating the desert in an attempt to expand their holdings. Maria Reiche had been a fixture here for over forty years. Before our flight this morning we had walked across the street to visit with her, but *La Doctora*, as the locals called her, was already out on the plains below us, laboriously removing debris from the soft pampa figures.

Later in the afternoon we caught a bus headed southward out along the Pan-American Highway, which then steered off-road, deeper into the desert to the ancient burial ground of Chauchilla. For a thousand years the cemetery, isolated in the dry Nazca desert, was used to bury the dead and mummified remains of the Nazca people. The area was littered with human skulls, bones, and broken pottery shards. Strands of ancient woven fabric, once worn by the dead, caught in gusts of wind and swirled around as we walked. It was a surreal landscape, pocked and cratered with the opened graves of the ancient wealthy and influential, their resting places now ransacked by tomb robbers. We looked down into the tombs. Mummified remains squatted there, wrapped in faded cloth and bound with rope. Skulls, some still with bits of straggly hair attached, stared open-jawed back up at us. I picked up a piece of broken pottery, its ochre-colored designs still vivid after a thousand years.

Back in town we stumbled upon an ancient ceramic vessel in a tiny dilapidated shop alongside the roadside. We had actually been in the process of changing hotels when we spotted a row of ceramics on a shelf as we passed by the open doorway. The shopkeeper, who looked as old as the ceramics she sold, told us they were from the sand-covered city of Cahuachi, twenty miles in the desert east of here. She explained that centuries ago the ancient architects of the Nazca Lines lived in Cahuachi and this pottery was from that era. Mary and I are both packrats and interested in the ancient cultures. We looked at one another and nodded. The piece Mary chose was small but elaborately decorated, with a catlike, human-headed animal painted in ochre, brown, and black. Carefully, we wrapped it in newspaper and safely stowed it in her backpack and continued on to our new hotel.

In the darkness of evening, under an eerie, yellowish wash of gas lanterns from the street vendors' wagons, we strolled along the edges of Plaza de Armas. We stopped and sampled hot roasted peanuts, rich chocolate, oranges, and even skewers of delicious-smelling barbequed meats. We asked about their origins, but never received an answer we understood. It was probably better that way.

Wednesday: Nazca

This morning we bused back up the Pan-American Highway to the *Mirador*, a lookout built the year prior under Maria Reiche's guidance. She wanted a way for people to see some of the lines without having to pay for a plane ride. We'd spotted it yesterday on our forty-minute plane tour. As we climbed higher, the patterns emerged. Perched on the platform fifty feet above the Ingenio valley we saw the branches of the Tree of Life scraped into the rocky floor below. They stretched out towards us, ending a few feet below where we stood. The roots were barely visible, and behind them huge, elongated triangles disappeared into the horizon. To our left, the enigmatic hands were clearly visible. The fingertips stretched away from us and emanated outward from some strange, amorphous, birdlike body

We scrambled down the metal ladder and walked up along the highway towards a large trapezoid cut by the highway and wandered up onto the slopes of two nearby hills. We overlooked the lizard, its body bisected by the highway, and its torso systematically destroyed by the tire treads of trucks and vans as they cut across the desert. All that was left of the giant reptile were the soft depressions of two webbed front feet and bits of its head and body. We walked down to the lines, careful not to disturb the rock patina. These lines were only about a foot wide, a simple depression in the ground.

To call this place a desert was a little misleading. There's no sand here. The plain that stretched out around us was in fact an incredibly large patch of rock-strewn soil. To make a single line like the one before us was pretty simple. Moving the dark red, iron-oxide-covered rocks revealed a lighter gypsum-rich soil underneath. Removing stones in a straight line was easy enough. To make the complex designs and biomorphs that surrounded us was a different matter. Ancient engineers, like sculptors, started with an empty, rocky canvas. Sculptors removed clay. The early people of Nazca removed rocks to create these incredible images in the plains.

Thursday: Maria Reiche

I knocked softly on the hotel door of room 132. Mary and I shuffled our feet. Both of us were a bit apprehensive about meeting this icon of Nazca research at her home in the tourist hotel, but we needn't have been. The door opened and there she was, the lady of the lines. Her face was creased with sun-aged wrinkles and framed with fine graying hair pulled back behind her head. A pair of heavy, round glasses with thick lenses perched on her nose, held in place with an elasticized strap. She smiled, and with a slight Teutonic accent asked us to come inside.

Perhaps we expected a sophisticated sitting room full of bookshelves, work desks, and storage cabinets jam-packed with years of research files. Instead, her room was stark and simple. The floor was cluttered with drawings and photographs; the only furniture was a small single bed, a card table desk, a tattered but comfortable armchair, and a tall wicker basket bulging with rolls of maps and charts. A trunk in the corner, I suspected, was for clothing. We followed Maria back inside. She dressed as simply as her lifestyle, from the rubber flip-flops on her feet to the simple cream-colored dress with faded brown circular patterns. Over it all she wore an unassuming and unbuttoned wool cardigan.

MATHEMATICIAN AND ANTHROPOLOGIST MARIA REICHE

Over the next couple of hours we chatted about her life and her life's passion: the lines of Nazca. Maria was seventy-four now, and she confided it was getting harder to get around. Born in Germany, she came to Peru in 1932 to teach in Cuzco. She teamed up Paul Kosok, an American anthropologist. Together they mapped and assessed the lines, convinced they were of some astronomical importance. When World War II broke out, people like her, of German decent, were detained in Peru, but Maria continued her work from her home in Nazca. She was a mathematician and she began to evaluate the construction of the lines with a mathematician's precision. Now, she revealed to us, she believed she had broken the construction code.

Her sight was failing, she told us as she rummaged through a pile of detailed charts; perhaps her vision was fading, but not her clarity of mind.

"Units," she said. "To measure anything we need units. Inches, meters—it doesn't matter, as long as we have units." She pointed at the chart on the table. The idea first struck her as she measured the head of the giant frigate bird, the same figure we saw two days earlier from the air. For years she had struggled with how the Nazca people created the arcs and curves so perfectly. The problem was that she just couldn't figure out the unit of measurement they used. She reached into her cardigan pocket and carefully pulled out a worn length of string. "Now," she told us, "I believe I have the answer." Maria held the string between her index finger and thumb and with her other hand stretched it across her body: 132 centimeters. "That's the primary unit. That's the basis for their measurements. All the forms and circles were somehow multiples or derivatives of this basic number," she asserted. Her mind moved with certainty as she patiently explained her theory, little arcs within arcs overlaying on her pencil drawings.

Maria joked that she often worked as a cleaning woman—a cleaning woman with a straw broom alone in the desert, sweeping the lines free of small debris. "It is an endless project," she said, "but it's the only manageable way to keep the lines intact." She mused that the locals kidded her that she was like a "witch riding out to the pampa on her broom."

We left her there in that little room, the string safely back in her pocket, hunched over the charts on her desk. As I closed the door I looked inside her little book *Mystery on the Desert* she had signed for us: *"To George and Mary Ayers, Nazca, best wishes from your friend Maria Reiche."* That morning with Maria was a moment worth remembering.

Friday: Arequipa

Our bus roared out of Nazca early this morning. It was another *autobus de lujo*, a new luxury bus, and by happenstance we'd snagged seats three and four, the front row across from the driver. The night had been cold sweater-weather, but the day held great promise. Out the front windshield a hint of the late September dawn was spreading across the desert horizon as we headed east towards the coast. For the first hour we drove through shadowed desert, between huge sand dunes and sprawling rocky wastelands illuminated by a morning sky caught somewhere between moonlight and nascent sunrise.

The sun was up by the time we closed on the Pacific and turned southward. Sunburnt soil and massive boulders led us down past the small farmland valleys of Chavina and Yauca. They were two tiny oases in the desert. Fields of onions and corn bordered the rivers that fanned out into the ocean. The cordillera swept down to the ocean's edge where the sea mists stuck against the rising slopes of flowering plants and grasses. We followed a narrow ribbon of roadway cut into its slope, with harsh rock and desert sands on one side, and precipitous drops to the rolling Pacific surf on the other.

Back in the nineteenth century, while California, the Yukon, and Australia boasted of their gold rushes with untold fortunes made, Peru bragged about bird shit. Here, along Peru's Pacific coastline, we passed hundreds of islands buried deep in white guano. Fortunes were made and lost amongst these islands. Last century, schooners plied the nearby waters, gathering nature's perfect fertilizer from the labyrinth of islands that dotted the coastline. These islands were renewable compost factories created by the millions of cormorants, boobies, and brown penguins that inhabited the area. The Humboldt Current made the water rich with plankton and fish. Below us, pelicans flopped into the water and countless flocks of piqueros circled above, squawking amid the chaos. On some islands guano was tens of feet deep, and in the days of the tall ships, even deeper. Back then all it took were strong vessels with large holds and a willing crew of anosmatic sailors. By 1875, the English-owned Peruvian Guano Company exported millions of tons of guano for the exhausted croplands of Europe.

The gold rushes petered out when the gold ran out. Guano was self-renewable. Unfortunately for the guano kings, technology and nature changed the equation. Large beds of nitrate deposits, potash, and saltpeter were being mined worldwide. It quickly replaced guano as fertilizer, and it had an added benefit as a key ingredient for explosives—which was a distinct advantage for European nations preparing for war. At the same time, something happened off the coast. The Peruvian government sanctioned anchovy overfishing. Removing anchovies changed the whole coastal food cycle. Without food, the vast bird populations migrated northward and guano production dropped. Without easy profit the trade dwindled, and like the gold rushes it just faded away.

Farther south, along the Pan-American Highway, we were blocked by drifts of blowing sand. Signs warned us: "*Zona de Arenamiento* ahead," they announced. Like snow in a Minnesota blizzard, sand piled across the highway stalling our passage. Road crews manned front-end loaders along the roadway and cut paths through the sand, allowing us to pass. The sharp, flinty sound of sand flecking off the windows continued until we curved inland and followed the sheltered curve of a deep bay inlet.

Along the water's edge we swept by little shantytowns and isolated houses on the beach. Virtually every home was constructed out of sticks and cornstalks interlaced with palm thatch and mud, their corrugated roofs strewn with tarps and tires. Wood was scarce here in the Peruvian desert. Homes and fences were built into rock facings and rubble, sheltered from the waves and wind. We suspected they were filled with fishing families that lived as close to work as possible.

We tracked the coast for hours. After a long mealtime stop in the dairy farming river valley of Camana, we passed through the fishing port of Cerillos and veered inland, climbing into the hills. Our bus wound up along steep faces cut through the passes. The road twisted upwards across iron bridges towards the high, flat pampas. Passing other vehicles around hairpin turns on these narrow mountain roads was a study in machismo—the driver's, not ours. And Mary and I had front row seats. There were few rules, but perhaps the most important turned out to be that the smaller of the two oncoming vehicles really ought to get out of the way of the bigger one, regardless of who might have the legitimate right-of-way. In case of a potential tie, use the horn. It didn't seem to matter how much roadway could be seen beyond lumbering trucks in front of us; we pulled out, honked, and passed. As the bus inched by our focus was torn between the road in front and the blank stares of the drivers we were passing. We watched help- lessly as oncoming traffic bore down at us. Making it even more exhilarating, our driver would honk, pull out, and pass on sharp hairpin curves without the slightest inkling of what was coming towards us around the bend. Countless times Mary and I held our breath and slouched down in our seats, but the driver always seemed unconcerned. Besides, he had the ultimate defense; he had the loudest horn. Somehow we always got back into our lane split seconds before catastrophe.

We climbed four thousand feet up along the Atacama Desert, broken only by the lush farmlands of the Vitor River Valley. By five that evening we had negotiated another three-thousand-foot climb and arrived up on the high Valley of the Chili River at the very edges of the cordillera of the Andes Occidentals and into the city of Arequipa.

The day had been a long one. We were up before dawn that morning, followed by a twelve-hour bus ride. The nervous energy of constantly stomping on imaginary brakes as our bus driver blindly passed in the winding hills had disappeared and was replaced with a fatigued detachment. We were tired as we made our way north up Calle Peral to Hotel Americano. Mary climbed under the covers, released a long, exhausting sigh, and lay still. I watched her for a moment, then found the lone chair in the room and sat for a while in the dark. I undressed and slid in beside her. Outside, somewhere on the street, a band was playing and people were cheering. Normally it might keep us awake, but tonight it just drifted around us.

Saturday: Arequipa

Staccato sounds of gunfire and heavy mortar rounds rattled us from sleep. *Mierda!* Shit! It sounded like it was happening just outside our hotel. In between explosions we stared at each other and then mouthed the word, "revolution." We were caught in the middle of a frigging *coup d'état.* (My journal recorded a more expressive vocabulary for our concern rather than "frigging," but my ninety-eight-year-old mom promised to read this book and she has very little latitude when it comes to the use of profanities.)

Peru had a recently turbulent political history that alternated between periods of civilian and military rule. Since 1968 the country had been under military rule. In fact, the last coup was only two years ago when General Juan Velasco Bermudez seized power. This year general strikes across the country organized by communist-inspired trade unions demanded radical social justice. The strikes and violent marches increased the friction. The unionists' stated goal was to replace what they considered a bourgeois democracy with a new democracy—whatever that meant. Military presence was ubiquitous. Everywhere we traveled there were military vehicles, armored cars, and squads of police.

When we finally gathered enough courage to peek out our door, expecting the worst, we were amazed to see the hotel manageress casually sipping tea in the colorful pasta-tiled courtyard. She just sat there cupping her tea, smiling and calmly listening to the explosions outside. Something was off. "What's happening?" we questioned. "Is it a coup?" She looked at us like we'd taken leave of our senses and shook her head in confusion.

"No es un golpe de Estado, es un fiesta nacional—Nuestra Señora de la Merced (It's not a coup, it's a national festival—Our Lady of Mercy). No need to duck," she said laughingly. The gunfire we imagined was merely fireworks and the mortar explosions were simply sky rockets. They were an invitation to an all-day party in the plaza just down the street. The manageress went back to sipping her tea. Gringos were such a strange bunch.

Lady of Mercy festivities were a weeklong affair. We had arrived on day one, the noisy kickoff. The order was created in Spain way back in the thirteenth century in an attempt to save the Christian prisoners from Muslim torture and starvation. It came to Peru with the mercenary priests who accompanied the conquistadors. The Lady has been parading around every year since. We caught up with the revelers south of our hotel close to the plaza. A large statuette of the Lady dressed in white ankle-length robes with her arms outstretched was carried on the shoulders of the devout. She rocked back and forth with the rhythm of the walkers as they made their way around the arcaded buildings that embraced the plaza, heading towards the Cathedral of the Company of Jesus. Some of the marchers wore chains and shackles, symbols of captivity, the poor, the downtrodden, and of the order itself. Their passage took them through other festival activities: craft stalls selling alpaca goods, makeshift restaurants, outdoor musicians, buskers, noisy fair rides, and hordes of people all jostling for space.

The crowd swept us along and we found ourselves under the archway of the heavy wooden doors at the entrance to the cathedral. Built shortly after the conquest, shattered by earthquakes, and rebuilt again and again, the church was an architectural moving target of mostly Jesuit influence. We stood under its incredibly intricate baroque façade made entirely of sillar, the petrified white volcanic lava that still defines the city. The mestizo artisans carved decorative romantic designs between the tall faux pillars above us.

Inside, we stared up at the polychrome cupola of the Saint Ignacio chapel. It was smothered with bright tiled murals of tropical flowers that blended with fruits and birds intermixed with warriors and angels. Mary was captivated. The color, the singsong chanting, and the familiar sweet fragrance of incense blended together in a hypnotic illusion of greater purpose and power. Slowly, we broke away from the spell of that incredible dome and walked outside.

Lunch at the San Camilo market, just a few blocks away, sounded tempting. The market was a huge, two-story square block of frenetic activity. We curled our way through the crowds amongst rows of guinea pigs ready for slaughter and down side aisles heaped with potatoes, giant avocadoes, flowers, breads, dried beans, and cheeses. We saw more varieties of potatoes than ever imagined. It was easy to get lost, and we did several times, haphazardly drifting through sections of live birds, tarot card readers, and beauty parlors. The food stalls were above us. As we approached the old concrete stairway that led up to the second floor, we were enveloped by aromas of hot grease, roasted meat, and novel culinary concoctions. Upstairs in the makeshift *comedors* we ordered what we thought were just innocent red bell peppers stuffed with a savory mixture of minced beef, raisins, garlic, and onions. The red rocoto rellenos sat invitingly on top of a big pan of pale, creamy *au gratin* potatoes. The dish looked fantastic and we each ordered a plate. Someone should have yelled, "Fire in the hole." What a shock! The innocuous-looking bell pepper turned out to be one the hottest peppers we ever ate. We both choked back tears as the heat caught up with us. We downed a second glass of leche and tried to act nonchalant as the staff snickered at our discomfort. We nibbled our way around the edges of the rocoto peppers, digging out the filling and mixing it with the potatoes. Our mouths burned. We knew what went in at some point would have to exit. We just hoped the spices would have mellowed before that happened. "Fire in the hole" could take on a completely new, and not a terribly subtle, connotation.

SILENCIO! Silence! It wasn't simply a suggestion—it was an edict, a directive carved in capital letters into the archway at the entry to the Santa Catalina Convent. The nuns of the Dominican Second Order meant business. There were fewer of them now, their numbers greatly diminished from the convent's zenith in the seventeenth century. Occasionally, we heard the quite rustle of their flowing white habits as they scurried in and around the cloisters of the adjacent living quarters. Once inside the convent, we virtually stepped back into the eighteenth century. It was a miniature town in the midst of a city. The buildings were constructed of the same white volcanic rock that gave Arequipa the nickname the White City, but the walls were bathed in painted shades of cinnamon and marigold and deep azure blue. We marveled at the simple lines of the architecture and aimlessly explored the narrow streets, the cobblestone alleyways, endless museums, and colorful plazas. It was a photographer's delight.

That night as we lay in bed we heard the staccato sounds of gunfire and the thud of heavy mortar rounds down in the plaza and smiled at our naivety.

Sunday, September 25, 1977: Arequipa

There's a certain day-to-day rhythm of traveling: accommodation, exploration, food, and transportation. But travelers need down days, too. Time to redirect thoughts, recuperate from bouts of stomach ailments, plan ahead, and just lie about; time to do nothing. This was one of those days, not tempered by great explorations or outstanding events, but rather recollections of the commonplace that constantly surrounded us. Three trivial matters caught my fancy today.

Never trust a sign in a cut-rate hotel that advertises *Agua Caliente*. Hot water was often an illusion. Water tanks were frequently nonexistent, abysmally small, or a simply a curious spider web of patched electrical wires that magically appeared out of a hole in the stall wall and attached themselves to a small immersion heater shower head. Hotel Americano had a tiny hot water tank. So when the hotel proudly boasted of hot water, what they really meant was the first person into the shower had hot water. The next person bathed in tepid water, the third shampooed with cold water, and the fourth person was shocked into a frigid state of near hypothermia by *al tiempo*—or whatever the outdoor temperature was at the time. I was fourth this morning. The water, like the air, was a frosty mid-forty degrees. Let me tell you, it's no fun showering fourth in line. As far as I could tell there was only one advantage: it was brief.

At the market, the vendor appeared a little miffed. "Of course its *pura* alpaca," our shopkeeper irritably intoned. She acted almost insulted by our question. "Don't be fooled by those other vendors who offer lower prices," she warned. Their alpaca blankets are mixed with sheep or llama wool. That's why they're cheaper. Her goods, she promised, were all woven with genuine, soft, and fine alpaca wool. It was a storyline repeated ad nauseam in every stall we visited here in the tourist section of the San Camilo market. The bottom line was that tomorrow we were headed for the high sierras, the Altiplano, with its sun-drenched days and brutally cold nights. Last night it was in the low forties, so we imagined our evenings another few thousand feet higher on the mountain plains would be even colder. We were neophytes. Neither of us knew how to distinguish pure alpaca from mixtures. All we knew was Arequipa was the center of the alpaca industry. We read that the wool from the alpaca's thin fibers meant woven clothing and blankets were warmer, lighter-weight, and softer than llama and lamb. In the end the decision was based on color, feel, and price. Mary picked the colors, I chose the softest from her selection, and we both haggled like crazy for the price. We paid seven hundred soles, or nine dollars apiece, for soft gray and yellow-patterned blankets that would keep us toasty during our voyage over the Andean passes to Puno.

For all the natural beauty and colonial architecture that surrounded us, quite frankly, Arequipa stank. Sanitation was not the uppermost item on the municipal to-do list. In the back alleys around the market we watched locals and peasants alike urinating on the walls and in the crevasses of closed doorways. Wherever we walked the side streets, dark, dried stains ran from the walls, across the sidewalks, and into the gutters. The smell of pee followed us. Was there a lack of public toilets in South America? Well actually, yes, and the scant *baños publicos* we found were fetid, soiled, and pungent. In fact, they were really just an enclosed and concentrated version of the sidewalk with additional delights of feces and soiled paper thrown in for good luck. We usually just dealt with the sanitary problem with pinched noses and eased past the pongy smell.

Monday: Arequipa to Puno

If you took a ruler, laid it over a map of Peru, and measured the distance from Arequipa to Puno it would be about a hundred miles. That's not so far if you were a bird, or if things moved in straight lines through the Andes. We weren't, and the trains didn't.

The PeruRail train station stood guard in front of the gaunt, sooty, railway yard just south of the Chili River, a brisk twenty-minute walk from our hotel. The station was a long, wooden building painted in soft yellow and chipped with age. The roofline glided out overhead to provide shelter from sun and rain. Filigreed-wrought iron braces gracefully swept up to the overhanging roof between rows of cathedral windows. It had elegance in its simplicity.

Our train boarded at seven-thirty. This time of year, PeruRail only ran it to Puno three times a week, down from the daily trips in peak season. The roads through the Andes were getting better and air flights more common. Soon enough there would come a time when train journeys would be simply an anachronism, some faded memories of old men. But today, the journey was ours. We bought a second-class ticket, threw our backpacks up in the overhead rack, gathered our blankets around us, and settled into our seats. It was a sunny 41°F out there that morning. Our tummies were already rumbling, and when the train pulled out of the station we headed to the buffet car that was just two tantalizing coaches behind us. Our five-dollar tickets didn't allow us to sit in the car, but we could bring food back.

Six weeks of lessons at Lord Twig's Language Academy back in Guadalajara Mexico last January provided us with a rudimentary Spanish language and the confidence to use it. Although, to be honest, our facile Spanish was decidedly primitive rather than conversational. We could, with great aplomb, stumble our way through virtually any situation with a barrage of mangled Spanish, which guaranteed to bring a puzzled smile to anyone who overheard us.

Verb tenses were a curse, although future tense was pretty simple. We just a put a *"voy a"* or *"vamos a"* in front of any verb, and *presto*—future tense. For example: *voy a* (I'm going to) followed by the verb to eat, to drink, to sleep, to go, to buy, or to fart. It was impressive. Everyone got it. Even we got it. However, present and past tenses and even verb meanings were constantly jumbled and intermixed with confusing results. Back in the buffet car we inquired about breakfast in a tangle of Spanish that left the staff with a look of perplexed concentration.

"We are the breakfast plate please," we buoyantly told our patient waiter. "You went to get the bacon and eggs? Oh, and I don't forgot the coffee. Thank you." It's a wonder we made it this far. In our defense, we were getting better by leaps and bounds. Our Spanish dictionary and guide to 201 Verbos de Español were already worn and dog-eared. Without a linguistic lifeline, there was an urgency to continously improve.

Back in our car, we huddled for warmth under the alpaca blankets and ate our breakfast while irrigated fields of soft alfalfa and wheat slid by. We watched as Al Misti slowly receded into the distance. The great snowcapped volcano was the heart and soul of Arequipa. It dominated the landscape and defined the city. It stood nineteen thousand feet above sea level, an incredible two miles above us as we wound our way north out of the city. The train coiled its way up the cultivated Yura Valley, across the Camara River, past the big granite plant in Yura, and then turned east and upward into the cordilleras that reached down towards us like stringy fingers from the high mountains. Through our windows to the right and left, far off at very edges of the Andean slopes, the massive twin volcanoes of Chachani and Ampato dwarfed the now-receding Misti.

The windy track seemed to wander in no discernable direction. It curved, following the contours of never-ending granite mountain slopes and deep canyons. PeruRail numbered each curve in the rail bed and we tallied them as we passed each one. By the time we reached the Altiplano, still high above us now, the little white placards we spied beside the track demarcated over seven hundred curves. The diesel engine growled as it pulled our cars forward, gaining speed on short straightaways and then slowing along each arc of rail bed. The train moved at a slow, deliberate pace, often in tight loops that backtracked our route at higher elevations, the rail bed traveling far below us. By the time we reached the tiny outpost settlement of Patahuasi we had climbed to the verge of the Altiplano with rock-strewn meadows of bunchgrass and lichen. Around us, tall rock formations stood like lonely wind-worn sentinels in a stone forest amongst the volcanic cliffs. We climbed over the next fifty miles, stopping in little pueblos with names like Sumbay, Culpa, Pucachanca, Piliones, and Vincocaya—tiny places, some no more than clusters of a few rough, earthy adobe huts nestled beside the tracks. Each one had a story, a history, and a reason for existence here on the edges of the Altiplano. There was always someone waiting to board or get off the train. But like wandering gypsies, we left each station without knowing the essence of the place. By the time we reached the gray, concrete stucco station at the summit of Cruzero Alto, we were 16,500 feet above sea level, the highest point on the wide expansive Altiplano. A frieze cut into the concrete above the weathered and wooden green station door told us we were 164 kilometers from Puno. From here all rivers flow eastward, down to the Atlantic. A short time later, we saw the first of the deep blue mountain lakes. In fact, for almost half an hour we wound between the margins of two lakes, Lagunillas and Saracocha, each ringed by low crags and visible out the opposite sides of the train. The mountainsides and canyons were dotted with llamas, alpacas, sheep, and the occasional tiny vicunas. We were like children, filled with wonderment for the first hour. We strained our heads to see every creature no matter how distant, and oohed as those near the tracks turned to watch the train pass by. As we descended down towards Juliaca, the rugged mountain scenery changed from desolate mountain peaks to fertile pampa as we stopped momentarily at the larger agricultural communities. We reached Juliaca at dusk. On the platform under vapor lights, market women spilled onto the tracks in endless layers of brightly-colored dresses, hustling equally bright knitted garments.

The train left Juliaca under a bright full moon that lit the tracks and the high pastoral countryside we traveled through. As we approached Puno and began our slow decent off the high plains to the shoreline of Lago Titicaca, the sacred lake of the Incas, moonlight reflected back at us off the cold black waters.

Puno station was a madhouse of activity. Hordes of hawkers waited at the gates and descended with full fury upon every passenger disembarking. They cried the names of hotels, restaurants, and transportation to nearby towns. No matter the situation, they promised there was an answer. They could help. We chose one taxi driver rather randomly. He looked friendly and aloof from all the others crowded around. Not much of a criterion, I suppose, but not one of the clawing hordes, either. He dropped us off at the Hotel Extra on Calle Moquegua up near the market. Of course, that's just a name. There was nothing extra about it. We got a ten-by-fifteen-foot, windowless, chipped stucco room with occasional multi-legged bugs scurrying up the walls. But it was home for the night and we gratefully crawled into bed.

Tuesday: Puno

We were eager to see the floating islands of the Uros Indians just a few miles offshore. After an early morning breakfast at the market, we headed along Avenida Del Puerto out to the docks that jutted into Lake Titicaca. Along with a group of Peruvians, Mary and I piled into a little powerboat. The old motor needed a lot of encouragement to start, but once underway our boatman puttered out into the bay. The bay was shallow and we were immediately engulfed in a forest of reeds. Small ducks, surprised by our sudden presence, splashed across the water and took flight. Our boat cut through channels cleared of totora, the marshy reed that was the lifeblood of the Uros people.

Two decades ago, the Uros were mostly isolated, preferring to remain alone on the islands, shunning visitors like us. Their entire history had been one of separation. The origins of the Uros were unknown but different from the Aymara and Quechua peoples who dominated the shorelines around the lake. Our boatman said they came from deep in the interior of Peru, and for defense and protection learned to live where others thought impossible: on the surface of the lake itself. Centuries ago their man-made floating islands offered safety and isolation from enslavement by the marauding Inca Empire and the Spanish conquest, and up until the last few years, from the proselytizing *evangelistas* and curious tourists. Our guide explained that the totora that surrounded us were the lifelines of the Uros; they used the small white tips of the reeds for food and medicine, and the long, hollow stems were woven into houses, bundled to make boats, or interlaced together to form the thirty or so small islands that ringed a wide sheltered canal.

We disembarked at a small island that supported two extended families. The women were laying down a layer of green reeds that the men had gathered from the outer edges of the lake. The light, hollow totora reeds floated on the water like corks. As sunlight aged and water rotted the plants, the island slowly sagged. Islanders constantly added new reeds. Stocks of freshly-cut reeds stood upright in piles around the perimeter. The islands' golden-brown surface gave way ever so slightly under each step, like walking on a mattress—it wasn't enough to alarm, but you knew you weren't just walking on dry land, either. In amongst the several homes was a reed chapel. It was decorated with a bag of coco leaves and a small ceramic statue of San Martin—offerings, perhaps, to an old deity and acknowledgements of new life.

The Uru men fished, hunted water birds, and even cultivated small amounts of potatoes on their reed islands. The women were consummate weavers, yet the Uros were the poorest social stratum of the area's peasant population. They had been so poor for so long that even their ancient Incan overlords demanded a simple tribute of the hollow reeds filled with rice. The Incans regarded them as *forasteros* (landless peasants) who had no communal land rights and so owed them only small amounts of tribute.

As the islanders went about their daily chores of gathering totora reeds, preparing meals, weaving, and caring for their children, I took photographs. They quietly accepted the oranges we offered in return for our intrusion into their lives.

AN OLD MAN KNEELS ON THE TOTORA, FRAMED BY
THE OPEN DOORWAY OF HIS REED HOUSE

An old man—in fact, the only man we met on this little island—
knelt on the totora, his body framed by the open doorway of his
reed house behind him. His clothes were typical of other Uros
on the island: worn to the point of being threadbare and heavily
mended. A small woven blanket pulled across his back kept him
warm from the cold wind that raked across the lake, and his matted
felt fedora shaded him from the strong rays of the high, thin air.
He was making twine. He patiently stripped the thin threads of
fiber from the reed and rolled them across his palms to create long
strands of coarse string. He worked intently and seemed oblivious
of our incursion into his space.

With her baby squirming on her hip, a young woman in her
early twenties walked up to us. She had a beautiful smile and an
excitement in her eyes that belied the harsh life she lived. Her jet-
black hair outlined a rounded face with dark mottled cheekbones
that had a fresh but wind-burned look.

URU MOTHER AND CHILD ON A SMALL FLOATING ISLAND IN LAKE TITICACA

"I'd like an orange too," she said meekly, smiling broadly and gesturing for us to take a photo. Her child wore a colorful woolen *chullo* tuque, which he continuously tried to remove. The kid wanted no part of these strangers and thrashed about to make his mom aware of his feelings in no uncertain terms.

An age-old woman—perhaps the matriarch of the island, since all of our tributes of fruit and vegetables seemed to be handed over to her—watched us carefully outside the closed doorway of her reed house. She spun llama fleece onto a little wooden drop spindle. Just in front of her, firestones ringed a blackened clay cooking pot for the *carache*, the small lake fish sun-drying on mats around her.

We visited three islands that morning. The second held another small communal family group much like the first, but the third contained a grouping of ten homes with at least fifty people. The island location was central enough to support a school. The only caveat was, like the island itself, the school floated too.

ESCUELA FLOTANTE ADVENTISTA, A FLOATING SCHOOL
ANCHORED AT THE EDGE OF A REED ISLAND

La Escuela Flotante Adventista was a floating school anchored at the edges of Santa Maria, the largest of the floating islands we visited in Lake Titicaca. The school opened just eleven years ago in April 1966 with sixteen students. It was a gift from the Seventh-day Adventists, an American faith-based Christian group that relished the idea of converting the false believers. Nowadays, the structure was a fully accredited primary school. Current enrollment exceeded thirty, with students in programs from kindergarten to the primary grades.

Children were the same world over. While the girls gathered and giggled, the boys roughhoused and shoved. They goaded each other closer to the edge of the reeds. A totora-reed boat poled into the island beside the corrugated gray metal school and dropped off another boy dressed in a blue sweater, which was the formal school uniform. He came from a nearby island and just made it to shore before the teacher came out of the school and waved in the children. It was time to start the lessons.

"Get 'um young," was the Seventh-day Adventists' motto. Why wait to convert the godless pagans to the true way—praise the Lord—when you could start with the youngest, most pliable minds? The school was both a blessing and a curse: a blessing in that it provided the basics of an education to a population isolated from the mainland school system, and a curse in that the true reason for the school wasn't really education. It never was. Education was secondary. The main reason was an excuse for the Seventh-day Adventists to strip the Uros of their cultural beliefs and convert them to the true faith and deliver them, blessings be upon Him, from their evil ways. One Adventist was still concerned that there were Uros who still didn't know God's saving grace.

"They follow the pagan religion of their ancestors," he told us, "praying to spirits for solace and guidance. It was the Adventists' mission to bring them into the embrace of the "one true God and shine light into their eternal darkness." Children would be the best candidates for the Kingdom. In addition to the basic Spanish primer equivalent of Dick and Jane and the repetitive one plus one equals two, the evangelists taught these fledgling newcomers to the faith that the Catholic Church was the Whore of Babylon, the Pope was the antichrist, and that listening to music, playing cards, dancing, and reading anything non-religious was inappropriate and bordered on sinful. These little children playing on the reeds at the water's edge had so much to learn.

It's not that American fundamentalists had any monopoly on sharing their distaste of the Uros' traditions. Way back at the time of the conquest, a Mercedarian friar, Martin de Murua, observing that the Uros ate sundried but raw fish, duck, and herbs, condemned them as being a "bestial, brutish, and uncivilized people." He proclaimed that "Eating raw food was a sin that needed to be reported in confession." Apparently the good Friar liked his steak well done.

I've always felt uncomfortable with some Christian missionaries in impoverished countries like Peru, the proselytizers who selfishly offered material inducements and sometimes the very basics of life—food, shelter, and education—to those who were willing to convert to their proffered faith. It seemed egocentric and petty and contrary to the whole Christian Good-Samaritan ethic of offering help without reward. So that day I found myself somewhat repulsed by what was happening to the youngsters on these small reed islands, and indeed, felt challenged not only by this current crop of scheming evangelists and those cruel friars of the past, but by the very precepts of religion itself.

Wednesday: Puno and Sillustani

The old bus rattled along at a snail's pace up the winding road out of Puno. In addition to ourselves, it was packed with locals and one chatty Australian. We were backtracking to visit the market at Juliaca some thirty miles north of Puno. As we climbed out of the city and approached the flatlands above the town, the wide expanse of Lake Titicaca spread out below us. Out our open window we watched the panorama of the lake with its massive reed banks and the distant floating islands of the Uros. Occasional reed boats poled through the maze of channels. Then, as we plateaued up onto the highlands, the lake disappeared behind us.

The early morning train from Puno to Juliaca ran beside us. Leaving town, the track bed had skirted closer to the lake, but now up here on the pampa we ran parallel only a few hundred feet apart. The train pulled ahead of us out of the Quechua town of Paucarcolla, its big air horn blasting a warning at every crossing. We could see it in the distance and we were gaining again. Up ahead, somewhere along the stretch of road between Paucarcolla and the next village of Caracola, we watched as another bus on a dirt side road perpendicular to the tracks rumbled along, throwing up a big dusty plume. The bus was headed towards the road we were on. To get to the roadway intersection it needed to cross the tracks. We heard the distant, continuous train horn signaling a warning, but the other bus driver didn't hear, or he simply chose to ignore the oncoming train. The train wasn't slowing and

neither was the bus. Neither seemed fazed by the impending possibility of a collision. Machismo: you've got a love it. Neither the
driver nor the engineer was giving way. We watched in horror as
the bus accelerated and headed across the tracks. Screw it; he was
going to beat the train. The bus just about made it across the tracks
before the train barreled through, but "just about" wasn't quite
good enough; the train ticked an edge of the back bumper and
the bus skidded upright diagonally across the road and stopped. It
wasn't a catastrophe, but you couldn't get much closer to one. The
train engineer never slowed to see what damage was done. What
was behind him was behind him and no longer his problem. Like
the engineer, our bus driver never changed speed as we passed the
intersection—although he did open the front door to get a better
look. Unperturbed, the train was still moving up ahead towards
Juliaca. Back behind us, in the stationary bus, I suspected every
solitary passenger was finally exhaling and wishing they'd had the
foresight to bring a change of underwear along with them.

We were tempted back to Juliaca by bowler hats and petticoats.
Virtually every Quechua or Aymara woman wore a felt bowler
hat, or as they called it, their *bombin*. It had been a traditional
part of their dress since the early 1920s, when women mimicked
the British railway workers who wore them. The bowler was the
perfect chapeau for the Altiplano women. The narrow, curved
brim shielded them from the sun and the deep crown assured
their hat didn't blow off with the stiff, blustery wind that swept
across the Andean plains. The decorative bands that festooned the
crown indicated marital status: brown (sorry, but I'm married);
black (I'm widowed); and white (take a better look, I'm single).

Just how many layers of clothing Andean plateau women wore
remained a mystery. Like a game, Mary and I looked carefully and

estimated the number of colorful skirts and blouses. Judging by
the girth of the women we saw in the market, they either dressed
in multiple layers or there were no thin women on the Altiplano.
We suspected the former. The air was crispy cold when the women
arrived at the market in the morning, but by midday it was
temperate and even a little on the warm side in the direct sun.
Towards evening it chilled again. So the women dressed for every
weather eventuality.

The collectivo we took back from Juliaca dropped us off at a
wide footpath that led up to the tall, cylindrical rock towers. It
was only 65 °F, but the afternoon sun warmed our backs as we
climbed along the red dirt path up to the crest at Sillustani. The
funerary towers of Sillustani dominated the high north peninsula
of Lago Umayo. The peninsula protruded out into the lake like a
giant rat's head with its ears flopped back, a thousand feet across
and two thousand feet long. The deep blue Altiplano sky arched
overhead. We could see forever: beyond the lake below and up the
rock-fenced banks of the far shore, across the endless sweep of the
Altiplano bordered by distant mountains. That's the way it was up
here in the high sierra plains. The rarified air was clean and crisp,
devoid of the soot of cities, dust of the desert, and the dark belch-
ing haze of diesel engines. Up here we were given a new piercing
clarity of vision, the common countryside suddenly awash in the
minutest detail. Distant mountains didn't simply fade into the
distant landscape; they stood there bold, clear, and defiant, taunt-
ing us to reach out and touch them.

Mary and I walked amongst the stone towers. Some were simply
latticed stones piled like arctic igloos, others tall majestic cylinders formed with intricate, pre-Incan stonework. The funerary
towers were from different eras, but served the same purpose:

repositories of the wealthy and famous of their times. Virtually all the towers and clusters of smaller burial *chulpas* had been looted for valuables over the centuries but burial chambers had been discovered during excavation of the few that remained intact. Those that remained stood proud and defiant after centuries of neglect, silhouetted against that brilliant blue sky. The area was littered with unending ceramic pottery shards, their faded geometric designs still visible after a thousand years.

Thursday: Puno to Cuzco

The two Argentine students who joined us for the seven-hour collectivo ride to Cuzco were running away. They were young, in love, and frightened. They had fled north through the high mountain plains of Argentina and slipped into Bolivia near the quiet border town of La Quiaca. Now they were on the move, desperate for the temporary sanctuary of Peru and with an idyllic dream of refuge in America. Two bulging suitcases on the roof rack were what remained of their life back home. They were running from Argentina's state-sponsored terrorism: the Dirty War.

A few years ago in Argentina, kidnappings, bombings, and assassinations by frustrated, left-wing radicals under the umbrella of The People's Revolutionary Army were commonplace. The Marxists attacked military installations and police. The military responded with equally murderous attacks on suspected leftists. The PRA ramped up the ante with bombings and violent armed attacks on buses, shops, banks, and restaurants. Last year, Isabel Peron, Argentina's President, authorized her annihilation decrees, the state-sanctioned murder of left-wing subversives.

Peron turned the military loose on them and then merely turned her back on the outcome. There were thousands dead and missing. Unionists and students were caught in an ideological whiplash as the politics ripped from far right to far left and back again. Then, just seven months ago, this past March, Peron was put under house arrest and ousted by a military coup. But the violence didn't stop; it escalated. The new junta closed Congress, and Argentina's elected government set up hundreds of clandestine detention centers throughout the country and then rounded up, jailed, and persecuted tens of thousands of its citizens. They zeroed in on trade unionists, student protesters, intellectuals, and human rights activists. By the time they were done, over thirty thousand were dead and missing. The Dirty War was a policy of genocide. The military governor of Buenos Aires, General Ibérico Saint-Jean, described the new ruling ideology as "first we kill all the subversives, then we'll kill their collaborators, then their sympathizers, later those who remain indifferent, and finally we will kill the timid." It was a terrifying admission, but the military regime was supported by the financial might of America, and its victims were unnoticed collateral in a global struggle of economic ideologies.

The Cold War was at its zenith. America and the Soviets were battling it out around the world: the capitalist imperialists against the godless commies. Fifteen years ago, four hundred miles off the coast of Cuba, they stood toe-to-toe, face-to-face and tested each other's resolve. The United States had secretly installed nuclear-tipped missiles in Turkey and Italy. The Soviet Union retaliated by attempting to set up missile sites in Cuba. The world stood still and held its collective breath while those two big boys, Kennedy and Khrushchev, blustered, blockaded, and generally threatened each other with total thermonuclear annihilation.

There was nothing more worrisome than two paranoid nations armed to the teeth with atomic weapons standing flat-footed and jabbing rhetorical fingers into each other's chest. Fortuitously, intelligence prevailed and political back channels between the two super powers resolved the Cuban conflict. Instead of war, each country promised to decommission and withdraw the missiles, the USSR overtly from Cuba, and the USA covertly from Turkey. Both countries recognized they had come within a hairsbreadth of disaster. Now, in the late seventies, instead of direct confrontation, they fought proxy wars and pressured governments within their sphere of influence: the Soviet Union in Eastern Europe, and the United States in Central and South America. Over the last decade, South America's industrialization and modernization came with a price tag. Foreign money and foreign corporate ownership filled the vacuum of the old colonial empires. Throughout South America, foreign capital and foreign ownership meant American money and dominance. The new land and business owners, their bankers, and government officials got wealthy and the workers got exploited. Market efficiencies gave way to large farms and forced thousands of small subsistence farmers off their land. Small local industry fell to larger, more competitive transnational ones. The unemployed and landless streamed into the cities looking for work and shelter. They rarely found it there. That was how unbridled capitalism worked. It was also how the radical left and revolutionaries recruited the disenfranchised and the desperate. The strongest instinct of the powerless is a compelling hatred of the powerful.

Our friends sitting behind us on our collectivo snuggled together, alone and frightened but free. They spoke in whispers as if lost in another place, another world. It was a world unthinkable to us, but one alarmingly prescient to both of them. The horrors and the heartbreak flowed farther behind them with every passing mile.

Collectivos, privately-owned passenger vans like the one we were on, were an economical way the locals got around. They were cheaper than taking a train or bus but they were passenger-dependent. The vans only ran when fully loaded with paying passengers. That meant that besides driving a fixed route, collectivos stopped any place and any time that someone signaled them down. Usually no matter how full, the driver could squeeze one more person on board. Up here on the Altiplano, fares included luggage, sacks of produce, critters heading out to or home from the market, and any number of other malodourous items stored up on the roof—or, more likely, in passengers' laps. It also meant if too many passengers got out at any one stop, the driver would pretty much stay put until the van filled with enough passengers to make it profitable to move on. So, unlike buses or trains, long-distance collectivos were often a bit of a crapshoot as to arrival time. Nonetheless, our driver was confident we'd be hoisting Pilsen beer in the ancient Incan capital of Cuzco by dusk.

Stones rattled off the undercarriage and a plume of dust bellowed out behind our collectivo as we drove along the packed gravel road across the Altiplano. A small river snaked alongside our route, meandering down through the flat high plains of endless, coarse grasslands. Alpacas and llamas framed by terraced foothills and distant snow-peaked mountains watched us with a detached curiosity. Local shepherd womenfolk spun wool or knitted, squatting in the scant shade of ancient stone fences that traced up from our roadway. Our collectivo frequently stopped to discharge or gather more passengers from little villages with narrow streets and brown adobe houses with rust-colored tiled roofs capped with broken pottery. A few hours out, those distant mountains closed in around us, squeezing down into the valley to the edges of the road. We stopped at the fourteen-thousand-foot summit of the La Raya mountain range with its peaks shrouded in mist and rain. The four of us stood for a moment in the eerie silence, staring into nothingness, the only sound the occasional metallic click of the van's cooling engine. We all climbed back in and began our descent into the fertile plains of the Cuzco Valley. All about us, agricultural terracing backlit by the dying sun left scars that wandered high into the mountains, the rock rises and long runs of crops accentuated on each step. The mountains towered over the deep valley and shadowed the Vilcanota River that flowed alongside us. Near the colonial town of Huambutio, the river plunged sharply into a deep gorge before it widened into the great Urubamba canyon. It was dusk as we approached the apex of the Watanay River Valley and Cuzco, which was surrounded by a knot of mountains and shielded from the harshest of the Andean winds. Our collectivo driver dropped our Argentine friends and us at the Plaza de Armas in the historic center of Cuzco, just alongside the great doors of the Santo Domingo Church. We hugged and bade them good luck, threw on our packs, and began the uphill trudge along the cobblestoned Calle Saphi to Hostal Familiar.

Friday: Cuzco

Cuzco's Plaza de Armas, the city's heart, laid down the cobbled street before us. In the cold valley sunlight on this flawless late September morning the plaza seemed like the perfect setting for the capital, the epicenter of the Incan realm. It was anchored by the great cathedral and bounded by adobe, stone, and red-tiled buildings that flowed through myriads of narrow streets and up onto the surrounding hillsides. It wasn't always so. In early Incan myth, the world was covered with darkness until the great god Viracocha emerged from Lake Titicaca, creating the sun (Inti), moon, and stars to light the world before sending forth a handful of humans into that new land. It was from that great light—Inti— that the first of the Incan emperors, the original Sapa Inca, was descended. Incan myth also foretold of a homeland where a sacred golden staff could be easily driven deep into the earth. Centuries later, the Inca, under command of another emperor, Manco Capac, migrated down the Cuzco Valley and, at the site of present-day Cuzco, drove the staff deep into the soil of the prom- ised land. But before they could make this valley their home, the Inca needed to defeat and subjugate the people who had originally claimed it: the Chankas.

The city was constructed on an ancient glacial lakebed sur- rounded by mountain peaks and laid out around the conflu- ence of three high Andes Rivers: the Huatanay, Tullumayo, and Chunchul. Cuzco may have begun centuries before, but it truly started to coalesce into a city befitting an empire under the reign of the ninth Sapa Inca, Pachacuti, in the 1400s. Swamplands to the north were drained and the heart of the city, where we stood now, took shape. The fortification of Sacsayhuaman, the north- ern defense perimeter, was constructed. Coricancha, the sacred complex dedicated to the highest gods in the Incan pantheon, was expanded, the massive walls of the complex built from large stone blocks finely cut and fitted together without mortar. A broad band of gold ran head-high, adorning the walls, and hundreds of thick, pure golden sheets covered the doors, interiors, and exteriors of the temples, and (if rumors were true) emeralds studded the inside walls. It was a city of immense wealth when Pizarro found it.

Now, the city embraced three cultures: Colonial Spanish, Quechua, and a contemporary, more cosmopolitan society, all intertwined. Music, architecture, language, and culture flowed together and sometimes collided headlong into a heady clash of the traditional and modern.

We felt it as we walked the narrow, cobblestoned backstreets and stopped beside a group of Quechua musicians playing huayno, a style of music so common up there in the central Andes. The melodies were simple and haunting. The hollow reed of the panpipe flute, the strings of the charango mandolin, and the wooden, half-pear sounding box and inlaid neck of the domingacha harp created the sounds of wind, strings, and percussion that echoed off the masonry stone walls of the ancient buildings around us. The songs, created from pipes of different sizes and tunings, were not soft or melodious, but rather wild and disputatious. After hearing this diabolically-inspired pagan music, you could imagine those early Christian friars troubling at these lost souls. Like early rock 'n' roll was to our parents, huayno was the devil's music to the friar's ears.

Back down near the main plaza, amid the clutter of small tiendas and restaurants, music stores with humungous speakers dragged to the front entrances blasted modern Cumbia tunes from groups like *Los Demonios del Peru* (The Demons of Peru) at full volume. Full of electric guitars, drum sets, and bassline riffs, Cumbia—or Chicha, as it was locally named—was the modern counterweight to the old traditional music. It incorporated some elements of huayno and then overwhelmed them with sheer volume. Cumbia was the music of the young and rebellious. Teenagers flicked through racks of cassette tapes, oblivious to the loud, chest-pounding, distorted bass coming from the cheap speakers that surrounded them.

Architecture was another of those contradictions that seemed overlaid. The central square, the Plaza de Armas, was the cultural center of the city. Up cobbled streets, radiating out from the plaza, and hidden behind tall, whitewashed adobe walls were the old colonial and red-tile-roofed homes, shops, and residences. They were mostly of Spanish influence with a graceful, flowing style that harkened of bygone times. The plaza was ringed with arched porticos overhung with wooden balconies. It was all so profoundly Galician. Beyond the north end of the plaza, far up on a distant hillside over a skim of roofs, stood the single tower of the San Cristobal church. In front of us, anchoring the square, were the great rival churches of Cuzco. One was the ornate Cathedral Basilica of the Assumption of the Virgin, with its huge main altarpiece carved in cedar wood and draped in gilded gold. Its renaissance façade was conjoined with the Iglesia del Triunfo, the earliest church on the square that was built just a few years after the conquest. Across the street was the Catholic's Jesuit competitor, the Company of Jesus.

Like every church in the area, they were built with stones pilfered from Sacsayhuaman or other Incan sites, and like every church, they were built on the foundations of existing Inca religious or government buildings. The church was never adverse in benefiting from the emotive power of pagan customs and places, even if it needed to be seen officially as distancing itself from them.

We visited the Church of Santo Domingo, built on the foundation and from the stones of the Inca holy site Coricancha, which had been gifted to the city by a dying Pizarro. Twenty-seven years ago in 1950, an earthquake here in Cuzco sent much of the Convent of Santo Domingo church crashing to the ground, exposing the Inca Temple of the Sun after centuries of being hidden. There, amongst the church-rubble, it stood virtually intact. The Spaniards built graceful, ornate structures, but many like Santo Domingo were hard-pressed to withstand the rigors of time and nature.

The tremors revealed a new appreciation for the great stonemasons of the Inca. Yet again, that cultural contradiction somehow found harmony. There was a power to the simple Inca stonework. As we ran our fingers along the stones that walled the House of the Chosen Women and the Palace of the Serpents, Mary and I both felt a visceral conduit to an earlier era and imagined a personal connection to that long-past civilization. Those stones relayed a potent force to all who reached out and touched them.

We walked the unassuming and narrow street of Hatun Rumiyok to perhaps the most prominent creation of all the Incan masonry, the twelve-angled stone. What amazed everyone about the Inca stonework was the precision cutting and shaping of huge granite blocks that were so finely fitted together without mortar. They simply sat like a giant jigsaw puzzle joined with gravity, the hewn edges so finely carved that even my knife blade couldn't slide between the blocks. I have no idea what lay behind the front edges of the stone. For all I knew, rough-cut rubble held all these walls in place and the only pure fit was the facing I ran my hand across. It didn't matter. These stone walls represented a powerful statement of the skill of the Incan masons.

Over the course of the day we wandered about Cuzco, up stone stairways in narrow roadways, down cobbled streets under tiled roofs, and past llamas shepherded by colorfully-dressed Quechua women. It was indeed an enchanting place well worthy of the Incan capital.

Saturday: Cuzco

We were warned about thieves in the San Pedro Market. Fellow travelers, locals, and even our *South American Handbook* all cautioned us to stay vigilant. The pickpockets were becoming audacious, more numerous, and better at their craft. Practice makes perfect, and the growing tourist population here in Cuzco gave them ample opportunity to hone their trade.

Inside, the narrow isles were bottlenecked with vendors, shoppers, farmers, chefs, and shamans who were each part of the market hierarchy. There was an established pecking order of inside versus outside, permanent versus makeshift stalls, and all were a stratum above those with their wares simply scattered around on the floor. The market was a bit like stepping into Aladdin's cave, full of rows of exotic herbs and spices, piles of strange produce (which included an infinite variety of potatoes), and a section of newly slaughtered animals whose heads, intestines, and innards swung on metal hooks, intermixing with the mysterious cooking odors wafting from small makeshift kitchens. It was crowded, noisy, chaotic, and the perfect setting for pickpockets.

Our pockets were usually empty with the exception of a few coins and the odd tissues. I kept my passport, traveler's checks, and money in a pouch looped to my belt and securely tucked down inside the front of my jeans. Mary did the same with a cotton pouch that knotted around her neck and hung down past her navel, tucked under her shirt. However, we were the only ones who knew this.

Peru was a country of abject poverty with a tiny elite society of economic predators that controlled virtually all of the country's resources. A few people controlled the power while most lived in poverty or, at the very least, rode on the rough edges of subsistence. On a purely intellectual level we understood why desperate people might find mischievous ways to exist, but the reality of being targeted and robbed was an entirely different experience.

There are probably hundreds of different techniques good pickpockets use, from deception, deflection, to bump-and-grab. But here in the San Pedro Market they seemed to work in pairs or groups and virtually all set up the ruse using the same system. Someone, a vendor or passing local, engaged us in conversation, usually by waving an unbelievable bargain in our faces. The aisle was always crowded as folks jostled to get past, bumping and shoving their way through the knot of people. The distraction, however momentary, gave ample time for the swift action of a wandering hand to inspect the inside of my pocket. It was usually quick. They were good, but having been forewarned, we were on high alert. Three times I caught thieves in my pockets. The first two—young boys, maybe twelve or thirteen—each got a reflexive elbow in the head and a dirty look. I caught the third, a teenager, with his hand still in my pocket. I grabbed the kid's wrist and held on, yelling "*ladrón, ladrón*" (thief, thief) at the top of my lungs. He pulled himself free but I followed him down the aisle shouting invectives at his backside as vendors laughed at the lad's misfortune to get caught. It was all jolly good fun, a diversion from the usual market action. But I was really annoyed and vowed revenge. In my imagination, I was determined to make certain that the next pickpocket paid dearly for his deeds. Over lunch in a market *cocina* I unfolded my strategy to Mary. I would sew a double-edged razor blade into my pocket and then just stroll around the market and wait. The next pickpocket would get the surprise of his life. "Whaddaya think?" I asked. I got that look husbands all around the world feared getting, an expression somewhere between disgust and discovering that she just might have married a raving psychopath.

"That's about the stupidest thing I've ever heard," she retorted. "You know what's going to happen? You're going to forget you sewed it in there, you're going to be the one to reach down to get something out of your pocket, and I'm going to be the one that has to take you to the hospital for stitches." She shook her head and turned back to her meal, leaving me to stew in my own devious machinations.

Sunday, October 2: Cuzco

Charlemagne, my little sister's pet guinea pig, was a miniature bundle of white- and caramel-colored fluff. Any time one of the family entered the room, Charlemagne's ears would suddenly animate and she'd let out a blast of short, wheeky sounds. Often after school, sis sat contentedly watching television with Charlemagne snuggled in her lap, the little critter purring and grunting away in pleasure. That was years ago. I only mention this because this evening we were drawn to try the infamous local delicacy—*cuy chactado*, the Spanish equivalent of roast guinea pig. There's a certain amount of bravado after downing a few jugs of beer and being goaded on by fellow travelers. So, with courage up and good sense obviously flagging, a bunch of us threaded our way along the cobbled side streets until we found a dodgy-looking *picanteria* with racks of skewered cuy cooking over white-hot coals.

We had seen live caged cuy in the San Pedro Market. Like a production line, someone would reach in, grab a cuy by the head, and just flick it, snapping the neck and killing it instantly. After a couple of deft cuts it was skinned like a rabbit, the fur slipping off like a glove. Once skinned someone sliced the throat and bled it out. Then the mouth was cut open and the critter gutted and washed in a plastic bucket of trickling water and skewered through and through. It was all matter-of-fact. No emotion—just idle chatter as they prepared the animal for roasting.

With other animals we'd eaten, what arrived on the plate no longer resembled the original proprietor of the body, whether it was a cow, pig, or chicken. There were no childhood memories attached to them, no sense of guilt, they were just things we called steaks or roasts or bacon or chops or drumsticks. Nothing—*nada*. No resemblance and no memories whatsoever. Those beasts we ate had already been processed, nicely packaged in neat little tubs wrapped in clear plastic with a price tag that told you how much it cost and how much you were buying, and then they were served on a plate with French fries. That sure wasn't the case with our little cuy. There was just no getting around it. No matter how much beer we downed, our guinea pig looked just like a crispy-critter version of Charlemagne, and it was sitting on a plate in front of me with its four legs splayed out as if it had been cruelly inter-rogated on some medieval torture rack.

"Turn that bloody thing around so it isn't staring at me," Mary scowled as she elbowed me in the ribs. "It gives me the creeps." Its little head—with its eyes burnt black, whiskers scorched and pointing in odd directions, and its mouth agape with two little front teeth—stared uncompromisingly and intimidatingly at her. "Move it," she commanded. I turned it so it faced across the table and ignored the throaty sounds of my tablemates as they viscerally connected with the roasted face. Now all I had to do was eat it.

Cuy wasn't some delicacy. It was perhaps *the* protein staple up here in the Andean countries. So it wasn't like only a few people ate it. It was everyday food for folks. That fact didn't offer any solace as I reached down, broke off a hind leg, and pinched off some meat. The most difficult part was actually putting it in my mouth. It smelled wonderful, but the skin was crispy and the meat was the color of the dark meat from a turkey leg. In fact, that's close to what it tasted like—although it was maybe a touch more exotic, so you knew you weren't sitting around your standard Thanksgiving Day table. The delicate bones made eating a slow process and it was only by a newfound intestinal fortitude bolstered by a seemingly endless supply of *bebidas alcohólica* that I finished off the little critter. No matter how much prompting from the server, I just couldn't crack open the head and eat the brains. I didn't care if it was, as he put it, the *"best part"*—there was no way I could even begin to rationalize making the obscene into something palatable. I had limits.

Later, lying in bed as I slipped somewhere between dreams and foggy consciousness, I struggled with visions of Charlemagne's cute, wiggly nose and the blackened gaping eyes of my last meal.

Monday: Cuzco to Machu Picchu

We reached the San Pedro train station across from the market on Cascaparo Street just after daybreak. The morning sky was clear and the air was bitterly cold, just above freezing. It was early, but already the station platform and the street in front of it were frenetic. In addition to the usual melee of vendors, we had pushed our way through a blockade of placards and angry shouts from striking rail workers who lined the station front. Theirs was a universal cry; they wanted more money, better working conditions, and shorter hours. PeruRail's response to their strike was to bring in the military. The army ringed the station and kept the protesters off the platform and away from the early morning passengers and curious tourists. Armed soldiers operated the train. As we slouched in our seats we wondered whether our new khaki-clad, gun-toting conductor would punch our tickets or simply fire a slug through them.

A few minutes out of the station the train began its steep run up Picchu, one of the high hills that surrounded the city. At each of the four switchbacks, soldiers disembarked, manually racked the switches as we alternately shunted forward, and then reversed up each of the steep inclines. We watched as Cuzco spread out below us, a wide panorama of whitewashed adobe walls and sway-backed, rusty-colored roofs surrounded by sprawling, worn red hills until we reached El Arco and the remnants of an ancient Spanish viaduct at the summit. Then we began our long, slow, sixty-mile decent along the Huallaga valley to the base of Machu Picchu and the Puente Ruinas railway station nearly four thousand feet below Cuzco.

There weren't many tourists on the early train. When we reached Puente Ruinas we all surged forward and shoehorned into one small minibus. Mary giggled with nervous excitement as we crossed over the river and up onto the five miles of the twisting, switch-backed Hiram Bingham roadway. The engine snarled in protest while at each of the fourteen turns we crossed back over the Camino de Herradura footpath, the original mule track that led up the mountain face. This morning there were only a couple of ardent climbers determined to make the ascent on foot. The rest of us smugly watched them disappear from view. We'd reach the summit in twenty minutes; they'd take an hour or more. As we wove back and forth, the valley floor dropped out from beneath us. At the top, while others dashed to the site entrance, Mary and I headed for the old government-run tourist hotel and checked in. Built in the late 1940s as a place for traveling VIPs, it had morphed over the years from a fancy hotel into a rundown wooden building on the cusp of being demolished. The hotel was small, with only eighteen rooms and beds for thirty-two tourists. We dropped our backpacks in our tiny room, locked the door, and rushed outside to explore.

Alone, Mary and I strode the last couple hundred yards from the veranda of the tourist hotel to the gates of Machu Picchu, under the archway, and then up the long, stone steps to the summit. Before us lay the summer home of Pachacuti, ninth emperor of the Incan dynasty.

It wasn't the thin, high mountain air that took our breath away. Those stone steps led us up to a place unlike any other on earth. We were overcome by the vision spread out before us; a purely mystical embodiment of space, time, setting, and silence. Up here the noise of our fellow travelers was strangely absent, muffled beneath a cloak of quiet that permeated the mountaintop city. No one was immune. In that first view, in that first moment, every visitor absorbed the essence of Machu Picchu in reverent stillness. In 1944, in his twelve-part epic poem *The Heights of Machu Picchu*, the remarkable Chilean poet Pablo Neruda declared, as he stood on this same spot, that this stone fortress "was the tallest crucible that ever held our silence." He was right. What meager words could we ever cobble together to express the imagery of this moment?

We angled towards the Temple of the Sun, along the dusty, trodden pathway, amid tiers of agricultural terraces that ascended and descended above and below. The walkway was beaten smooth by a million visitors who came before us. Like those past visitors and the countless millions who would follow in our path, we felt as much as saw the city unfold. The city of gray-white granite was architecturally powerful and geographically staggering, suspended on a vast saddle between two great peaks and set against a backdrop of lush green mountains that spiked up from the deep ravines of the Urubamba Valley. Machu Picchu was dominant, incorruptible, and massively powerful. Hidden from sight on its mountain perch, it survived the gold lust of Pizarro's marauding conquistadors, the capricious whims of Christianity, and even the violence of nature itself. Now perhaps its greatest hazard was modern curiosity.

There was a gravitational force that drew us to a rise above the *Plaza Sacrada* (the Sacred Plaza). The Intihuatana—"the hitching post to the sun," an enormous granite ritual stone sculpted out of the peak of the mountain saddle—was the enigmatic center of the city. It sat elevated above the Sacred Plaza, overlooking the Valley of San Miguel with Urubamba winding below, framed to the north by the massive peak of Huayna Picchu. Incan carvers had shaped it into three steps that led to a rectangular stone pillar at its center. While Mary, lost in thought, sat on one of the steps that led on to the flat, stone platform, I ran my hand along the cold, granite sun pillar that rose skyward from the surface. It was smooth and warming up in the morning sunlight. For a moment I could imagine the High Priest of the Sun caught in some abyss of time, arms upraised, wrapped in ceremonial robes and towering over me, his chest adorned with sun discs of beaten gold, summoning the sun on some past equinox morning. In that brief, mystical moment, through the power of this very stone and at the priest's command, *Tayta Inti*, the great sun, stayed tethered to *Pachamama*, mother earth, and for a moment, stopped its northward movement in the sky. It was a moment repeated throughout Incan history and across the reaches of the empire at each spring and fall equinox, directing the planting and harvest.

The sun god was a common thread within Incan mythology, and the Intihuatana a central construct to that belief. Early on, the Spanish realized this ceremonial stone held such sway over the lives of those they chose to convert that they destroyed every Intihuatana within their reach. How could the Catholic priests allow these great altars to remain intact? After all, it was their Christian God, no one else's, who created heaven and earth and then said, "Let there be light, and there was light." Through these stone altars, the locals believed they had the ability to stop the very creation of God himself in its tracks and hitch the power of the sun to the earth. The Intihuatana was heresy. If their idolatrous ways were seen as more powerful than God's will, these great ceremonial stones must be destroyed. Once broken, all its power to bind the sun at the Incan priest's command was released and gone forever. Once broken the stone could never hold that authority again. Very few altars survived the Spanish. One of the few that were spared was the sacred Intihuatana, hidden here at Machu Picchu.

Beyond the Intihuatana, the ruins of Machu Picchu contained staircases, terraces, temples, tombs, palaces, fountains, and towers. We explored them all, guidebook in hand, poking through doorways, wandering grass flatland, climbing stone stairways, always inspired. Machu Picchu was more than the sum of its parts, more than simply the agricultural district with its terraces. It was more than the urban district with its irrigation canals, fountains, and staircases that led from building to building, more than the simple setting of the Temple of Sun with its exquisite, circular wall and ritual stones. Machu Picchu exuded synergy. No matter where we sat, no matter what we explored we were forcibly drawn back to the sum of the whole, that majestic vista, and the words of Pablo Neruda.

MACHU PICCHU WAS ARCHITECTURALLY POWERFUL

AND GEOGRAPHICALLY STAGGERING

Tuesday: Machu Picchu

A light mist skimmed across the cradle of Machu Picchu this morning, cloaking the surrounding mountain peaks in a gauzy white haze. It was lifting early, evaporating in the morning sunlight. Above us, up a stone stairway, a lone llama framed by an ancient gate grazed quietly, unperturbed by our presence.

No other travelers had ventured out so early and the guards had simply smiled and looked the other way as we edged past them. In silence and alone we retraced our steps along the terraces, past the Temple of the Sun, through the Sacred Plaza, and under the faint shadow of the Intihuatana. Like an apparition, Huayna Picchu appeared and vanished in the mists that hovered and swirled above us. We caught ephemeral glimpses of its steep mountain walls and the sharp razorback that linked the royal city to its massif face. Over the next hour we investigated and explored our way through the city to the giant Sacred Stone that guarded the mountain, Huayna Picchu, which was now bathed in sunlight, its slopes awash in infinite shades of jungle green. A small, handwritten and weatherworn wooden arrow pointed us to the narrow pathway that led to the cavern-like Temple of the Moon perched near the summit.

Ahead of us, as we maneuvered our way down across the razorback ridge that linked the city to Huayna Picchu, the sheer walls of the mountainside looked impassible. Disjointed, spidery trails crisscrossed the face as we cautiously picked our way along the narrow stone steps still wet and slippery with cloud condensate. On either side our trail fell away precipitously, fifteen hundred feet down to the valley floor. We listened to the soft resonance of the Urubamba far below as it washed along the foot of the mountain. Then suddenly the trail pitched up and we scrambled up steep narrow rock steps cut into the mountain centuries ago. At some spots, as we practically clambered on our hands and knees, it felt more like mountaineering than hiking. The steps were treacherous, many broken and uneven, and there were no modern conveniences such as railings, lines, and ropes to help. Instead, we searched for handholds of rock and roots along the stone face beside us and worked our way along—one step up, then another, then another. Our breath was coming in gulps now. I thought we were in good physical shape, lean, fit, and adjusted to the high mountain air, but this climb challenged our limits. Forty-five minutes later we reached a resting point beside small stone buildings and terraces that appeared glued to the very edges of the mountain. We stood there red faced, huffing, and puffing, trying to catch our breath while leaning against a rough stone wall that overlooked a distant Machu Picchu, wondering aloud if we could go on.

Mary decided. She smiled, abruptly turned, and headed up the next tract of impossible steep steps. We followed like obedient lambs, although we felt more like mountain goats as we climbed the narrow steps and glanced down past our feet at the steep drop-offs. As we climbed we tossed two questions back and forth. Looking down we wondered how many people die on this climb every year. We were constantly reminded of our mortality. We agreed that as long as they don't report three gringos missing today, it didn't really matter. And, how many steps to the summit are there? Mary said a couple thousand. My guess was a couple jillion, and right then, listening to my heart thumping and labored breathing, I felt I might be underestimating.

Within another half hour of spectacular scenery and riveting climbing, we reached the ruins of the Temple of the Moon. We climbed across overgrown agricultural terraces that once were part of a sacred garden of herbs and sweet-smelling flowers. Stone masonry structures rose up around us, half hidden in a shallow, open-faced cave. More stairs cut into the temple walls allowed us to ascend beyond and around the mountain. We crawled into a narrow tunnel opening in the wall, squeezed through, and then moved up more rock steps on the other side. We wedged through a gap in the rocks and out onto a boulder-strewn summit. On three sides below flowed the tiny sliver of the Urubamba, and on the forth side, looking south, lay Machu Picchu, resembling a child's toy in the distance. Down there, tourist buses had finally arrived from the train station at Aguas Calientes and a new group of maybe thirty tourists wandered antlike along the terraces, simply dots of color moving along the dusty path. We had not met another single soul ascending this morning. Huayna Picchu was ours.

OUR TRAVELING FRIEND LOU, GEORGE AND MARY PERCHED ATOP HUAYNA PICCHU

Up here on the mountaintop the mists were a memory and white clouds mixed with a deep blue sky above. We sat on a giant boulder, rested our bodies, and refreshed our minds while swallows, wings whistling, glided above us. I balanced my camera on a nearby rock, set the self-timer for fifteen seconds, and ran back up onto the boulder, cautiously squeezed by and posed behind Mary and our hiking companion Lou. My heels were inches from the edge of a straight, sheer drop and I didn't dare look down, even after the shutter clicked.

The climb down was mental intimidation. The descent off the mountain was not for the faint of heart. On the ascent at least we could stare at our feet and the next solid rock step and pretend there was solid ground all around us. That comforting illusion wasn't there on the decent. Try as we might to focus solely at our feet and the next uneven step, our eyes were constantly drawn beyond and down the insanely steep pitch. It was slow, laborious, and careful work. Oftentimes we were caught between holding our breath and nervous giggles as we climbed back along the unprotected drop-offs.

Finally, as we headed for the undulating safety of the razorback, we met the first group of climbers since we started this morning. We had been on the trek for almost four hours, they for less than half an hour. Already they were huffing and short of breath. There was no kindly greeting. Their first words weren't "hello." They wanted to know how many more steps to the summit. We smiled and answered: "a few, just a few more!"

For the rest of the day we wandered the silent, stone structures of Machu Picchu, oblivious to the guidebook's directions and not caring anyway. The sheer amount of printed and spoken information was overwhelming. Most of it was probably outdated or

wrong, the result of few tangible facts and overactive imaginations. We might never understand this place, but we could fully
appreciate how it tugged at our souls.

Wednesday: Wiñay Wayna

Five hundred years ago, a twenty-five-thousand-mile road and
bridge network linked the Incan capital of Cuzco to its sweeping
kingdom. It carved skyward across immense mountain regions,
swept through deep valleys, cut across snowfields, snaked down
coastal deserts, wound past vast swamps, and alongside raging
rivers. Scores of east–west lateral spurs fused into the main north–
south highway system that ran from Quito, Ecuador, southward
past Santiago, Chile. It was an engineering marvel unparalleled
in the New World and with few equals in the Old. Unlike today's
interstate highways, traveling the roadways was restricted to the
official business of the realm: the emperor and his court, soldiers
protecting the kingdom, caravans moving food or trade goods,
and of course tax collectors.

The Inca Trail that linked Cuzco to Machu Picchu was a cobblestone pathway that clung to cliff sides with steps and tunnels cut
into solid granite walls. In the Sacred Valley out of Ollantaytambo
it was wide, but up here, high in the mountains, it was scarcely
more than a couple of feet across at best. Early morning dew
coated the grass bordering a narrow dirt footpath that led up from
the southern edges of the Incan city. The condensation left our
pant legs damp and cold. The pathway was really nothing more
than a simple depression, a slender link along the meadow above
Machu Picchu to the old Inca Trail and Wiñay Wayna, a small

sanctuary of terraces, fountains, and buildings some five miles distant. We traversed the remnants of agricultural terraces along the edges of the site, past the latticework of restoration ladders that clung to the House of Caretakers and the massive Funerary Rock, and began our climb along the Inca Trail. The trek along the trail provided few flat stretches. If we were not struggling uphill, we were descending down knee-jarring drops. For forty minutes we pitched up steep steps cut into the granite mountainside, twisting and turning as we worked our way upward. The rises and runs continually changed, challenging our energy. Maybe it wasn't as steep as yesterday's ascent up Huayna Picchu, but our lungs burned with each labored breath that seemingly never drew enough air. Then, mercifully, through a narrow passage in the crevice of the mountain above, the walls of the *Inti Punku* (the Sun Gate) appeared with its magnificent view of the great city. It was another one of those moments where we were caught up in the mystery and elegance of the city as we stood on the edge of the precipice and looked back in stunned silence. Centuries ago, the Incan leader Pachacuti, nearing the end of his journey from Cuzco to his great mountain-top retreat, stood right here and admired his creation. You could feel his presence. Archeologists found no gold here, no silver. But there was incomparable treasure: the beauty of the city itself.

From the Sun Gate we edged along the narrow stone pathway, the Vilcanota River below us. We switchbacked along never-ending broken steps under the deep jungle canopy as we worked down the mountainside and across two wooden bridges balanced between outlying precipices. We reached a section of the trail that had been destroyed by recent landslide. Massive boulders, old Incan roadway rock, and trees and roots torn from the mountainside obstructed our path. There were two options. Climb high above the slide, maybe for an hour or so, or work our way across it. We chose the latter, knowing one misstep and we'd cascade off the edge and bounce a thousand feet down granite and trees. We toiled our way cautiously, grabbing handholds of rock and root, sliding, catching footholds, and moving across.

Finally, there it was before us: the rugged, white-gray skeletons of bygone buildings, the site of Wiñay Wayna. Two clusters of stone houses—which were overtaken by scrub grasses interwoven with flowers and connected by a long, precipitous staircase—sat nestled amongst ancient agricultural terracing. It was a beautiful setting. Looking down from the trail way above, the ruins seemed to hang at the mountain's edge, soft wisps of mist holding them magically suspended above the deep drop to the valley floor. As we climbed down through the terraces, past the gracefully curved balconies of the upper buildings, we marveled at the effort to create these sites that were so far from the major urban centers of the day. They had been built with so few tools and the results were both delicate and powerful. The structures literally followed the harsh contours of the mountain and danced to the very edges of the crag. In the local Quechua language, Wiñay Wayna meant *"forever young,"* and that's the way we felt looking around us. We breathed in the clean mountain air and listened to the whir of hummingbird wings as they skimmed from orchid to orchid. Although the buildings were crumbling and the terraces long forgotten, the sheer beauty of our surroundings harkened back to a time long ago when people toiled here, lived here, laughed here. Together, as we sat looking through stone windows down into the sweep of the great Urubamba Valley, we could sense their presence and feel their energy. As we absorbed the city's spirit surrounding us, it was easy to imagine that we too would be forever young.

Sunday, October 9: Pisac

Even after yesterday's frenetic evening train ride back from Aguas
Calientes station at the base of Machu Picchu, we arose early and
invigorated. Sunday morning was market day in the small town of
Pisac in the Sacred Valley, a short bus ride across the highlands.
While our early morning bus wound out across the Altiplano,
above us long, lateral, terraced farmland stepped down to the
roadway. An hour later, as we switchbacked down the mountainside, Pisac swept into view from across the Vilcanota River
a thousand feet below. Our bus dropped us off on the outskirts
of town, along a dusty commercial backstreet lined with vendors
selling llama and alpaca wool out of rusty trucks beds or from
tarps spread along the roadway. It was the rougher side of the
Pisac market. These were the no-nonsense farmers and herders
with their families, down out of the surrounding hillside villages
to sell raw wool and gather supplies for the coming week. There
was a tinge of discontent amongst the indigenous populations.
These stalls fronted a backdrop of graffiti-scrawled walls and door
frames that, like giant bulletin boards, proclaimed dissatisfaction
with the central government. The previous federal government
had actually converted a few private land holdings into agricultural cooperatives, nationalized some private industries, and
mandated profit sharing for private workers. Last year the new
military regime promised a transition to a civilian government,
even holding out the possibility of a full participatory democracy.
The problem was that those were all lowland successes. Not many
of the Andean locals were exposed to or could take advantage of
agrarian reform. So as we traveled up here in the highlands of
Peru and while everyone greeted us with smiles and friendship, we

knew there was an undercurrent of anger that would someday find a release in violence and insurrection. These Andean people we saw around us in the market today would soon be caught between a right-leaning government and a violent Maoist insurgency. They would become the fodder in the clash between those two conflicting ideologies.

We wandered the local market, amongst makeshift wooden stalls and blankets spread on the ground with piles of produce, animals, clothing, and utensils. It wasn't only a place to buy and sell; it was a meeting place. Despite the hand-scribbled protest slogans the air was full of laughter, conversation, and whispers of the latest gossip. Vendors sat in long rows by sacks of peppers, piles of lettuce, heaps of carrots, mysterious herbs, and mounds of potatoes. They bartered with buyers and giggled amongst themselves. Dye vendors with bags of brilliantly-colored pigment squatted next to coca leaf and limestone ash sellers.

Mary and I had been experimenting with coca leaves pretty much since we arrived at high altitude. We had our stash with us today. Chewing coca up here in the Andes is a lot like drinking wine in France or beer in Canada—everyone does it. We just pulled off the leaf stems and squirreled a few away inside our cheeks. Before long, the leaves had formed into a soft, saliva-drenched ball which we activated by popping in a pinch of flavored limestone ash. That mixture activated the alkaloids in the plant. Mary complained it numbed her mouth, but beyond that, the leaves seemed to give us more climbing energy and helped a lot with the altitude. As the ball in our cheeks lost moisture, we added a couple more leaves every once in a while and the mild stimulant effect lasted for hours.

Up in the plaza, under the shade of a magnificent, centuries-old pisonay tree with its sunny orange flowers, the tourist market was in full swing. Every forgettable, over-priced and poorly-made souvenir was on display. So were the tourists; there were well-coiffed, well-dressed tour groups from the big cities sporting expensive cameras, and ragtag hippies who seemed oblivious that their adulteration of Andean clothing and torn jeans didn't exactly sit well with the locals. And then there were veteran travelers like us who liked to believe, maybe even with a little seasoned arrogance, that we fit in a tad better. In the markets everything and everyone was on display. While we eyeballed and rubbernecked the clothing and manners of the local peoples, the locals in turn stared and gaped at us. To paraphrase lyricist Matt Dubey, we were all part of a mutual admiration society.

To escape the crowded market we headed out to explore the Pisac Ruins atop a mountain spur at the entrance to the Sacred Valley. We wound up out of the village along a footpath and across the long, graceful, golden curves of the agricultural terraces that swept along the southern flank of the mountain. It was a brutal climb up diagonal flights of granite stairs and cliff-hugging footpaths. As we labored past strategic and ancient stone guard posts with sightlines high above the valley floor, we passed a young Quechuan girl as she sat on a terrace edge, quietly admiring the town down below. Typical of the locals, she wore a broad felt hat to shield herself from the sun, and her layered clothing kept her warm in the cold Andean mornings. She smiled as we rested and offered a greeting in a language we didn't know. In a brief moment of connection we smiled, paused for a while to enjoy the view with her, nodded our heads in recognition, replied in a language incomprehensible to her, and then pressed on. The path took us up into what appeared to be a military complex, including structures with sightlines both up and down the valley, set at the very edges of the mountain and back from them. They were possibly housing for the hilltop guardians. With one final push of energy, we climbed up steep stairways and niches carved out of the mountain face, through a narrow archway, and onto the flat ground of a long-abandoned ceremonial center. Like six-foot-high stone skeletons, just the remnants of the buildings were left. Inside a circular stone masonry wall, the Intihuatana—the sun calendar—waited the coming of the equinox, chipped and broken but smoothed with age and constant touch. Climbing still farther, we were rewarded with a glorious view of the ruins perched above the Sacred Valley.

The afternoon bus amid lengthening shadows brought a tired collection of travelers back to Cuzco. Mary and I had one more group of ruins to explore before our departure tomorrow, a late afternoon climb to the hilltop fortress of Sacsayhuaman. I looked back toward the Plaza de Armas and the cathedral framed through the narrow alleyways of white adobe, across the red-tile roofs of the city bronzed in the failing twilight. Sacsayhuaman was built a millennium ago, long before the Incas conquered the valley. According to legend, Cuzco was laid out like a puma: the tail was where the Huatanay and Huaccolo rivers entwined, the body was the central plaza, and high up here on the plateau overlooking the city was the head of the beast—the fortress of Sacsayhuaman. The stones of the citadel were far more massive and impressive than those of Machu Picchu. Three parallel fortress ramparts towered above us, zigzagging continuously over a thousand feet. One massive stone interlaid into the wall weighed an estimated seventy tons. It seemed impossible that it was dragged here, but it was. Cut from a quarry over two miles distant, it must have taken herculean effort and incredible engineering to move it into position. While Mary and I irreverently relaxed on emperor Pachacuti's massive throne carved out of a single piece of giant rock, an American acquaintance named Charlie approached. He dug three old and frayed beanbags out of his rucksack and started juggling. As soon as the bags went into the air the locals, even the guides, started gathering around him, drawn to Charlie's performance like iron filings to a newly energized electromagnet. All eyes were on Charlie, and the Incan fortress was now simply a backdrop to a simple bit of entertainment as old as Sacsayhuaman itself.

The sun was cautiously slipping behind the mountains, and Cuzco already lay in shadow as we descended back into town and the sanctuary of our little hotel. Our bed was going to feel good tonight.

Monday and Tuesday: Cuzco to Ayacucho

It was a cool, hazy morning under a sky of low clouds as we maneuvered out of Cuzco. The supposedly short bus ride down the Apurimac Valley and then up through the winding highlands to Ayacucho turned out to be a bit of a marathon. By plane it was a quick half-hour flight, but by bus—the cheapest and therefore our most common mode of transportation—it was a tad longer. In fact, it turned out to be a tiring, soul-consuming, teeth-clenching, thirty-one-hour adventure that took us through some of the roughest and remotest terrain of our entire journey. The first hour or so passed easily enough. Our bus climbed up across the hills that rimmed the city and then down onto a wide plain of fields and farmlands that stretched out around us, passing through valley towns with quixotic names like Pucyura and Izcuchaca. Then two hours out, almost on command, the cordilleras muscled in on our comfortable journey and we began the first of the endless, dizzying ascents and descents around the hairpin switchbacks cut into jagged mountainsides. We seemed to be caught in some vortex where time and distance had no meaning. Maps were utterly useless for gauging how long it would take to get somewhere, as the vertical ups and downs of the mountain roads added an amazing amount of time and distance to our journey.

We had planned to overnight in Abancay, the rustic capital of the Apurimac Department. Now that we were off the bus we had a look around, figuring that unwinding with a relaxing day would be just the ticket to prepare us for the longer bus ride to Ayacucho. For all we knew Abancay might have been paradise, but here around the bus terminal things certainly weren't on-board with the whole tourism thing. This section of town was a squalid, dirty, bustling madhouse. Bus terminals were magnets for bars, brothels, cheap hotels, and restaurants. It was late afternoon and we were hungry as we searched for a nearby *comedor*. The hunt didn't take long and we plunked ourselves down in a rather forlorn-looking place amongst boxy speakers that blasted out tinny Cumbia music at full volume.

Flies buzzed around the restaurant. They were drawn hypnotically to the dirty tableware and streaks of old spilled food that had been indiscriminately wiped clean with a rag of doubtful cleanliness. The local patrons smiled bemusedly as we flicked and shooed the little pests in a futile attempt to rid them from our table. To be honest, the flies looked an awful lot like the black fragments in the *comida corrida* afternoon lunch special. Mary suggested the specks actually added a little *je ne sais quoi* to the unappetizing bowl of achromatic, cornmeal-like gruel parked in front of us. Her answer to our culinary quandary was to leave the table in search of transportation out of town. Mine was to push my spoon around the bowl in a non-committal, delaying tactic.

She was back minutes later with startling news. "There's only one bus line that runs to Ayacucho, and there's only one bus scheduled today. The driver said he's leaving here in about fifteen minutes. The next bus to Ayacucho doesn't leave until Thursday. That's two days from now. I bought us tickets. Let's go." The anxiety in her voice was a good indication of how she felt about staying in Abancay for two days. Looking around, I couldn't fault her decision one whit.

The bus was crowded, indicative of the sparse travel options. Over fifty of us packed on board, jostling for seating and rack space. Our packs were lashed up top along with a rather disconcerted goat that, judging by its constant bleating, was apparently very dissatisfied with its newfound accommodations. By the time we left, every square inch of that bus was overflowing. Seats designed for two often had a third rump parked at the edge, overhead racks were jammed with bags, and produce along with some locals stood resigned in the aisle. It was no matter; once past the *Guardia Municipal*, the local police checkpoint, we wound our way up into the mountains and on to and our next adventure.

Now, a packed bus bouncing over unpaved roads at ever-increasing altitudes—coupled with the constant swaying back and forth around hairpin turns—gets a little disorienting. Judging by the unsettled looks on the faces around us, it affected the locals on board as much as us lowland gringos. It wasn't long before the first passenger succumbed to a noisy round of nausea. The smell added to the mélange, triggering reactions in others and, within a few miles, we had a smorgasbord of vomit wafting through the cabin. It didn't matter how many bus windows were opened, the smell now on the floor and clothing was sickening. And we had hours to go until the first major stop in the town of Andahuaylas, where we were scheduled to change buses for the next, more challenging section of the overland route. As night approached we just hunkered down, wrapped warmly in our wool blanket, and stared out the window at the precipitous drop-offs inches from our tires. The constant hairpin turns along a narrow, gravel roadway high in the mountains were as unnerving as the smell was pungent. Out the front window, through the silhouettes of fellow passengers, we simultaneously caught glimpses of the narrow road ahead and the driver as he concentrated between shifting gears, braking, and honking as we rounded the blind cliff-side curves. Looking out our window we rarely saw the edge of the roadway as our bus pushed through a landscape that looked like crumpled paper. All of us were frightened, the total control of our very existences in a stranger's hand. As we negotiated curve after vertiginous curve, the question creeping into everyone's thoughts was when—not if— we'd skid off the road and plummet down into some long, dark abyss below. Conversation turned to religion. Not for philosophical reasons, but for self-preservation. Surely, even if we weren't true believers, it was safer to make our peace with God and let Him watch over us. We weren't the only ones applying a vigorous religious code to our situation. As we looked around the bus passengers crossed themselves and offered silent prayers for a safe journey. If everything went horribly wrong, at least we'd have gone out prepared. The driver, who was wrestling with the steering, brakes, and gearbox, was unperturbed and chatted away with a fellow driver who would take over on the route from Andahuaylas. It was only about six in the evening, but the approaching night sky with only a small sliver of moonlight brought one blessing: the darkening landscape slowly disappeared from view.

You'd think a bus change in Andahuaylas would change our luck. Not completely. The nauseous odor was gone—just a distant, mental aberration—but the new bus wasn't in great mechanical condition, which is kind of a requirement on roads like these. The next morning found us still poking along through remote mountain passes, all alive and well. We were on a single-lane road that alternated travel direction depending on the day of the week. The roadbed was treacherous: wash-boarded, potholed, muddied, and broken by occasional creeks that seeped from the rock faces. The bus threw up a big plume of caliche dust that engulfed those foolish enough to travel this path on foot. On the bus, we'd made our peace with God and weathered the night uneventfully. And other than the infrequent stops at the small Andean towns and villages along our route where dogs awakened from their evening slumber to chase and bark at the village intruders, we had slept fitfully while slumped in our seats.

Everything was going well until we heard a loud, hollow clunk followed by the whine of the left-side rear wheels scraping in protest against the fender skirt. We stopped; the driver exited, surveyed the damage, and returned. "Everyone off," he commanded. We all gathered around him at the rear of the bus, forty-five would-be mechanics staring over his shoulder. He knew what the problem was right away. The U-bolts that held the rear axle to the leaf springs had jarred loose. The axle had slipped forward off the main springs, the rubber pads that separated them worn down to nubbins. The bus wasn't going anywhere without sliding what was left of the pads back in place, resetting the axle under the springs, and retightening the U-bolts. The question was how to fix the problem out here in the mountains in the middle of nowhere. It could be hours or even a day or so before another vehicle passed, and even then there was no guarantee of assistance. Everyone had advice, but no one had solutions. Inspirationally, the driver fixed it in typical Andean fashion. Over the course of the next hour using a large spanner from under the front driver's seat he loosened the nuts and slipped off the U-bolts, gathered a couple of large boulders from the edge of the road, and dropped them in front of the back wheel. He got back into the bus, gunned the engine, and just drove over them. That more or less slammed the axle back up into place. He replaced the rusty U-bolts and cinched them tight. *Voilà*—a little mechanical magic coupled with a bit of misplaced confidence, and we were on our way.

The rest of trip was spectacular. We crossed rugged mountain chains with blue summits, drove along high sierras of rolling grasslands, and forded rivers over narrow bridges built decades before along roads that flirted with the very edges of disaster. At every stop vendors poured on as passengers disembarked for home or simply stretched their legs and enjoyed pee breaks. The Andean air up here (over thirteen thousand feet at times) was clean and bright, the blue skies so free of pollution that they darkened in the distance to the deepest indigo. We would never see sky or distance like this again. By early afternoon, as the bus began the descent through gently rolling hills, we spotted Ayacucho nestled on the plateau down ahead. Although it seemed within reach, traveling on Peruvian time and Andean distance, it would take us more than two hours before we were on the plateau and heading into the city.

It was nice to be on flat ground again, even if it was a lung-sucking 9,500 feet above sea level.

Tired, we searched out a hotel and found a little gem, the Hotel Colmena. It was a beautiful, old building across from Colegio San Juan, along the narrow Avenida Cuzco, and just a stone's throw from the plaza. We walked through the open courtyard and up the stairs to our little second-floor room, a simple affair with a delightful balcony that overlooked the street below. Best of all: it was stationary. Mary and I slipped out for a quick open-air dinner in the plaza. We sat and ate the local *puca picante*, a dinner of potatoes, onions, peanuts, garlic, and lumpy pork belly all marinated in a bright red *aji panca* pepper sauce. And of course we drank beer, maybe even more than we should have. After supper, emotionally drained, the sensory overload of the bus trip seeped away, leaving us exhausted. By four in the afternoon, we had tucked into bed and fallen into a deep sleep that carried us late into the next morning.

Wednesday to Friday: Ayacucho to Huancayo

The gauntlet had been thrown down and the race was afoot. The two drivers with clutches depressed and each with one hand on the gear shift revved their engines. They eyeballed each other through the open windows, exchanging taunts and suggestive gestures with their free hands. Moments later, at some unseen signal, the back wheels spun, caught, and two plumes of road dust and rocks billowed behind as both drivers rocketed towards the narrow, solitary gravel roadway that led out of Ayacucho. The forty-five-mile battle down the Lauricocha valley to the town of Huanta was enjoined.

We were passengers on the heavily-laden, fully-packed El Andino bus that led past the post marker to the outskirts of town. The competing bus was glued to our back bumper, eating our grit. One of the great things about being right up front across from the driver was that you got to see all the little nuances and expressions, such as the sweat and the bits of spittle around the edges of his mouth. The only negative was that you were right up front, in the epicenter of any crash zone—*número uno*, as it were, to bite the bullet. No matter—we passengers were being treated to a textbook demonstration of Latino machismo. There would be no quarter given and no prisoners taken today. The competitor's bus pulled out and passed, head held high, horn blaring, and fingers pointing skyward as he skidded by us just in time to slam on his brakes to avoid the road rubble of a recent landslide. All along the way pedestrians cowered off the road, and cars and trucks sensing danger had the good sense to get over as far as they possibly could as we approached. The skirmish wound through river valleys, up into the sierras and back down once again on to the high flatlands as each bus jostled for position. Our driver—and vicariously, of course, us passengers—won the battle at a narrow bridge. Both buses were roaring two abreast as we approached the narrow, one-lane bridge. Both drivers braked at the very last second. Our bus just happened to skid onto the actual bridge way, such that it was. The competition ended up perched off-road at the ravine's edge, his front bumper just a few feet from disaster. While he reversed, we sped forward with cheers of victory that rang through the bus for the last few miles to town. We were never to be challenged again. Today's trophy was ours.

The road got worse north of Huanta on the way to Huancayo, but the scenery became more stunning. Each hour of our journey took us higher into the Andes as the bus followed the course of the Mantaro River upstream towards its source. The roads were narrow, cut in mostly above the river floodplains, at times resembling more of a trail glued to sierra ridges than an actual roadway. The bridges on some of the river junctions were so fragile and narrow we had to be guided across. Over one crossing I stretched my arm out the bus window and let my fingers scrape along the concrete retaining wall mere inches on either side.

Midnight found us snuggled under our alpaca blankets in soporific oblivion, unconcerned with the rattling vibrations of the bus, the sound of some underpowered, staticky, local Andean radio station, and the omnipresent bleating and baying of animals hidden under the seats or above us in the luggage racks. A woman leaned over and pointed out the window at the barely-visible, distant mountain profiles silhouetted against the night sky. "The Inca called these mountains *Apu*," she said. "It means spirit ghosts. Don't they look like it?" We watched them for a while, letting our minds float a bit above reality, lost somewhere between wakefulness and sleep where the sounds that surrounded us comingled with elements of dreams. Why shouldn't mountains have spirits?

Nocturnal travel usually meant fewer stops. However, at these hours, even at scheduled stops, everything including the terminal was locked up tight. That created a busload of full bladders. While our bus driver had to hold some Olympic record for the biggest bladder on earth, the rest of us squirmed in our seats knowing that relief would come when—and only when—the driver needed to wiz. Our constant pleading was of little consequence, and he seemed content to motor on indefinitely. Maybe he had a malicious side and relished in our discomfort. On those rare occasions when he did stop, his ticket-taking companion would jump out and pile rocks under the back tires to prevent the bus from rolling off the road and into oblivion while the rest of us unabashedly surrounded the bus, standing or squatting and letting it fly. Forty passengers could trace the entire outline of the bus in a urine-soaked roadway in a matter of seconds. A good forensic scientist could have tracked us right across the Andes by the smell alone.

Saturday, October 15, 1977: Huancayo

A group of Peruvians energetically celebrated my birthday today. Unfortunately, it was three in the morning when the festivities got under way. The revelry was on the street two stories directly below our hotel room. They were all liquored up and ready to party while we were deep in sleep and trying to stay that way. That combination really didn't encourage mutual participation. Raucous laughter and loud, drunken voices woke us up. It was amusing for a few minutes, but the noise just went on endlessly. I opened the shuttered window and hollered down to them to quiet down. There was a less-than-polite response and the racket continued. We were secured in our little room two floors above them and the hotel door was firmly locked for the night and so the solution seemed simple. I picked up a cup of last night's tea from my bedside table. Fearing that I had somehow discovered my inner psychopath, Mary objected. I leaned out the window and poured cold tea over their heads. "Get out of here!" I yelled. They did, but only after an agitated dialogue that included a lot of new, colorful, feces-based colloquialisms. The drunken melee slowly retreated down the street in a full Spanish rage with occasional angry outbursts focused back at our window. Birthday wishes were probably not included in any translations.

The Chupaca weekend market, a half hour east of Huancayo, was in full swing by the time we arrived by collectivo mid-morning. We wandered aimlessly, following the market around the central square as it snaked down back alleys and into every nook and cranny imaginable. Like all local markets, Chupaca was noisy, colorful, odiferous, and constantly in motion. It was a glimpse at Andean life. Most women wore thick woolen leggings surrounded by layers of skirt, colorful blouses, and cardigans, usually topped off with a tattered felt hat. Most carried market goods tied across their backs, occasionally with children wrapped in the striped, coarse, woven cloth. More than once I mistook a baby for a sack of potatoes. Mary snickered, but it wasn't simply my nearsightedness. At times the only clue as to what was in the bag were two tiny feet that dangled out the bottom, visible only after they passed by. Mary and I wandered down aisles of herbs, flowers, and chickens, past sacks of corn and piles of potatoes, amidst the constant, blaring music from loud speakers and the bartering shouts of vendors. Women sheltered under umbrellas and makeshift tarps sat on blankets amongst their wares. We heard livestock braying from the backs of trucks. Farmers traded sheep, pigs, and donkeys along a backstreet. For us the market was a bit of whimsy, something novel to experience and enjoy up here on the Altiplano. Most of the locals here were rural and the market was a necessity, a way to pick up the essential food and household items for the coming week. Most had a long trek ahead of them out of Chupaca and back into the countryside.

In the afternoon a noisy, crowded bus took us a half hour north out of Huancayo, through rolling hills to the little farming community of Cochas Chico. Our bus sped past fields of harvested barley stooked together amongst the stubble. We motored along the dusty dirt road into the village between the soft brown adobe-block homes. Women, their hair braided in double plaits and backs laden with bags of produce, plodded through town. From October to February the focus here was on agriculture. According to locals we met on our walk along the town's only major street, March was a month of celebration that apparently included a lot of drinking. Gourd carving was in full swing in April and July. We missed the drinking part, but there were still a lot of gourds around. Chico was the undisputed epicenter of *Mate Burilados*—the pre-Incan art of carving gourds.

A family stopped us outside their adobe home in front of a little flower garden planted in metal cooking oil buckets that rested on a square of concrete blocks. The woman's name was Delia Maria, and like her parents and her grandparents, she was a carver. Her five- or six-year-old son Ramon stood there at his mother's side dressed in a soft green wool sweater with long pants rolled up at the cuffs. Head bowed, he was lost in thought as he nonchalantly played with a piece of string. His younger sister, just a baby really, hopped impatiently by his side. Delia invited us in to look at the mate gourds she had carved. We passed beside a heap of broken, cracked and discarded gourds near the doorway and went inside their home.

There, along a shelf, reminiscent of all the other artisan shops and homes we had visited this afternoon, stood a dozen or so mates. She showed us every one, positing the artwork and the intricate carving, encouraging us to buy just one. Nothing engaged us. We had seen so many similar carvings that they all began to blur together. The artistry was wonderful, but so were so many others we saw. We simply couldn't make up our minds, and as gracefully as possible we exited and walked back out into her little flowered courtyard. As we passed the scrap of discarded gourds, one caught my eye. It was a large sectioned gourd, maybe thirteen inches in diameter and intricately carved. I pointed at it and Delia exclaimed *"esta en ruinas—basura justo"* (it's ruined—it's just garbage). Sadly, Delia Maria said she had worked on it for almost a month, carefully etching the hard surface of the gourd with her thin-bladed *buril* (chisel) and rubbing oily charcoal into the intricate cuts. Then one morning, she recalled, while she was busy at the market, her son, wanting to showcase his young talent, proudly carved two large, crude fish and two feathered circles into her work at the edges of her mate. There had been harsh words and reprimands—maybe even a thrashing. Her elaborate work, now seen as worthless, was thrown with other cracked and mis-shapen gourdes into the scrap pile. Delia's month-long effort was for naught. Hopes of a well-earned price, a reward for all her talent and time, were dashed.

Mary picked it up and ran her fingers along the boy's crudely-scribed figures. His cuts were wider, deeper, and darker than Delia's finely-worked figures. He used burnt embers from the fire pit to darken the mate skin. But his work also told a story. His primitive figures were an insight into something this little boy wanted to express in his own simple, artistic way. The gourd was now not only carved, but it also held a tale of family intrigue, a tale he might one day relate to his children as they watched him carve. Besides, this piece was both beautiful and unique.

What Mary held wasn't simply a carved gourd. This was a thirteen-inch silent narrative of the very essence of peasant life here in the mountain plains. At the top Delia had carefully scribed a church with two tall belfries that surrounded a large ornate door like bookends. A pastoral scene anchored the bottom of the gourd. Farmers in the ploughed fields guided wooden shears pulled by teams of oxen, while the women beside them stooped and planted potatoes. In the distance, far behind the fields, a line of Andean mountain ridges poked up into the sky. In the center of the gourd, a simple wooden corral penned in wool-laden sheep. Surrounding the corral and out to the very edges of the gourd, hundreds of intricately-carved figures celebrated traditional village and country life. A string of musicians with harps, mandolins, drums, flutes, guitars, and violins marched behind a line of smiling dancers. Peasants, their backs bent with sacks of produce, together with alpacas laden with trading goods walked to the market. All across the gourd, filling every space, villagers celebrated the harvest with folkloric dances and feasts around the church in the main square. It was an engraved celebration of traditional and everyday life here on the high sierras.

Delia was confused. We had chosen a piece of work she had discarded as worthless. We offered her the Peruvian sole equivalent of fifteen dollars and her face lit up. That was probably close to the value of her original untouched work. Perhaps Ramon would be forgiven after all.

Sunday, October 16, 1977: Huancayo

Huancayo was an old market town and the heart of the Mantaro Valley, populated mostly by Indians but owned, it seemed, by mestizos and immigrants. It was an odd paradox. Every Huancan resident we saw either ran some tiny household enterprise or worked in one of the endless number of small *tiendas* and *talleres*. They were also the petty traders, the artisans, and the farmers from the surrounding hillsides who brought their produce and goods down to the Sunday market.

The *feria*, the market on Calle Huancavelica, was capitalism in its purest form. Perhaps no one better described the market than A. Hyatt Verrill, an American zoologist, explorer, and writer who had visited here some sixty years ago and wrote about his impressions. Little had changed and his words written decades ago still captured the vibrancy that we experienced that day.

We had planned to reach Huancayo for the Sunday market, and now as we stood there, nowhere on our journey had we seen anything that equaled it. For the locals it was as much of a fiesta as a business matter, and for centuries—since the untold years before the days of Columbus—Huancayo had been the center of Indian commerce and barter and weekly get-togethers.

Hyatt wrote,

At dawn on Sunday they began to arrive. Dressed in their best, the women staggered under enormous bundles on their bent backs, with tiny children carrying loads heavier than their chubby selves, the men urging on plodding llamas and tiny burros. All seemed happy, laughing, shouting, and chatting in their Quechua languages.

From sunup to sundown the market stretched four stalls wide, down Huancavelica for almost a mile, with an unending variety of vendors. There was some order to the packed roadway, however. Each outlying village specialized in some commodity, whether it was artisan crafts or food crops, and by age-old custom they were each allotted their space in the endless rows. We moved through sections of yeasty-smelling breads and down through the exhaustive vegetable areas with endless piles and varieties of potatoes.

Again Hyatt penned,

There were the pottery sellers with their wares, great earthen cooking pots, fat-bellied ollas, graceful and ornamental water jugs, pitchers, plates, saucers and figurines of every shape and color. Squatted at the edges of ponchos and blankets were the hat vendors with their colorful headgear spread before them. There were sections of the street where nothing but rawhide goods are displayed—ropes, halters, whips, reins, bridles—all beautifully and skillfully made. Other sections were restricted to sandals and shoes.

Like us, Hyatt found a section of weird and wonderful medicinal herbs and "bits of bark and roots, the dried bodies of fetal llamas, desiccated lizard, frogs, snakes, pills and powders, charms, and talisman." He continues:

But the most colorful, the largest of all sections of the Huancayo market is devoted to textiles. Of all the native arts and crafts the weaving of cloth is the most important and reaches the highest perfection. No one has ever equaled the textiles woven on the crude handlooms by the Indians of Peru. Although today, none of the cloth approaches the beauty and quality of their pre-Columbian work, and the textiles of the back strap loom woven from hand-spun cotton, llama, vicuna, or alpaca exceeds the work of modern machinery.

Scattered amongst the textile-sellers were the dye merchants. Their tables were lined with piles or bags of bright homemade dyes and pigments with colors from deep indigos, brilliant reds and scarlets, to ochre and gold and green. They did a brisk business, their dyes measured out by the spoonful onto a folded piece of torn newspaper and sold by the equivalent weight of an old Peruvian coin.

Towards the end of the long market day we rested for a few minutes and sat silently out of sight, sheltered behind the canvas roof flaps of a neighboring food stall while sipping Inca Cola and watching a young vendor working his tiny open street stand. His only products were a table of disposable razors and knotted plastic bags of mothballs carefully arranged in little displays. With a fist full of razors in one hand and a bag of white mothballs in the other, he engaged the endless passersby, shouting encouragement to stop and buy. No one did. The best he ever got were curious glances. He was my age. I turned to Mary and expressed aloud what I had pondered many times before at market scenes like this: "How can my life be so full of promise, so full of future, and so full of confident successes, while his is just an endless loop of mere existence?" I felt a little ashamed at my good fortune to be born in a place of so much opportunity, education, and wealth. As we moved out and passed his stall I glanced back and, for a just moment, wondered if I could ever have the strength of character to be him.

Monday: Huancayo to Lima

There's a certain romance about riding the rails. Perhaps it was just nostalgia that drew me back to my childhood when I watched passenger and freight trains rattle through our tiny village in central Ontario. Even then I wondered where those trains went, what they carried, and who was on board. Rarely stopping at our lonely wooden station they just passed by, full of people reading newspapers, sipping thermos coffee, or simply daydreaming, staring absently out at the passing countryside. There was something about trains that let you slip into a bygone mindset where time and distance had no real meaning and the journey, not the destination, was the true adventure.

Like buses, trains in the highlands were filled with locals, mostly women still burdened and bent with bulging cloth bundles slung across their backs. We watched as they boarded, sporting an assortment of homemade hats of styles and colors that would have made a big city milliner proud—high-crowned, round-crowned, narrow-crowned, wide-brimmed, broad-brimmed, made of felt, straw, and cloth and of every color and endless combinations thereof. Perhaps women here were like women everywhere when it came to hat fashions. You could almost hear the teenagers whispering, "Oh my, that two-inch brim is *so* last year." Blouses were decorated with embroidery and brightly-dyed mantas woven from alpaca wool draped across their shoulders. Reaching almost to the carriage floor were wide, capacious skirts of orange, mauve, cerise, or blue, made even more voluminous by countless petticoats patted smooth as they plunked into seats around us. No matter how great their load, the younger women always had space for wide-eyed and hungry babies who snuggled into their arms or were carefully cradled atop the cloth bundles stored at mom's feet.

The Central Railway of Peru was no express train. It was the long-distance diesel equivalent of a commuter run that paralleled the highway up through the Mantaro Valley, past fertile fields of barley, alfalfa, and cash crops. At every small town junction passengers disembarked while vendors of every stripe, with a cadenced singsong and an eye on the conductor's whistle, darted on board selling fruits and candies, empanadas, handmade breads, and homemade cheeses. We bought heaps of individual foodstuffs, making a kind of do-it-yourself brunch that we nibbled on as the countryside drifted by.

Beyond the town of Hauripampa, we left the fertile farmlands and ventured along a narrowing valley with steep granite walls flanking the rail bed while the Mantaro River's current gained strength along our gentle climb. For the next hour we passed the snow-covered summits of distant mountains towering two thousand feet above us. There was another unexplained stop along the track (although it seemed that all stops were unexplained in Peru). People just waited around until things started happening again. By ten in the morning we rolled through the gritty slag fields, past the tall, ugly smelters of the Cerro de Pasco Copper Mining Company, and into the rough outpost town of La Oroya.

Upon reaching La Oroya, we had been on board for almost four hours with another six or seven more in front of us. We'd traveled at such a leisurely pace that we felt part of the landscape rather than cut off from it. Travel was so laid-back aboard. We leaned out the windows of our carriage and stood on the open metal platforms between the cars, watching the scenery as it rolled gently by.

The big diesel engine strained out of La Oroya, heading westward against the Atlantic flow of the Yauli River. A century ago, Henry Meiggs, a New Jersey engineer, was tasked with the daunting feat of building a rail line from Lima up through the impassable Andes to La Oroya. Meiggs swore he'd "run the rails wherever the llamas go." True to his dream, twenty-three years later the rail bed stretched from Lima, across the Andean passes, over deep gorges, along impossible cuts across the mountain faces, and under tunnels blasted through granite, all the way to La Oroya.

Within twenty miles we had reached the first of the twenty-one steeply-graded switchbacks along the route to the summit. It was amazing to see how quickly the train was handled at these reversals. Train staff jumped off, changed the points, and climbed back aboard as the train reversed up the steep incline. At the track's end they were off again, manually changing points then scampering back on board as the train diesel ramped up power and moved forward. For almost three miles we zigged and zagged, gaining nearly a thousand feet in altitude. By the time we slipped into the 3,800-foot darkness of the long Galera tunnel we were at one of the highest points of our trip—15,600 feet above sea level. The tunnel cut through Meiggs *Montaña* rising at a one percent grade and gracefully curving inside the contour of the mountain.

Up here in the high mountains the air was thin. Chewing coca leaves helped, but just sitting quietly our breathing became harder and more strained. Even with deep breaths oxygen intake was minimal. Our conductor passed through the coaches, offering puffs of pure oxygen from what looked like a giant leather ball. You just raised your hand, and as he passed by he would give you a little whoosh of instant energy. Ah, that felt good.

A mile or so out of the tunnel and back into daylight we reached Ticlio Junction, the first stop on the Pacific side of the Cordillera Central watershed, a breathtaking 15,800 feet above our destination of Lima.

Over the next few hours we cut across a myriad of bridges over deep ravines, through scores of tunnels that turned day into darkness, and wound down dizzying switchbacks along the edges of rough, rugged mountains, counting down the elevations marked at the station junctions: Casaplaca, *altura* 13,623 *pies*; San Bartolome, 4,965 feet; and Chosica, 2,800 feet. We finally reached Lima, just a few hundred feet above sea level. We had come back down to the coast along the rails that took us "wherever the llamas go."

It was late afternoon when we disembarked into the madhouse of Lima's Desamparados rail station and worked our way through platform crowds and city traffic to our little Hostal Roma on Jirón Union. We had left that comfortable hotel over a month ago. The proprietress offered us back our little room that overlooked the street. She smiled and teased us that she'd saved it for us all this time. It was like coming home again.

Tuesday: Lima

This morning we had a firsthand peek at Peru's socialized medical system. Fellow travelers at the hostal suggested, in advance of our journey down the Amazon, that we get a gamma globulin shot as a precaution against hepatitis. It seemed reasonable, but we thought it appropriate to seek out some medical advice before we got injected, and what better place for advice than a hospital. Hospital Nacional Dos de Merced, a major general hospital, was only a few blocks away, near the university. We walked under the arched portico, through the front doors, and smack into a milling crowd of hundreds of people loosely formed into four lines. So we stood in one of them. A doctor moved down the line asking for names and symptoms. We explained why we were here and he assigned us a case number. As the line shortened we were confronted by a contentious matron who demanded our medical history for the hospital files. That was normal enough, I guess, although her combative nature and her endless forms were a bit over the top. This hospital—and quite possibly every Latin government bureaucracy—operated on the premise that infinite volumes of paperwork and corresponding sheets of carbon paper were incontrovertibly the most vital part of the entire service. When she finished her interrogation, she assigned us a room number where we were to report. As we approached the assigned room it appeared that everyone else in the city had been assigned the same number. Undaunted, I gave my chit to the nurse stationed outside.

"Nope," she said as she blocked the door, "you need to buy a hospital admission ticket before I take your forms," and pointed down the hall. We were back in line again. This time I mustered up a little Latino spirit and wormed and muscled my way forward to the front. I expected howls of protests but instead I got requests to more buy tickets from those behind me. I made an extra ten soles right on the spot. Forget about teaching English as a second language; I could have turned aggressive queue-jumping into a lucrative, full-time paying job. Admission tickets in hand, we retraced our steps back to the appointed room where the sentry nurse opened the magic door to another crowded room. After another two hours of waiting, a cotton ball pressed tightly to our arms, we finally exited the hospital and worked our way home.

This evening, beneath our balcony, we gazed down upon an endless crowd of believers celebrating Lima's *El Morado* (Purple Month). The smell of incense curled up towards us as we listened to the steady drumbeats and heard the continuous shuffle of feet on cobblestone. Purple was the color worn by the faithful who followed the processions winding through Lima's colonial center. They were celebrating one of Peru's most venerated religious icons—*El Señor de Los Milagros*, the Lord of Miracles, a three-hundred-year-old replica of a mural of Christ that had been painted by a freed black slave on a wall of an unassuming building where the newly converted *negros* gathered to pray. Legend has it that the building housing the artwork was flattened in a 1655 earthquake, all walls crumbling except one—the wall on which the frieze was painted. It became venerated in the black community, and despite attempts by the Catholic bishops to paint over it, it survived and was finally given into the care of the nuns of the Nazarene. Every October 18 since 1670, a replica of the mural has been taken out of the home church of Nazarene and paraded through the streets of Lima to the Church of La Merced. Intrigued, we followed amongst them up the street to Iglesia La Merced, where we joined a purple-robed brotherhood laboring under the weight of their revered two-ton artifact, shuffling slowly up the church steps and into the basilica.

Miracles aside, it was a great evening to street grunt. Hundreds of tiny food vendors lined the edges of the procession and crammed into every street corner. For us it was like one enormous, nonstop buffet and we munched our way along, sampling every concoction dipped in batter and fried in oil. Mary's favorite was turrón, a traditional cake-like pastry topped with candies that tasted like graham crackers. She devoured them with true religious enthusiasm.

Wednesday: Lima

Just down the street from the Lima Cathedral was the seminal seat of Catholic power in Peru: the Court of the Inquisition. A holy place, where in the late fifteen hundreds the heretics were tried, condemned, sentenced, tortured, and sometimes executed. It was a side of the Catholic Church hidden from Mary. Her rural Minnesota Catholic upbringing had taught her it was the Christians that were brutally ravaged and ripped apart for sport in the Roman coliseums. However, in the Court of the Inquisition, it appeared as if the Catholics had relieved the lions of their duties and then found even crueler methods to torture and murder in God's name.

In the court we stood like the accused in front of life-sized models of our inquisitors, the ultimate judges of the defendant's fate. The troika comprised two ranking members of the church, a scribe, and a jailor. The judges sat below the great seal of the church and stared back at us with accusatory looks. The petitioners, those who accused, were hidden from view. The defendant had no defense other than to agree with or deny those accusations. It didn't really matter, anyway; burden of proof or innocence rarely mattered when issues of heresy and the soul were at stake. The court devised a macabre method to acknowledge the accused's fate. A crucified Christ figure on a wooden cross was mounted in such a way that his head could be manipulated by a series of cords from a secret room. If Christ shook his head, the accused was freed. If Christ nodded, the accused was guilty and suffered all the consequences of that culpability.

Below us were the torture chambers, the racks, the iron shackles, manacles, masks, and spikes with gruesome scenes of torture and human degradation that chilled the heart. Holes drilled in the ceiling allowed the court to hear the suffering and the screams of the tortured.

Mary was visibly shaken. The very foundation of her faith she practiced was the good will and community of the church. Here was the reverse of that coin. Religion, regardless of its name, was often used to divide and separate, to control and manipulate, to convert and subjugate non-believers. It seemed that the core belief of every major religion was that it and it alone was the one true path to salvation and eternal life, and as such had a divine obligation to bend all others to its following. We spent the afternoon sitting on a comfortable bench in the *Plaza de Armas*, our backs to the Lima Cathedral's massive wooden *Portada de Perdón*—the Door of Forgiveness, talking about religion and reflecting on faith.

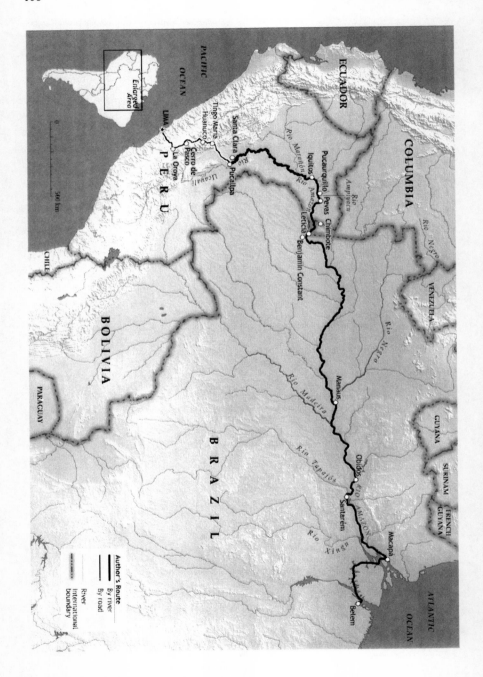

AMAZON

Thursday, October 20: Lima to Cerro de Pasco

We were down at the central Desamparados rail station in the heart of Lima early in the morning. The old station sat on the south bank of the Rimac River only minutes from our hotel. We trooped inside the three-story building under an ornate clock tower with two carved figures of justice. One figure, fittingly, held an old black steam locomotive in the crook of her arm. Mary and I crossed through the bright symmetrical patterns reflected onto the marble floor from the station's beautiful glass skylight above and purchased our tickets.

The train to Huancayo was filling with passengers, mostly locals but a few travelers like us, as well. Our destination was La Oroya, a small mining town up on the Altiplano some two hundred and fifty kilometers distant.

The vermillion-colored passenger cars with their distinct, wide, yellow pinstripe—the colors of Empresa Nacional de Ferrocariles del Peru—waited patiently in the cold morning air. The smell of diesel in the air mixed with the sounds of the yard. Railway stations were always a magical step back in time. Our car creaked as people boarded and tucked their luggage into the overhead racks. Then with a shout and a whistle from the conductor, the diesel locomotive powered up, the couplers between the cars hammered together, and our car shuddered forward. We were on our way out of the station. We were excited for our reverse journey of a few days ago, back through that remarkable landscape. Just this past Monday we had come down off the Altiplano. Now we were heading back. Ahead of us was an impressive highland passage with its fifty-nine trestle bridges, sixty-six tunnels, twenty-two switch-backs, and nine zigzags through the mountain passes. Of course, we anticipated that strange, mustached, rotund conductor with his magic leather ball of oxygen. We would not be disappointed

Seated a couple of spaces over across the aisle was an American traveler named Michael, who had a clipped New England way of speaking. He was absolutely bursting with energy. It radiated out of him. His clothes were new, clean, and pressed. His shirt was starched, his pants held immaculate straight creases, and his walking boots were freshly oiled. By contrast our clothes were old and worn. Our packs had little rips sown closed, and my scruffy beard accentuated Mary's long and not always shampooed hair. We mostly talked to the locals in Spanish, and usually only when they engaged us in conversation.

Michael, on the other hand, pushed up his window and ener-getically waved to and smiled at every boy and girl who looked at the train as we departed through the rough edges of Lima. The conductor and waiter on board received smiles and a big *gracias* for every passing remark they made. As we edged our way out of Lima towards the cordilleras and the ride up into the massive Andes, every outcropping or adobe house brought new loud exclama-tions of wonderment. As we watched and listened to Michael, we smiled. It was like observing us some seventeen months ago when we started our journey. Now we enjoyed life around us without the excessive emotion of a new traveler, perhaps more seasoned to the varying landscapes and its people. In a way, I envied his enthusiasm. Michael informed us he planned to travel for six months. We quietly wondered aloud if he would still feel this energetic and enthused at the end of his journey. Perhaps his karmic energy would shield him.

Within half an hour we meandered out of the mosaic of pastoral flatlands of Lima's suburbs and into Chosica, the small Andean foothill town. We had climbed a mere 2,800 feet in elevation, but already the mountains were closing in with rough pastel shades of purple. Those barren mountains were dotted with thorny cacti and small trees. Just out of the station we moved through the first of the several zigzags ahead. The train pulled forward onto a siding until the tracks ended. Rail employees jumped off the train, changed the points, and hopped back on. Within seconds we reversed up a steep grade on parallel tracks, stopped, and then reversed direction once again as the process played out over and over. We had moved up significantly in elevation over a short rail distance. It was a difficult maneuver, but it allowed the train passage over restricted mountain terrain. Converging mountains shadowed the valley and hemmed in our course ahead. Only the most vertical streaks of sunlight penetrated the narrowing valleys flanked by steep granite walls.

From Chosica the average grade was over four and a half degrees. Within a few miles at Cupiche we crossed the first of the great iron bridges that spanned the river gorges. The rail bed clung to the irregularities of the mountainsides and our locomotive strained along sharp cuts across the face. The tracks were laid high above the winding roadways and rivers, moving through tunnels blasted into the rock face and across the high trestles of painted iron bridges. The train whistle blasted our approach to every small station and jolted us back to attention. We watched the elevation markers at stations like San Bartolome (5,200 feet), San Jermonimo de Sucro (7,500 feet), and San Mateo (7,800 feet). For a short stretch beyond San Mateo the tunnels came in such quick succession that we seemed caught between night and day. We emerged from a dark tunnel into the light and crossed the Puente de los Infiernillos Bridge that spanned a chasm one hundred and fifty feet below us. By the time our train reached Ticlio Station, the highest point of our journey, we were at 15,800 feet above our starting point. Along the railway the high passes displayed magnificent pastel colors of mauve mountains, deep blue skies, and occasionally the soft greens of the hardy mountain grasses in folds of rock.

Our officious conductor had been busy over the past hour. From San Mateo station onwards he strolled through the passenger cars offering his snorts of oxygen. As he passed each seat a simple raised hand or verbal invitation resulted in a squeeze of the ball and a whoosh or two of fresh oxygen in the face. Soroche, or altitude sickness, was a common malady on these trips. The air was thin up here. Shortness of breath, nausea, and headaches abounded for those not used to thin air. No matter how good our health back in Lima was our blood needed oxygen and at these mountain altitudes, oxygen was in short supply. We breathed faster and shallower. Michael looked positively ashen and welcomed the respite of pure oxygen. But even as his face turned a milky, translucent white, that enthusiastic smile never disappeared. It just appeared a little lopsided.

We decamped at Ticlio Station during a scheduled stop and saw firsthand the potential dangers on these mountain railways. Across the track bed, twenty feet below the station, a diesel locomotive lay crushed. Its sixteen iron drive wheels faced skyward towards us, and its engine and cab lay crumpled under the weight. It perched tentatively on a narrow rock outcropping just beneath us, but far above the roadway and river farther below. I suspect the engineer never had a chance when it derailed, went down, and flipped on its cab. In general, the roadways in these mountain passes are more dangerous than the rail. Every year scores of people die, clipped by trucks and private vehicles as they walk along the roadside or ride in buses on narrow roadways above deep gorges with overzealous and ill-trained drivers.

We re-boarded for the short hour-long journey up to La Oroya. We were on the Altiplano now. The mountains pulled back and the valleys widened. The locomotive strained a little less as the grade softened, and we made La Oroya by early afternoon. That's where our luck ended.

The station at La Oroya was a simple affair. Like the town itself, it was surrounded by barren hills covered with ugly slag heaps that seeped down from the lead, zinc, and copper mines above. The mines were run by the state-owned Empresa Minera del Centro del Peru, and the company made no effort to clean up the tailings from its mining operation. The smelter stacks belched deep sulfur dioxide plumes that rose and floated across the town, layering it in gritty ash. It was a morose and damaged landscape.

We waited over three hours in La Oroya, along with twenty other Peruvians, trying to hitchhike out. No intercity buses operated at that time of day. No private trucks would stop. We despaired having to overnight here. Evening was approaching and the sun began to set behind the town. Bad luck abounded until a local in-town bus driver saw our plight and stopped. He was at the end of his shift and heading home. Twenty paying customers and two obviously rich *Norte Americanos* were just too good a payload for a hometown boy to pass up. On the spot he initiated a new route to Cerro de Pasco and we all clambered into his timeworn bus. Our route took us up along the Mantaro River valley road, through narrow canyons to the wet and mournful Junín pampa plains. As night quickly overtook us and the temperature turned bitterly cold, Mary and I huddled together for warmth. Mists slid down the mountain and like opaque curtains slowly covered the granite walls. In the darkness of a half-moon, the landscape became fantasy. As we sped along through the cold Altiplano air we tried to envision where the mountains and mist began and ended.

Two hours later our driver dropped us off near the little Santa Rosa hotel in the center of Cerro de Pasco. Our room was colder than a Canadian winter. We slept entwined together, shivering under the weight of five threadbare woolen blankets. The damp cold penetrated us to the bone. We swore never to complain about the heat again.

Friday: Cerro de Pasco to Huánuco, Peru

Mary and I awoke from under the pile of wool blankets to sunlight bursting through the cracks in the wooden shutters overhead.

Last night we arrived in town under moonlight. In daylight Cerro de Pasco was bleak, inhospitable, and disturbing. It has been mining central ever since the days of the Spanish conquest in the mid-sixteenth century. Copper, lead, zinc, silver, and gold are extracted from the ores mined across this area. The terraced McCune open pit copper mine started production in 1902 and expanded deeper and wider over the years. The pit has now migrated to the very edges of the town. Cerro de Pasco is perched on the very rim of the huge, muddy mining abyss. McCune threatened to, and surely will, swallow everything in its widening path. Mining conglomerates own this region. Mining companies dictate where and how fast the mines expand. Cerro de Pasco is in the way. Inevitably, the town will be destroyed and its population, including the very miners who work in the pits and live in the town, will be forced to resettle elsewhere.

After an unappetizing breakfast with bitter instant coffee, we searched for a bus to Huánuco. As we walked the streets we heard the throaty rumble of explosions deep down inside the mine pit.

We never found a bus. Instead, we discovered the Mixto, a homemade contraption of half-truck and half-bus. It was a mythical being. The first fifteen feet back from the cab was a multicolored, crude, open wooden bus shell with simple slatted wooden seats inside. The last eight feet of the vehicle was just a flat bed of an open-aired cattle truck. We paid a privileged fare and got seated under the protective wooden shell, along with several other well-to-do locals. It took an hour or so to load that last eight feet with cargo. Boxes, large cloth sacks, pails, and barrels of cargo were loaded, reloaded, shuffled, and reshuffled to get maximum volume and value. Then more passengers climbed on top of the cargo. Above our seats, lashed in the wooden carrier rack overhead, unwashed lamb and llama wool and skins and passenger luggage completed the payload. After three trial runs around the market square to test the weight and load security and to announce our destination to any stragglers, we were off on the rutted road that led out of town.

A short way out, we were slowed to a crawl by a procession of brightly-costumed men singing and dancing on either side of the

road. It was a parade of sorts—or perhaps at the very least a practice for a parade. For a better view I climbed out of our enclosure
and up onto the roof rack as the procession slowly parted to allow
us by. There were maybe thirty of them formed into two straggly marching lines, many wearing huge blackface papier-mâché
masks with grotesque bright-red lips and open white eyes. They
represented the *Negritos*, the blacks of Huánuco, slaves freed by a
decree in the mid-eighteen hundreds. Over the years the freed
black population dwindled and disappeared but their memories
were fêted.

Born of the minstrel shows a century ago and honed in vaude-
ville, blackface back home in America was used by whites to parody
and mock the early plantation slaves and freed blacks alike, mim-
icking the worst degrading and ugly stereotypes: the big white eyes
of horror, thick lips, unruly hair, unintelligent-sounding pidgin
speech, and impulsive behavior. Black women were shown as fat
and lazy mammies and the children as pickaninnies,

We grew up with the mocking stains of tar baby and Brer Bear,
but here the locals wore blackface in celebration of a rich black
past and marked that day of freedom in revelry and dance. Most
wore sombrero-like hats adorned with colorful pom-poms or
iridescent feathers, not to mock black culture, but instead that
of the wealthy slave owners. Everyone on parade carried and
played musical instruments of some sort, ranging from cymbals
and drums to horns and small mandolins. They parted to either
side of the road to let our Mixto pass, then waved and sang to us
as we slowly edged our way through. It was an enlightening cultural contradiction.

In my absence the passengers had shifted below. As I climbed
back down I realized I was part of a major passenger relocation

project. Every spot along the two rows of benches were full. Mary smiled and shrugged as if to say "I tried to save it." Resigned to my fate I climbed back up and made myself comfortable on the bus' roof rack amongst the luggage and skins. I found a pack of sheepskins lashed together and used them as a backrest. A pile of lamb's wool warmed my feet and a heavy canvas tarpaulin provided relief from the cold winds. Refreshing temperatures kept me alert and I enjoyed the beautiful Andean peaks *al fresco* as we descended sharply some eight thousand feet into the Huallaga River valley.

There was something pleasant about being thrown back and forth as the truck braked and swayed along the road. It was like riding a lurching roller coaster at the county fair, except this ride never seemed to end. Scars of white switchbacks led up into the mountains from our roadway. They seemed to end without reason high up above us. We traveled beside the Huallaga, from its nascent birth to its roaring rapids down the valley. An hour into the trip, the sun rolled out from the dark clouds and dispelled any possibility of rain. My trip atop the truck, snuggled amongst the skins under the tarp, was quite pleasurable. Another brave soul climbed up from below and joined me. Together, we laughed at every bump and violent sway of the truck as it sped on along the narrow road of the widening valley.

We arrived in Huánuco on the Upper Huallaga River by mid-afternoon. It seemed like a pleasant Andean town with its two ancient churches of San Cristobal and San Francisco, but today we were too tired to attempt much sightseeing. We found a room at Hotel Imperial at Calle Huánuco 581 just above the fast-flowing river and collapsed on the beds for a needed rest before dinner.

Saturday: Huánuco to Tingo Maria

Huánuco is an old city. Two millennia ago, long before the Incas annexed the town into their elaborate empire and made it a way station on the overland route from the imperial capital of Cuzco, the Kotosh cultures called this land home.

This morning we were in for a pleasant but unexpected surprise. We sat at the edge of the old, circular fountain in the Plaza de Armas, engaged in one of our favorite pastimes: talking to the shoeshine kids and village miscreants that lolled around the town square. Initially, they tried to figure out how to get money from us, but eventually they succumbed to our poor Spanish vocabulary and grammar. Our language proficiency was even worse than theirs. Instead of being dismissively ignored, they were suddenly elevated to teacher and counselor. That meant instant friendship and laughter with odd bits of pleasant derision. They quickly gathered around us, grew in numbers, poked fun, and corrected our pronunciation. Everyone thoroughly enjoyed the game of thrust and parry. Mary and I always felt a quiet sense of humility surrounded by these kids. They had so little yet always were eager to engage.

The surprise part came in the form of a *Guardia Turistica*. Recently hired by the town council, he sauntered over to see what all the noise in the square was about. The kids scattered, throwing barbs at the newcomer. He just smiled, watched them disperse, and introduced himself. Jorge was one of a kind—a bit of an experiment, really. Huánuco council wanted to boost tourism. Jorge was hired to encourage travelers to visit around the area. His job, it turns out, was to show us around.

Jorge was our age. His police uniform was crisp and clean. A new gold-braided lanyard ran down the right side of his short-sleeved shirt. He had a pistol tucked inside a newly whitened web holster and belt and held a guidebook in his hand. Apparently the pistol was for difficult tourists.

We found a truck headed north towards La Union out along the upper river basin of the Huallaga and climbed on board. The Kotosh ruins were just a few kilometers out of town. Our driver dropped the three of us off at the side of the road overlooking the site. To get to the ruins we crossed a rickety abandoned suspension bridge over the brown water of the Higueras River. Jorge led the way. Half of the bridge's wooden floor planks were missing and we edged our way forward, shimmying across the heavy suspension wires foot over foot, hand over hand until we reached a section where the planks had not been ripped out for firewood.

Guidebook in hand, the three of us explored the ruins. The site was partially excavated by Japanese archeologists in 1963. Kotosh was a ceremonial center, not a major population center. It lay mostly abandoned now as simple primitive buildings with crude attempts at restoration. Under a sheltered tin overhang on the walls of the partially restored Temple of the Crossed Hands was the plaster relief of two crossed arms, surprisingly intact after two thousand years. We felt a sense of discovery here alone amongst these ruins, most still overgrown and covered with dirt and loose stone. We stood on the narrow site caught between the Andes above and the river below.

Back in town, we gathered our belongings and went out to the Guardia Control post at the edge of Huánuco to wait for a ride to Tingo Maria. The Guardia was a type of security force, not quite army, not quite police. They were tasked with guarding the frontiers and remote outlying regions of the country. We had passed through numerous checkpoints on the outskirts of towns and villages and randomly along the roadways as they examined documents and cargo. The force was well armed, assertive, and in some cases, ruthless. Today they were simply friendly. Two young foreigners represented no threat to national security and we were allowed to wait under their shelter as we attempted to thumb our way towards the Amazon rainforest.

After two hours of waiting, a giant yellow Volvo transport lumbered to a stop and following a cursory inspection by the Guardia, the driver offered us a lift. He was headed all the way to Pucallpa through Tingo Maria. Our driver was from Tocache in the central highlands. He ran his truck from Lima to Pucallpa and back every week. The central highway took us down the Churubamba Valley and steeply up ten thousand feet and through the small town of Acomayo on the Carpish heights. Then we headed sharply down again into the lush green vegetation of the Amazon jungles. The paved road turned to gravel just after the tunnel exited the highlands. We were on the face of the Cordillera Azul, the front range of the Andes that led up from the jungle. Hundreds of little waterfalls cascaded from the mountains around us. The Huallaga River got stronger as we moved downstream. About a half hour out of Tingo our driver stopped beside a roadside waterfall, stripped down to his underwear, and had a shower. The water teeming with rotted jungle organics was an unappealing yellow-green. We turned down his invitation to join in. For the last hour, down from the cordilleras, it rained. Our dirt road became a mud bath. Every vehicle we met was covered in red sticky mud. From the cab we could see parts of the roadway washed away by the fast-flowing river. A recent landslide and washout slowed our progress and the truck edged through the rock and debris. Our driver dropped us off on Calle Raimondi, the muddy riverside street at the eastern edge of Tingo Maria, and bade us farewell. Mary and I looked at each other. We were sweating. It was decidedly hot.

Sunday, October 23, 1977: Tingo Maria, Peru

Tingo Maria was nestled in the broad river basin where the sierra highlands swept down to meet the jungle selva. The landscape around the city was striking. The town itself was like a child's imagination, a place found in frontier novels about the Wild West. The thoroughfare of Avenida Raimondi had more slick mud and deep puddles than usable surface, yet cars, trucks, motorcycles, and even horses passed by. Cars were parked haphazardly at the edges of the street on solid bits of earthen islands amongst the puddles. Townsfolk shuffled along the wide, elevated boardwalk on either side, keeping their boots dry. Small retail businesses lined the roadside, such as a tire repair shop, Chinese restaurant, bus depot, and Cine Central. It seemed that every business along this street was next to a bar.

That morning we were up by seven. Hotel Raimondi had been an active place last night. Saturday night was not the night to have a hotel room that overlooked the main street in town. The music, in typical Latino fashion, pumped out of the restaurants and bars. Latino music can only be played at full volume; anything less just isn't macho. Couple the music with the mechanical concerto of motorcycle engines and energetic horn honking, and sleep becomes a frustratingly distant pleasure afforded only to the hard of hearing.

We walked along Calle Lamas through the Plaza de Armas to the end of the road, and then wound our way up a steep hillside path between tiny wooden shacks covered by rusty corrugated iron roofs. The true beauty of Tingo Maria lay below, its rutted, muddy roads and its rugged-outpost ambiance set between the jungle and the mountains. At the town's edge the river separated us from the rough Huallaga Valley. Once the roadway from Lima is paved this town may lose its settlement feeling, but the setting will certainly always be here. By the time we finished our walk, the mud of this remote city caked the bottom of our shoes.

In the late afternoon the cocaleros, the small independent coca growers, streamed down from the hills and into the little bars that lined the main street. One of the cocaleros we shared a beer with boasted that a NBC television correspondent would arrive tomorrow to interview both growers and refiners. He said the old cash crops of coffee and cocoa were disappearing, replaced with coca and the illicit cocaine trade. The climate was ideal for multiple harvests, and the trade was too much of a pull for the locals who simply saw it as a way to feed their families. The cocaleros we encountered on the streets and in the bars were unarmed, polite, and sociable. Virtually all sold their coca leaves to Peruvian drug traffickers who refined the leaves into *bruta*, or paste. Those local drug traffickers conducted business in an outwardly pleasant and friendly manner, but within a year that would change. Easy money would soon bring in organized drug cartels—the brutal *Sendero Luminoso*, the Shining Path guerrilla insurgency—and the predictable violence. Within a year the Tingo Maria would be known as the "snow capital." Guerrilla groups would extort cocaleros in the Huallaga valley and threaten and kidnap locals and travelers alike.

Within a year the murders would begin in earnest, and this route would not be safe passage for anyone.

There were gypsies camped behind our hotel on a rough, muddy ledge of ground fronting the river. The caravan contained four large ragged and striped canvas tents held up by wooden poles anchored with frayed rope looped over rocks and metal spikes. In the heat of the day the canvas sides were tied back to reveal small cooking fires, boxes of kitchen tools, and baskets of clothing. Chickens roamed freely, pecking at tiny morsels of treasures scrapped off plates. An old yellowed cloth sign splotched with red paint and handwritten with bold, black block letters stretched out across the side of the leading tent. "Attention to the polite people of this city," it read. "Now, for the first time, meet the famous mystic. Her hands are the mirrors of the soul. Her brilliance is the reality of her existence. No one can say astrology does not exist. Do you suffer from illness? Do you have an unhappy home life? The teacher can solve all." Small red and blue stars and crescent moons cut from cloth were sewn on the canvas side to alert passersby that this tent housed the clairvoyant.

I snuck out in the evening; Mary declined, and walked back into the encampment. The gypsy women wore colorful, bright, flower-printed cotton blouses tied over long, flowing skirts. I wanted my fortune told even if it was in a language and with words I didn't fully understand. An older woman agreed and for a few coins she began. We sat in a circle with other gypsies under candlelight and drank herbal tea brewed over a small nearby fire. She smelled like mildew and smoke. It was a salient combination. After several attempts at a nuanced verbal explanation and with each burst of fortune met with a furrowed brow and perplexed look, she simplified my future. Exasperated, she foretold my future with unsophisticated words and basic hand gestures: "happy travels and a long life."

The rain started again. Within minutes it was deafening as it pounded on the canvas. We watched as the streets turned slick with mud and puddles. Stooped against the deluge, I sloshed my way back to the hotel.

Monday: Tingo Maria to Pucallpa

By virtue of our travel budget Mary and I often found ourselves surrounded by the less fortunate. Both she and I grew up in middle class families; we were always well fed, well clothed, well-schooled, and rarely deprived of much. I'm sure we felt deprived at times, especially as teenagers; every teenager I knew felt deprived of something. But here the reality was so obviously different. For the past several months, starting in Central America and moving southward, we lived with the local population. We traveled in local transportation, stayed in inexpensive local hotels, and ate unpretentiously in small local restaurants. And yet even with our modest means we lived so far above so many around us. Over half of Peruvian families survived below the poverty line. A quarter of the population lived in utter destitution. Hopelessness and despair was ordinary. So many wondered when the next meal would be eaten or where the next place was to shelter overnight. Serious schooling was beyond reach and only the most menial of jobs accessible. To so many there were no luxuries to life. To them there were no grand dreams. To them each day's mission was simply survival.

Traveling as we did, we were constantly approached by those in need. Mostly they asked for money. Sometimes they pleaded with us to buy their simple homemade fares or inexpensive goods. Sometimes while we ate they implored us for food. You couldn't look at the frayed clothing, the desperate expression, or hear the soft laments without compassion. But the enormity of it, the never-ending stream of need, created a kind of numbness. Over time we began to see the poverty as if in a waking daydream or some out-of-body feeling. We experienced it with a sense of separation. It was real. It surrounded us. And yet it existed somewhere beyond our concern, beyond our ability to fix it. We, like tens of thousands of others, hardened to it. Perhaps it was the only way to keep some sanity. A hardened heart didn't mean we didn't occasionally still hand out coins to those that asked. It did mean we began to be selective and sometimes indifferent of those that sought us out. And sometimes when the world weighed more heavily on us, after a long travel day, a poor night's sleep, or just from a weariness of spirit, we lashed out when someone pushed the limits of our generosity. That happened yesterday evening.

Last night we ate in the Café Rex, a small, simple restaurant between the Cine Central and the bus line office right on Raimondi and close to our hotel. The menu, hand-stenciled on the window, promised local Peruvian and cheap Chinese fare. Mary ordered *anticuchos* marinated grilled chicken on a stick slathered with garlic sauce and served with French fries. I tried the stir-fried *Lomo Saltado*. It had some kind of beefy-looking meat sautéed with tomatoes, peppers, and onions blended with soy sauce and fried potatoes with a pile of rice on the side. It was not a dish for the carbohydrate faint-of-heart.

A young woman came into the restaurant and wandered to our table. She was younger than Mary, but maybe not so much younger. She approached and extended a hand. *"Por favor,"* she pleaded, "can you give me some money?" No! Hardly glancing in her direction we waved her away with a dismissive hand. She didn't leave but instead pointed to our meals and softly mumbled something indecipherable. The intent was obvious; she was hungry and wanted food. *No.* We dismissed her again. She reached down slowly and with an extended finger touched a small piece of chicken on Mary's plate.

I never saw Mary react so quickly. We both exploded with anger. Mary jumped up and threatened to deck the woman. She had a hold of the woman with one hand and the other arm ominously cocked back with her hand clenched in a fist. The waiter scurried over and interceded, shooing the poor woman roughly out the door. If he hadn't, I truly believe Mary would have bodily thrown her out herself. She shook with anger as we finished our meals. The waiter, eager to smooth things over, apologized again and again.

We had alternatives to what we did. Our kinder, gentler nature might have prevailed. In a compassionate moment we could have given her a skewer of Mary's chicken, given her some change, or offered to buy her a meal. These were all simple things. They were all within our reach.

Upon reflection we saw a woman hungry and desperate. No one wants to beg. No one wants to demean themselves. She was driven to plead for the very basics of her life: food. I don't know what she did when she was thrown out of Café Rex. Perhaps she went on to the next bar or restaurant down the street and begged again. Perhaps she found a quiet spot and just wept. We thought we were desensitized to all of this. It was just an illusion. Even today it lingers, a question of morality that I have never been able to sidestep. Memories have a way of piercing the soul. I still feel the weight from the sadness in those eyes.

By early morning we were seated comfortably in a long-distance bus operated by the La Perla bus line over near the east end of town. We managed to snag the front two seats on the right side, across from the driver. That was a coup. Those seats were usually reserved for the driver's wife or girlfriends. Apparently, neither was coming along today. The big bus windshield provided an unobstructed view. It was like looking out through a picture window at the approaching landscape. We eased through Tingo and out onto the wide Huallaga valley plains. A few miles out of town the road branched and we continued east. The route took us back up over a stunning and treacherous mountain pass, through the Cordillera Azul, and between the Huallaga and Ucayali rivers. We drove down through beautiful valleys full of crystal waterfalls. The river beside us carved strange and fascinating shapes into the red rock face. Everything was crowned with lush jungle foliage. We were traveling at the front edges of the rainy season and the gravel roadbed was frequently washed out and broken. The tires pounded through the ruts and runoff, but the bus' big springs evened the ride. In sections, workers labored over equipment at the edges of the gravel. A new road was being built to replace the more difficult narrow bridges over river canyons.

Even on this well maintained, newish-looking long-distance bus we were surrounded by two of the constants we always found as we traveled: animals and produce. Today we were accompanied by a dog, three hens, and a parrot. The dog lay contentedly, nose in paws, near its young owner on the floor near the rear. Neurotic

hens housed in a wicker basket under a seat a few rows back periodically objected with raucous cackles at the rough vibrations of
the washouts. Directly across the aisle, a green parrot perched
cautiously on its sleeping master's head. Occasionally, the parrot
turned to face us. It would cock its head lower, half turn, and stare
at us for minutes on end with a single beady, unblinking eye.

Entertainment was where you found it. A couple of hours
from Pucallpa, as we crossed the winding San Alejandro River, a
small boy, thinking himself in private, had climbed a tree to take a
dump. Just as he was comfortable and enjoying his perch, our bus
rounded the corner. He squatted just above us in the tree, mouth
open in horror, pants down around his ankles, perfectly exposed
to the laughter and our wild applause.

We reached Pucallpa in the late afternoon. Long shadows
washed out over the wide dirt road as the bus headed through
the commercial wasteland towards the central station. We waved
goodbye to the driver and packed our way down Calle Ucayali to
the little Hotel Comfort. We were just a few blocks off the water,
too far to see it from street level, but close enough to smell the
activity along the wharves.

That evening, from the sheltered balcony of our hotel, we
watched the thunderheads roll in and lightning streaks as they
stretched across the river, illuminating the darkened sky.

Tuesday: Pucallpa, Peru

Chaos! The waterfront was simply chaos. Looking down at the
river, Pucallpa seemed like the town where civilization ended.
We had walked over from our small hotel in hopes of finding

transportation downriver to Iquitos. We expected to find boats moored to docks along the river. We stood motionless on the muddy bank above the river and stared down in disbelief. Below us, stretching off in either direction were colorful boats of every size, shape, and description and in various states of disrepair, haphazardly crowded together, bows pointed shoreward. Lanyards lashed the crafts to the shore and thick wooden gangplanks joined each boat to land. Longshoremen, their backs aching under the weight of rough-cut mahogany, gasoline drums, or bags of sugar wore empty burlap sacks across their heads and shoulders to ease the pressure of their loads. Above the boats a barrage of trucks parked randomly along the muddied road, waiting to pick up or discharge loads. Vultures perched everywhere and watched. In fact, one of our first lingering impressions of river life was buzzards and bananas. It seemed both of those things were everywhere. The vultures stalked the dock area, lurching at the last second out of the paths of workers who loaded heaps of plantains and lumber on board. Rows of these big birds perched atop the wooden sheds and houses that served as restaurants, bars, cheap rooming houses, ramshackle homes, and brothels. Shouts from the longshoremen, the throb of boat engines, rumble of truck diesels, and the steady voices bargaining for goods unloaded and loading all blended together into a cacophonic symphony.

We walked along the shoreline amongst the discarded produce and mud, dancing around the longshoremen amid the tangle of ropes and gangplanks and cargo. Within two hours we had talked with scores of boat captains and crews as we tried to determine who was going downstream and when. The morning temperature rose; so did our disposition. We picked our way through this bedlam, communicating in a language we didn't fully grasp and being passed from longshoremen who pointed to crew who then deferred to the captain or owner. Sometimes just finding anyone in charge seemed impossible.

After three hours of searching we found two boats heading downstream that day: an archaic peque-peque and a decrepit lancha.

The peque-peque, a mainstay of Amazon River travel, was a motorized, wooden, dugout canoe. It was the most common mode of river transportation and scores of them were nestled in and around the larger barcos and lanchas. Peque-peques came in all sizes, from small dugout canoes to longer and wider wooden homemade boats. They all had one thing in common: an unsophisticated two-cylinder gasoline engine bolted on a swivel to the rear transom. The engine was mounted to a long, enclosed metal propeller shaft. The boat we spied had an old corroded Briggs and Stratton engine mounted with bolts and a rebar welded to a ten-foot propeller shaft. A brown rusted rectangular gas tank strapped against the cylinders counterbalanced the muffler on the other side of the contraption.

The owner steered the craft by maneuvering the engine and propeller shaft left and right through the water. He could also raise the shaft in low water. It made for an ideal craft down shallow tributaries. The peque-peque before us was a crude thirty-foot boat with three rows of basic, unpadded seats up front. Overhead a white tarpaulin covered a simple, open, wooden skeleton of bracing. The hull seemed to be painted haphazardly in faded red and aquamarine with white flashing along the gunnels. Supporting crossbeams struts were cut from a thick, discarded advertising sign for some local cola soft drink. The captain invited us on board and we sat and negotiated the rate. The trip would take eight days, he told us. We'd stop frequently at villages and tributaries, but we'd sleep on open beaches. We'd have to bring our own food and water for the journey, but not too much. There wasn't room. The expression on Mary's face as he extolled the virtues of the trip told me how to respond. No!

The only other barco we found to be leaving that day was the *Nautilus*, a two-deck wooden craft that looked like it could sink into the water at any moment. The crude lower deck was cargo. It was already jammed full of oil and gas drums, coarsely sawed wooden planks, produce, and cases of soft drinks. We gingerly edged back to the stern and climbed up a ladder with damaged rungs to the second deck. Local passengers squatted on the floor under the tarpaulin roof and squinted at us as we walked to the wheelhouse up front. It was crowded and filthy. By the time we arrived at the wheelhouse we'd changed our mind and retreated. The peque-peque was bad, but this was worse.

We made one more attempt to book passage on a nice, sturdy-looking wooden launch named the *Hilpar*. The skipper told us he wasn't leaving until Friday and he was hesitant about taking on passengers. He showed a row of yellowed teeth, but I don't think you could call it a smile. His demeanor reminded me of Captain Bligh on an off day. "See me tomorrow," he said and abruptly turned back to his work. The morning provided us with a glimpse of the frustration of finding and negotiating river transportation for the three-thousand-mile journey ahead.

That afternoon, Pucallpa lay completely still on the Ucayali River in the Amazonian lowlands. The heat was intense and everyone with any sense or any excuse was out of the sun. We slowly retraced our steps back to the edge of the wide brown river and looked upstream.

Eight hundred miles upriver as the crow flies lay the source of the Amazon River. On a snowcapped peak called Nevado Mismi, north of Arequipa in the high, thin air of the Peruvian Andes, water trickled downward. The Amazon, the largest and most powerful river system in the world, started its life as insignificant runoff from glacial melt. Down the mountains and through the Amazon's lowlands, it joined with over a thousand other tributaries on its journey to the Atlantic Ocean—farther than the distance from New York to Paris. The tiny rivulet gathered strength as other melt waters flowed into it down off the summit. The river coursed almost two hundred miles down through the Andean mountain valleys, joining with other tributaries to form the Apurimac river system. Broadening and deepening, one hundred miles later it merged with the Mataro River to form the Ene. Within another hundred miles the river left the Andean valleys and flowed out onto the westernmost part of the Amazon floodplain, with its low, densely forested banks. Finally, the Ene fused with the Urubamba River to form the Ucayali and the waters that flowed past us as we stood on its shore. It was now almost a half-mile wide with a slow, constant current that pulled silt and sediments from the banks and turned it into a gritty, muddy brown. Downstream in the direction we meant to travel it meandered with crooked, gnarled turns around low, flat islands until it disappeared from view. The Amazon River's discharge was larger than the world's next seven largest river systems combined. By comparison, the St. Lawrence River was a garden hose. Our goal, the Amazon's Atlantic estuary, was still some twenty-seven hundred nautical miles away.

As we stood overlooking the Ucayali, perspiration tickled as it rolled down our backs. Our shirts were discolored and sticky with wet, salty sweat. It was like we were being marinated in the air. We retreated back to the relative comfort of our hotel to shower and lay naked under the cooling arc of the big ceiling fan in our room.

Wednesday: Pucallpa, Peru

We were up with the sun, determined to bargain and cajole our way downriver towards Iquitos. We were amateurs. Once again, we ran head first into the inconsistency and nuanced bedlam of Pucallpa's riverfront.

The derelict *Nautilus* had not departed, its schedule still unknown. The captain of the *Hilpar* had not rescinded. He didn't want the added distraction of passengers. Two strikes and we had barely started the morning's game. We retraced our steps somewhat dejectedly with guarded strides among the cargo, longshoremen, mooring lines, and garbage, scarcely glancing at the maze of riverboats. "*Oye, estás buscando un barco?*" (Hey, are you looking for a boat?) The baritone voice carried over the waterfront clatter and we turned to find it. There on the bow of a big barge stood a tall, rotund, leathery-faced mustached man with his arms folded. Every buttonhole on his white shirt was stretched to the breaking point. "I saw you poking around yesterday," he said. He knew we were heading towards Iquitos, his destination a few days downstream, and we were welcome to come with him. "Come on board and let's talk." We warmed to his smile immediately. The barge was named the *Siempre Adelante* (*Always Forward*). She was maybe one hundred and fifty feet from stem to stern with a twenty-five-foot beam. A long, rusty, corrugated iron roof splotched with sealing tar covered the forward cargo hold. The back third of the boat comprised a partially enclosed two-story structure with a covered wheelhouse and open rooftop up top. Immediately below the wheelhouse on the main deck were four small, whitewashed, wooden crew's quarters. Aft of them was a galley with hanging pots and stacks of empty, straw-filled cages along with a large solid table and a raft of chairs. Across from the galley at the stern was a small head with a makeshift shower arrangement that, as the cook explained, *"funciona algúnas veses"* (it works occasionally). We boarded her and sat down with the captain for a breakfast of bananas and fish. While we ate he extolled the virtues of his boat. He pointed to the space in between the crew's quarters and promised us we'd have our own little area for sleeping on deck. "You'll need hammocks."

He swore Cookie was the best cook on the river and the meals would be the best cuisine ever. She was also his wife and was within earshot. "The *Adelante*," he said, "is leaving tomorrow morning." He wanted twenty-five hundred soles, or about twenty-three dollars apiece. The journey would take a few days, the exact time dependent on loading and off-loading cargo and the weather conditions along the way. The price seemed high and we wavered, uncertain to whether we could find a better price for the journey. "No matter," he said as he clapped me on the back, "if you change your minds you'll always be welcome."

By ten thirty on the waterfront we were emotionally drained and looking for an alternative activity to reenergize. We decided to walk out to the Guardia Control and catch a bus out to the rather ramshackle town of Puerto Callao on the shore of Lake Yarinacocha, just a few kilometers northeast. The lake was home to several scores of Shipibo Indian settlements scattered throughout the Ucayali river basin north of Pucallpa.

It was an easy walk to the Guardia Control. Several khaki-clad officers lounged around, stopping vehicles as each passed through a simple checkpoint in and out of town. They were searching for drugs, contraband, and thieves. There were moments when this was not the most hospitable part of the country. As we sat and waited for a bus, a young sergeant came over. He was curious about my green Canada T-shirt with its stylized maple leaf logo. Before long we were engaged in negotiations: his khaki army shirt for my t-shirt. We would swap, but not before he removed his rank from the shoulders, name plate from the front pocket, and police identification sewn into the collar. After a few snips and a not-too-subtle attempt to remove the police insignia we made the trade. He was now a smiling Canadian tourist. I was a veteran Amazon explorer in my well-worn, short-sleeved khaki shirt. The intrepid explorer and his fragile blond wife boarded the bus on their next adventure.

We clambered off the bus at Puerto Callao in time for lunch at a little open-aired pallapa restaurant at the lake's edge. Small lake fish grilled over charcoal and served on rice and beans were followed by a desert of *picarone*: deep-fried donuts of sweet potato and squash.

An hour-long ride out on the placid oxbow lake in a rickety, makeshift passenger peque-peque brought us to the Shipibo Indian village of San Francisco. During the rainy season with the water up, the lake is part of the river. When the water is down it becomes an isolated lake. Throughout the trip over we navigated around scores of local fisherman in dugout canoes, spearing and netting fish as well as other small boats like ours that carried supplies and passengers. Mary and I walked up the pathway from the shoreline, into a cluster of primitive wooden houses that were raised a few feet above the ground on wooden poles. The population of the village must have been over a thousand. Standing at the top, surrounded by Shipibo women, and near what appeared to be a local craft workspace was a man who introduced himself as Bill Zolkowski. He said he was an American who owned a small import retail store in Ann Arbor, Michigan, called Baobab that bought and sold Peruvian art and crafts, amongst other things.

"Shipibo are a matriarchal society," he told us. "Until recently, the Shipibo economy was one of subsistence, with the men fishing, hunting, gathering, and planting root crops like manioc and potatoes on small plots of land. While the men hunted and fished, the women cooked, managed the family, and produced all the woven goods and pottery. Now, the textiles, beadwork, and pottery are renowned and valued and are really the only real revenue source in the village. The women control that trade, and thus the money. Money provides the ability to trade outside the village and culture."

Just west of us, along a narrow path through shoulder-high grasses and flooded meadows, was the small, less touristy village of Santa Clara. We followed Bill over narrow footbridges built of worn-down two-by-ten boards loosely nailed and lashed to wooden pylons driven into the mud. We occasionally paused as women balancing fish or supplies in wicker baskets on their heads wiggled precariously past. The jungle pushed in tight and clouds of tiny gnats circled us, looking for bare skin. By the time we reached Santa Clara each of us was scratching the swelling red welts on our arms and necks.

Santa Clara was simply a grouping of primitive, open-sided, and thatched huts raised on stilts. There was no electricity, no services, and no stores in the village. As many as four generations within two or possibly three extended family groups lived here. A grandmother with sun-weathered skin sat cross-legged on the dry dirt behind her granddaughter and squinted into the sun's glare. The two of them giggled and chatted as grandma ruffled through her hair, picking out lice and crushing them with her fingernails. Her nails clicked sharply as she carefully probed and crushed. *Click, crack*—her nails snapped every few seconds and another louse went to lice heaven. The grandmother, maybe in her fifties, was deeply wrinkled around her eyes but had jet black hair—like that of her granddaughter's—which hung long around her shoulders. Artful, maze-like geometric patterns we'd seen on pottery and fabrics tattooed her cheeks and throat. Both women were barefooted and each wore colorful blouses of bright yellows and patterned reds with bands of ruffles stitched across the front. Occasionally, during fits of giggles, the young girl looked up at us with undiminished curiosity. Mary's long, corn-yellow hair fascinated her. Surely her grandma could find a juicy louse or two in those tresses.

In a large open-sided lodge, several young Shipibo women wove and decorated pottery. Above them, long, billowing, white streamers of mosquito netting were tied off from poles around the edges to beams in the center. They were stored in the rafters and lowered around hammocks at night to provide some protection from the creeping, crawling, and flying insects that emerged from the jungle.

The shapes that adorned virtually every crafted item were ritualistic. Patterns covered women's clothing, woven textiles, pottery, and even faces. Paddles, canoes, spears, clubs, blowguns, and the bows and arrows used by the men were decorated with similar designs. The patterns were drawn from the mind's interpretations of nature, dreams, mysticism, and shamanism. A few hallucinogenic drugs such as ayahuasca, a Shipibo psychotropic tea, induced the shaman to communicate directly with the surrounding plants and animals and reptiles. Their spirits spoke through him to the villagers. The patterns mimicked the flow of rivers and patterns of anaconda skin. Most were a symmetric geometric design within three levels. Broad, straight, and curved patterns were drawn on a white- or sand-colored monochromatic background. Then parallel, smaller, more elaborate fine lines were scribed within the borders of the first, followed by hair-sized, intricate filler lines. Lines within lines within lines resulted in geometric patterns that were pleasing and uniquely Shipibo.

YOUNG SHIPIBO WOMEN WEAVING AND DECORATING TRADITIONAL POTTERY

A number of villagers, a mix of older and young women and their children, sat in the lodge on the palm-wood slat floor, laughing and gossiping as they worked on pottery. Their colorful clothing was streaked with drying clay. We watched as the wet, gray clay mixed with bark ash, and tiny fragments of broken pottery was worked and rolled into thin coils and slowly wound together to form a bowl. The coils were carefully worked with flat wooden scrapers and supple fingers until the thin sides were seamless. Scattered around us, outside in the warm sun, were pots that were in varying stages of air-drying. After several days in the sun they would be slowly cured in a wood fire. Women applied ochre and black pigments from boiled bark for the geometric designs. A final resin from tree sap gave the pottery its unique organic glaze. The pots were so lightweight that they felt incredibly fragile. But the process makes them pretty robust, and we decided to buy two pieces and backpack them down the Amazon with us. Bill helped us pick out some pieces, his keen eye looking for small flaws and more complex shapes and designs.

Later that evening, our stash of Shipibo pottery carefully wrapped in discarded newspaper, we ventured out with Bill again to a local Pucallpa waterfront bar for some serious drinking. Getting Bill to talk about his adventures was like asking my father-in-law Eddie to talk about the war. Mary and I were lucky we had nowhere to go.

"The Shipibo, like many other native peoples," he said, "still practice shamanism. The faith healer's relevance is declining, but it is still an integral part of the medicine practiced in the jungle regions." Bill related his strange, almost mystical revelation in the jungles of the Darién.

A few years ago, he and his business partner started selling the colorful reverse-applique molas of the Kuna Indian women from the San Blas Islands off Panama. The molas became a staple of their retail and wholesale business. The search for more relics drove them southward into the Darién and into the tribal areas of the Wounaan people. The women produced woven baskets made of palm fibers and organic dyes. Eye-catching with striking motifs, some baskets took months to weave. The Wounaan curandero (or shaman) practiced healing with intricately-carved wooden curing sticks. Curing sticks became a focus for Bill. He loved the idea of their magical influences and the native's belief in their curative powers. The sticks were carved to represent the nature of the needed remedy.

Foot travel in the Darién was virtually impossible. There were no roads or passable trails through a very hostile jungle. The only ways in were the rivers. Bill, his partner, and a local guide went in by motorized canoe along the Chucunaque, a small tributary of the Turia River. An hour or so upstream Bill arrived at a small settlement. They inquired about curing sticks and were directed to a house of an old, fragile woman. Her husband, now dead, was a curandero. The woman pointed to five sticks that lay in the open rafters. Most were carved with animals and figures. One was an intricately-carved as a pregnant woman. She agreed to sell them for dried beans, other foodstuffs, and household goods that Bill and his partner had brought with them for barter. Money was not a currency this deep in the jungle. She was reluctant to part with them all, but Bill was insistent. She wanted to keep the stick with the carved pregnant woman. In the end she agreed to part with them all, but only after the sticks had been touched by the new shaman to remove their healing powers.

Bill, his partner, and their guide left the village and headed back downstream. Along the way they picked up a hitchhiker. No one was left stranded on the riverbank if there was room in the canoe. The passenger asked to be let off in a large settlement near the mouth of the Turia River. An hour later, they let him off and started to push away when they heard the cries from the village.

"Stop. Wait!" They turned back to see the old woman who sold them the curing sticks waving at them. It was impossible. There were no trails through the jungle and no other canoes had passed them on their journey down the Chucunaque. How could this be the same woman? She came closer and pleaded with him to give back the curing stick with the pregnant woman. Without hesitation, Bill reached down unwrapped his bundle of sticks and returned it to her. She smiled at him and then turned back into the village and walked away.

"To this day," Bill said, "I believe the woman's mystical appearance at the village so far from her home—downstream and through impassable jungle—was a measure of the intrigue and power of the curing stick, as well as the myths of the shaman that still resonate here with meaning."

He spun more tales of adventure late into the night as we drank cheap Peruvian wine fermented from the purple berries of the acai palm.

Thursday: Rio Ucayali

Shamefully, we rose rather late this morning. We had more wine than good sense last night. It was close to midnight before we and Bill parted company, found our way back to Hotel Comfort, and collapsed into our bed. The old Spanish saying *"noches alegres, mañanas tristes"* (tipsy nights bring gloomy mornings) suddenly felt very relevant. Now it was nine-thirty and my head still hurt as we hustled over to the steep banks of the river waterfront.

Their heads appeared first. They looked forlorn. As they moved up the bank it was obvious they were travelers like us, returning dejectedly from their search for river transportation. The woman was dressed in a long-sleeved sweatshirt and baggy sweatpants with string ties. The man was tall and lanky. His long brown hair receded off his forehead. He wore big round glasses and had a full dark beard. He must have baked in his heavy blue jean jacket and patched bell-bottomed pants. They both looked European.

They were Dutch he said, and introduced himself as Frits and his partner, Wil. Their English was broken but understandable. Wil said they couldn't find any boats leaving today. Frits repeated "No boats!" Like us they were headed downstream, their ultimate destination Manaus. We invited them to come with us and talk to the skipper of the *Siempre Adelante*. Over the course of the previous afternoon and evening we had decided the *Adelante* was our best option out of Pucallpa. Now four of us walked along the waterfront and boarded the *Adelante* in search of the captain.

Jovial as usual, he told us we were welcome to come with him, and of course there was room for two more passengers. "Oh, by the way," he said, "we're leaving in an hour!"

We all shook hands in agreement and charged off the boat. We had to pack, check out of the Comfort, get money exchanged, and buy hammocks within an hour. We all split up. Frits and I searched out a local waterfront store and bought hammocks and some rope. Mary had the forethought yesterday to buy some river supplies so she made a beeline for a money exchanger. We all met back at the Hotel Comfort, then packed, checked out, and hastily headed back to the *Adelante*. Time was running out. We made it just before the deadline as we raced breathlessly up the gangplank.

Our first clue that the timetable was amiss was a misplaced captain. He was nowhere to be seen. "Don't worry," a crewmember told us. "Stash your gear over there between the crew quarters. He'll be back soon." One delay followed another: a little more cargo or another passenger, perhaps a few more supplies. We would leave on Peruvian time, or more precisely, exactly when they felt like it. By two in the afternoon there were a total of eight passengers. At three o'clock, almost five hours after we boarded, the big diesel engines fired up and reversed. The propeller wash churned the water white and we cautiously backed our way out of our entanglement with the other boats and barges. The captain was beaming. We were off on our expedition down the Rio Ucayali towards the junction of the Maranon River, about a day south of Iquitos. There, the two rivers merged to officially become the Amazon.

The five-hour delay provided lots of time for snooping around. Drums of petroleum and mangos were the main cargo of this trip. Petroleum powered the generators in the little villages and settlements along the river and up the tributaries. The bulk of the gas was destined to Iquitos. The mangos we weren't sure about— perhaps barter for supplies along the way. Mary, Wil, Frits, and I made our quarters aft on the starboard side in the little open-air space between the crew's cabins. It was comfortable and a little crowded. Our packs were stowed around the edges and our hammocks strung between the wooden structures. I had the outmost hammock hooks and was almost hanging over the wooden railing at the edge. I could look down at the water flowing by a few feet below.

We climbed up to the wheelhouse and stretched out on the roof. It was fascinating to watch the greens of the jungle as we wound our way around the bends in the river. The green canopy was broken by an occasional thatched house high on stilts, or by small settlements tucked into the jungle. By dusk we passed the Rio Aquayitu, a small tributary that blended its water with the Ucayali. We watched huge logs and endless saplings; full-grown trees and even flowers carried by the current drifted by us as we moved along the river. Freshwater dolphins frolicked briefly beside the boat, guiding us on our adventure.

Tonight's luxury dinner was rice, plantain, and *carne guisado*, a meat and potato stew. No one knew or dared ask what was actually in it. Cookie, a short, hefty woman, stood guard in her galley. She worked the stove in a tight short black skirt, her big black bra noticeably visible underneath a gauzy white see-through blouse. The entire outfit was set off with her stunning choice of footwear: knee-high rubber boots with Day-Glo orange reinforced toes. It was a fashion statement for the crew and travelers. She was, after all, the captain's wife. She'd been busy in our absence. Three live chickens nestled in the straw-filled cages hanging over the table. Everyone acknowledged that fresh chicken would be nice. Each of us pondered when there would be only two.

By seven we settled into our hammocks and drifted off to sleep with the thumping drone of the diesel engines and the rattle of propellers somewhere below. Ahead in the distance, lit by a ghostly-white full moon, dark thunderheads rolled across the jungle, spitting down streaks of lightning softly reflected by the river.

Friday: Rio Ucayali

Last night was a long one. Our sleeping quarters were cramped and the hammocks were hung short. That meant we couldn't lie diagonally across them and were continually doubled up, almost fetus-like. But the hammocks held and swayed with the motion of the boat. Although the sleeping arrangements were a little tight, there were no mosquitoes or other insects to bother us. That was a big concern. Malaria was a constant worry in the jungle.

We had started taking our Chloroquine tablets two weeks ago. Our doctor had provided specific instructions. Start a week or so before we entered a malarial area, continue once a week on the same day for as long as we were at risk, and then continue another six weeks after we left the zone. Friday mornings were our dosage day of choice. In theory, the medication was supposed to kill off any malarial parasites in our blood. The down side was that no matter how we tried to disguise the taste, the tablets left a lingering metallic flavor in our mouths. Ironically, the original organic base for our modern medication was discovered by the Quechua Indians right here in Peru. They ground the bark of the Chinchona tree into a powder, mixed it with water, and drank it. It stopped them from shivering in the cold air of the Altiplano. Hopefully, it would stop any parasites in our bloodstreams and livers dead in their tracks.

At first light, around four thirty this morning, the *Adelante* put in to the Shipibo village of Contamana on the eastern bank of the river. Surprisingly, we all felt well rested as we moored along the shore nestled between canoes and small barcos. Two crewmembers made a dash into the settlement looking for fish, fruit, and eggs. The other two helped villagers offload a dozen drums of gasoline, rolling them off the ship, down wooden ramps, and onto the soft, muddy shoreline.

The eight travelers onboard sat around the chipped wooden table and toasted each other with tin cups of bitter dark coffee. Cookie followed the coffee with a hearty breakfast of boiled bananas and eggs. Always conscious about her appearance she had changed clothes again. She now wore a loose-fitting sleeveless red dress. In fact, over the next day or so, she changed outfits frequently. The only constant to her clothing were the black rubber boots with the Day-Glo orange reinforced toes. Cookie was a fashion diva.

While Frits, Wil, Mary, and I traded travel stories, Cookie gutted fish on the table at the stern. She seemed mildly interested even though she didn't understand a word. She smiled and gutted, throwing the entrails over the stern. *"Mas comida para los peces"* (more food for the fish), she said. The gutted fish were taken to the tin roof up top to dry, open-air style.

Frits was twenty-nine and Wil two years younger. They didn't have a camera and traveled light. Wil said they didn't want to look like tourists. They wanted to blend in. Well, that was a problem; they stood a good head and shoulders above everyone around them, spoke only limited Spanish, and wore clothing unlike anything local. Like all of us travelers they screamed of "foreigner." The best they could do was not look *Norte Americano*.

Their journey started with a visit to Wil's sister, who lived in Sao Paulo, Brazil, and had recently given birth to her second child. Wil had just finished her studies and was scheduled to start work in a few months. They visited her sister and then followed the Gringo Trail through Salta and La Paz, Bolivia, down to Lake Titicaca. They continued into Peru touring Cuzco, Machu Picchu,

Nazca, and up into the Andes to the source of the Amazon. Now they focused on traveling downriver to Manaus and then a flight to Recife, Brazil, by the end of November to reunite with the family.

Frits, it turns out, was a movie star—well, at least a documentary star. A few years ago, he told us, he was a major character in a Dutch film production called *Rudy Schokker Huilt Niet Meer*. I don't think we ever got a good translation—maybe *Rudy Schokker Cries No More*. It was a docudrama spoof about a baby named Rudy born just as a big jet passed low and noisily overhead. The piercing noise of the engines frightened the newborn, and every subsequent time he heard a jet he screamed in fear. The father, our fellow traveler Frits, searched for somewhere in Holland where the baby could live free of jets. The saga was finding that perfect but impossible location in the small country. We were traveling with a Hollywood celebrity.

Noon found Cookie back at the table serving lunch. It was a scant change from breakfast with bananas, beans, rice, and fresh fish. Rice and boiled bananas, we discovered, were cooked in river water. From the first meal onward we never got used to the gritty sound of silt as we chewed.

In the early afternoon the captain put in just beyond the town of Orellana. While the crew offloaded cargo he, Cookie, and a local friend took us along a small dirt path that led out of town and into the jungle. Twenty sweaty minutes later we emerged at the edge of a large lagoon. Across the water, a tiny unmarked settlement he called Jose Ollajo pushed out in a clearing under the jungle cover. The skipper pointed at our transportation. Three dugout canoes rested on the bank in front of us. They were obviously local, carved thin from a single piece of marupa wood. He and I would take the smallest one, he said. The rest would make do with the remaining dugouts. He and I would cross first and speak to the elders. The other canoes would follow.

I knelt on the keel in the bow, knees resting as far apart as I could for balance. Our captain pushed off and settled onto a wooden crossbeam behind me. We each had paddles, although it was immediately obvious I would be the one paddling while the skipper directed. The canoes were shallow-keeled and unstable. The captain laughed and bellowed orders as we careened to one side and then the other, taking in water over the gunnels. I assumed we would sink long before we crossed. We'd be just ripples in the lagoon before we were found. I was relieved and delighted to hear our dugout bottom scrape against the sand at the village shoreline. The screams and nervous laughter behind us meant the others were closing in. The canoe approached, its gunnel mere inches above the water and overloaded with the captain's paddling friend. Behind him Frits, Mary, Cookie, and Wil held on with white knuckles and looked thrilled to be safely across.

The village was *mestizo*, a mix of Spanish and Cocoma native blood. Their skin was a coppery color like mahogany, accented with jet-black hair and dark eyes. They had virtually no facial or body hair. Villagers dressed in western clothes that were practically indistinguishable from those worn in the little town of Orellana out on the river. Well, virtually everybody, except for the young children who raced around barefooted in all states of undress. Some of the older girls, dressed in school uniforms, were returning home from the morning classes.

Every house was constructed on stilts with wooden poles buried in the ground that acted as foundations and supporting frames. The homes were mostly open living quarters, some with simply a thatched roof and low stick walls. Others, more elaborate, had open porches and stick walls that ran right to the roof. We peeked inside at the storage and drying racks, cooking pots, baskets, sleeping mats, and the odd blanket. Kerosene lanterns made out of discarded coffee tins provided light in the evening. There was no electricity or generator here. Most had a cooking fire out front, the coals still warm from the noonday meal. Behind the village were small garden plots, cut and burned to clear back the jungle. They grew corn and cassava, sweet potatoes, and beans. Around the gardens was a green wall of banana and plantain. These people were mostly subsistent farmers and fishermen. They lived off the land and river. Some of the men were employed in menial jobs in Orellana.

As we looked around we realized we had more material wealth in our backpacks than those that surrounded us now. They wanted to show us their village and homes. They were proud of both. They had no way of making the comparison with our lifestyles, but we did.

Late that afternoon a quick, torrential rainstorm hit the river. We scurried to help Cookie bring the sun-dried fish off the tin roof and then hustled to move our hammocks and packs away from the edges of the *Adelante*. The rain pocked the water around us and sprayed us with a fine mist as it splattered along the railings of the boat. We sat around the table at the stern drinking tea and silently watching the river flowing out behind us.

Saturday: Rio Ucayali

It was a delightful, relaxing night. We rearranged the hammocks using different hooks that gave us more length and easier rest.

Mist on the river provided a pleasant sleeping temperature. The fog got so dense we put in to shore in the middle of the night and anchored within feet of the bank.

I awoke to the faint green of the jungle as the morning light angled through the mist on the water. Mary awoke to mosquito bites. It was one of those vagaries of traveling. Mary had twenty-five on one leg and twenty on the other. The other seven of us passengers had scarcely three or four welts between us. The crew simply accepted the hordes of insects with both stoicism and composure. They were a natural irritant beyond their control.

River traffic was sparse, save for the dugout canoes and peque-peques moving between the many settlements along the river. Some of the villages were nothing more than a few weatherworn huts scattered by the geometry of dirt paths and overgrown grass. By ten-thirty that morning we passed the town of Iberia and without many stops we would make Iquitos sometime tomorrow.

All eight passengers slept, read, or simply passed time lazily, watching the river settlements as the *Adelante* slowly worked its way northward, offloading drums of gasoline at small settlements. The captain kept us about a hundred yards from shore—deep enough for safe passage, yet close enough to watch all the activity in each village we passed. Brightly-colored macaws burst out of the trees by the hundreds and looped and swirled in aerial displays before disappearing again into the jungle. Large white cranes huddled along the shoreline while pink-tinged river dolphins occasionally edged around the boat. There was a light rain. Big droplets, constant and warm, peppered the ripples in the current around us. Everyday has beauty, and midday's dark, cloud-lit sky gave the greens and browns of the jungle subtle shades and nuances that would be lost in sunshine.

The big diesel engine thumped along rhythmically. River travel can be hypnotically boring, and I drifted in and out of awareness. It was a soft and peaceful day. At that moment, the river matched my mindset as we followed the meandering water around bend after snaky bend. It was ideal for reflection. In the late afternoon the rich golden sunlight infused everything and turned our moving landscape into a work of art.

Down in the galley the cage was decidedly emptier. That morning two chickens hung plucked and cleaned by the railing. Boiled bananas, rice, and yucca were served in the evening with freshly baked bird. There would be fewer eggs tomorrow.

Sunday, October 30, 1977: Iquitos, Peru

Cookie's see-through blouses aside, she and the captain had been gracious hosts on board. They both eagerly engaged every one of us passengers in conversation, providing instructive tidbits about life on the river. Language differences mattered little to them. Hands took over where language failed. The captain, potbellied and mustached, delighted in watching our naivety about fixed schedules, local village customs and lifestyles, and the new birds and animals we spotted along the river. He and his wife explained each new discovery with simplicity and grace, even as each sentence seemed to end in laughter. They made our journey easy.

Over the last few hours we had put in at two new villages, Genaro Herrera and Saquena to offload more drums of gasoline and pick up crates of vegetables and fruits. At seven this morning we rounded a low island and caught sight of the dark brown waters of the Maranon River. The rivers joined, but for several miles the waters of the Maranon flowed beside the light brown waters of the Ucayali. For two miles or more the edge between them was razor sharp. Slowly over the next several miles the two flows merged and shifted, the dark Maranon waters lightening and the lighter Ucayali flow darkened until they were one. The Maranon dumped a lot of rubble into the river system. Suddenly, we were navigating through debris fields of trees uprooted from the shore during recent storms as logs, branches, and bits of flotsam and foam from the lumber mills upstream in Nauta drifted down with the current. It kept our captain alert and focused. We were now officially on the Amazon River, a few hours south of Iquitos.

Around noon we navigated around a huge bend in the river near Padre Island and Iquitos came into view. We steamed in close past the Belen slums built on the floodplain near the river. The rainy season had started and hundreds of houses made of dreary wooden boards and rusty, corrugated iron roofs perched on stilts above the water or simply floated on rafts. Instead of roads, channels of water wove through the shantytown, creating a chaotic maze of canals. Canoes and small boats were lashed to ladders that led up to homes. The area reeked of stagnant water and sewer waste. Boat crews' unloaded cargo along narrow planks laid across the mud. Longshoremen straining with their loads waded waist deep in the soupy water. Animals were simply thrown from the boats and floundered ashore as best they could.

The backdrop to Belen with its shanty homes and innumerable vultures was modern Iquitos. The buildings were new and high and clean. The roads that led down to the docks were paved. The *Adelante* carefully picked its way through the channel and slipped into shore, tied off, and cut the engines. We were here. The first three hundred and fifty miles of the Amazon were behind us. We bade farewell to the captain and Cookie with handshakes and hugs and set off to find a hotel.

With a population of nearly two hundred thousand, Iquitos was the busy capital of Peru's jungle region of Loreto. It had paved streets and plenty of automobiles, even though every road that led out of the city petered out to footpaths a few scant miles from town. It was one of the largest cities in the world without road access. Air and the river were the only two ways out of or in to Iquitos. We expected that finding a hotel here would be a snap. We were wrong. We went down the list of every hotel in our handbook and every one was full. While Wil and Mary hung out in the Plaza de Armas near the Iglesias Matriz and guarded our backpacks, Frits and I wandered the city, registering at every hostel or guesthouse that had vacancies. We finally chose the cheapest, the Hospedaje San Antonio, on a small back street called Jirón Lima close to Plaza 28 de Julio and the Iquitos cathedral. We settled in for a shower, even if it was only a trickle of water. It was the first in four days on the river.

A trip to the Bellavista-Nanay market at the northern edges of Iquitos restored our sense of the frontier. The four of us rode a crowded, purple, windowless bus up a potholed street to the very last stop right at the edge of the Nanay harbor. The waterfront whirred with the sounds of passengers and water collectivos that transported locals upstream to villages along the Nanay and Itaya Rivers. There was a steady flow around us as scores of people came and left on these boats. Villagers brought goods to sell in the market just feet from the riverbank.

Bellavista was a madhouse of activity, even in the late afternoon. The market was a mixture of open-air stalls surrounded by dilapidated tiendas, cheap restaurants, and seedy bars. It fit right into the folklore of the Amazon. We watched as two fishermen, in tandem and overloaded by the weight of a pirarucu, struggled in with their catch. At up to ten feet long and four hundred pounds it was possibly the largest river fish in the world. Pirarucu were car- nivores and fed on fish, birds, wayward monkeys, and, if rumors were true, the occasional human. The one the fishermen had caught wasn't four hundred pounds, but they struggled under its weight. We followed them into the fish stalls, held our breath, and looked around. If nothing else it was a testament to the diversity of river fish and a cavernous mausoleum of the soon-to-be-eaten.

Small wooden tables covered with palm fronds or cheap color- ful plastic held fish of every size and description. Women shooed flies with fans made of newspaper away from the tortoise meat and gonads, river snails, and even chunks of caiman. A man waved back at us as he shaved off fish scales with a wire-bristled brush. Evil-looking payere, nicknamed the "vampire fish," stared back at us with two-inch curved fangs, daring us just to reach out and touch them. There were buckets of piranha and racks of dried fish. It was a busy, noisy market.

We ate at a riverside restaurant, the water nearly lapping at our chairs. Our meals, we were assured, had absolutely no gritty rice and not even a trace of boiled bananas.

Monday: Iquitos

This morning we began our search for transportation downriver towards Leticia with a fancy breakfast in the grand old state- owned Hotel Turística on the Malecón Tarapacá. The hotel was a fifty-room, three-story building with wrought-iron railings that encircled the balconies overlooking the Amazon. In earlier years it might have been a showcase. Now a fan clicked monotonously beneath a custard-colored dining room ceiling made of beaten tin, and the fixtures seemed a little sad and worn. But it was still a starting point for travelers on the Amazon and we were drawn there.

Moored alongside the dock that fronted the hotel we spotted an impressive ship named the *Adolfo*. She was metal-hulled and maybe a hundred feet long with a beam of almost twenty feet. Three decks high, she was newly painted white and looked beautiful. We boarded her and sought out the captain. Turns out she was a tourist ship headed to our next destination, Leticia. There were ten private rooms on the main deck, crew quarters below, and a sort of dining room sitting area on top. The *Adolfo* was a ship from the rubber boom era, large and grand. "She'd take six days," the captain told us, "exploring tributaries and Indian settlements, river life, and customs along the way." We'd be welcome. They hadn't filled the cabins. Elation turned to dismay when he told us the price. The voyage would cost three hundred and fifty dollars per person. Frits looked dumbstruck. We all must have looked equally astonished. At our current rate of spending, that was the equivalent of forty days of travel. We shook our heads, smiled, and disembarked as gracefully and quickly as circumstances allowed. I'm sure the captain chuckled as he watched us go.

Locating the *Adolfo* was just too quick and too easy. We spent the rest of the morning walking the docks, inquiring, beseeching, and most of all questioning our decision to find the cheapest river transportation. The Latino mentality of keeping someone happy for the moment was frustrating: "Yes, there are boats. Just not here—over there is better." Finally, we decided to break the trip up into stages. First we would get to Pevas, a small settlement a hundred miles downstream. From there we would travel on whatever we could find. We needed to be flexible and luck would follow.

We found a small commercial cargo boat named the *Mirauta*. She sat six inches above the waterline with a beam of six feet. Rough boards encased her entire thirty-foot length with cargo openings every several feet. A corrugated tin roof that ran from stem to stern covered us from the elements. *Mirauta* was powered by a peque-peque engine. She was decidedly a step down from the *Adolfo*, but the fare was within our price range. We picked out our spot, marked our hammock hooks, and arranged payment. We'd sleep here on board tonight and depart in the morning.

MIRAUTA, OUR RIVER TRANSPORTATION FROM IQUITOS
TO PEVAS WITH MARY, FRITS AND WIL

The rest of the day was administration. We needed local currency and so traveler's checks were cashed on the black market in a darkened hotel room. When we entered Peru the exchange rate was eighty soles to the dollar. Today it was a hundred and five.

Travel was getting cheaper. Iquitos was the last big city in Peru before we got to Leticia. Consequently, we needed to get our passports validated to leave the country. Our next port of entry was Leticia Colombia. Our passports were stamped and our exit visas removed. We were now non-entities in Peru. Not that it seemed to matter in this part of the country.

We gathered our packs from the hotel and returned to the *Mirauta*, slung our hammocks, and arranged our supplies. The evening cooled the air. The mosquitos never circled. It was a good night for sleeping.

Tuesday: Iquitos to Pevas

My dreams abruptly ended with a sharp air horn blast from a heavily laden fishing boat sliding in beside us. The loud bargaining over the catch and its obviously inflated value brought the four of us out of our reverie and back into the real world around our little floating hostel. Besides, after a couple of drinks last night, our bladders were full and we needed to find a head.

Finding a toilet around town is not as simple as it might seem. Unless we were willing to buy something, *los baños* were *no se pueden usar*. It was a pretty hard and fast rule. As minutes passed, our search took on a new urgency.

One thing was certain. Never pee in the river. This warning was given to us more than once by local residents. We never decided whether it was tongue-in-cheek or dead serious, although to be honest, every bit of urine and feces either directly or indirectly ended up back here in the river. There were definitely no water treatment plants or septic tanks in the outlying village settlements, and even in the larger towns any treatment technology was at best dubious. But the "don't pee while in the water" advice seemed worth heeding. Travelers might think the river's most treacherous creatures were the carnivorous piranhas, the cold-blooded caiman, or the massive anacondas. From local gossip the most feared was the candirú, a nearly invisible, blood-sucking, toothpick-sized parasitic fish. It lingered in the murky depths, hidden and waiting to stalk prey. It targeted not by sight but by the scent of urea and ammonia expelled from the gills of fish. The tiny candirú silently bides it time. When the fish exhales, it dashes up the urea and ammonia flow and darts into the open gill. Within a fraction of a second it unleashes an umbrella of sharp barbs to anchor in place, rips a hole into an artery with needle-sharp teeth, and sucks the blood that gushes out. Engorged and swollen it lets go and sinks back down into cover while its prey spews blood and dies.

Urinating in the river releases that same scent and activates that same trigger for the candirú. Only instead of fish gills, it heads towards more personal orifices. Once inside, the barbs and needle-sharp teeth wreak havoc. In such a narrow space the parasite can't back up and escape. There is only one direction of travel: forward and farther into the host. Peeing while swimming in the water, we all decided, was not a smart idea.

Instead we found an abattoir at the top of the hill above the docks. It was dirty and smelly, but the manager said we could use the baños in the back out past the cutting floor. Seeing that much butchered meat so early in the morning was disturbing. The toilets to which he pointed made the slaughterhouse floor seem positively pleasant. They involved squatting over one of the two eight-inch holes cut into the concrete floor. The stench of sewage overwhelmed us as we lined up one behind the other, ready for our turn outside the small, unventilated rooms. The tank was already virtually full. Gazing down into the hole I watched as gray slime-covered rats climbed around and treated themselves to a delicious meal of feces. They were close enough to see the glistening hairs on their bodies. I could almost hear their little lips smacking. I could very definitely hear them scurrying around underneath. I pulled my pants down, squatted, and crapped right on top of them. My gag reflex nearly triggered and it was all I could do to stay composed. One by one we each took turns. One by one the reaction was the same. Wil said she looked a big rat right in the eyes and just let it fly. Mary came out with pursed lips and shook her head as if to say, *what the hell am I doing here?* Over the next month, we would all learn the art of the iron sphincter.

By mid-morning our three crewmembers had loaded fifty cases of beer on board. The cargo area was full. If we ever got stranded, we were going to be very happy travelers. Just before we pushed off another paying passenger descended on the *Mirauta* and immediately took command. "String my hammock there," she demanded as she elbowed and pushed her way through. When she opened her mouth it sounded like someone had switched on an electric carving knife. Her voice had a grating, metallic quality that abraded the ear as it sliced its way through the conversations. It was like a badly dressed Queen Victoria had stepped on board. Her bellowing and complaints, initially irritating, became a source of amusement to both fellow passengers and crew. She quickly got the nickname "the Loudspeaker." Over the next twelve hours she competed with the noise from the two-cylinder engine as we thumped our way downstream.

The river was wider now, nearly half a mile across in some sections, and the current was energetic. A couple of hours out of

Iquitos the craft turned up a tiny tributary, the jungle mere feet on either side. The captain was looking for potable water. We weren't ready for non-boiled river water just yet. Our guts weren't that strong. Lack of sanitation and drinking un-boiled river water accounted for most of the gastrointestinal diseases in the jungle. Worms, amoebas, and parasites from river water had a devastating effect on both locals and travelers alike. During the rainy season with flooding and worsening sanitary conditions, bouts of vomiting and diarrhea were pretty common. Deep in our hearts we knew we shouldn't drink water. But as we pressed farther into the Amazon basin the alternatives were rather unattractive. Boiling water was sometimes impossible, halazone tablets tasted awful, and there was only so much Inca Cola a guy could drink.

Our only other stop was at a small native village at the mouth of the Napo River to disembark a teacher. By evening we watched a marvelous Amazon sunset, comfortable in our hammocks as other passengers sang and played cards around us. The *Mirauta* reached Pevas at the mouth of the Ampiyacu River by midnight and while the Pevas-bound passengers scurried home, the four of us slept onboard, secured by lanyards to the wharf.

Wednesday: Pevas

At five this morning our crew unloaded the beer. The clanking bottles didn't come with a snooze setting and so we were roused unceremoniously out of our shelter. Our dockside floating sleeping quarters were no longer exclusively our own.

A local family took pity on the four rather unkempt foreigners who labored up from the water. We were invited to their home for a hearty breakfast of fried plantain, eggs, bread with strawberry jam, and some pretty palatable coffee. Even more remarkably, the daughter's older parents graciously volunteered their house for as long as we stayed in Pevas. We grabbed our packs and the elderly couple escorted us back down to the edge of the river to their home. The huts that edged along the river were elevated on stilts to deal with the flooding during the rainy season. Elevation also served to keep the rats and venomous snakes from becoming part of the family. A long wooden ladder led up to the living area ten feet or so above the soggy ground. The front faced dockside and an orange-railed veranda lined by big open windows provided us with a splendid view of the river. It was one of the few painted houses near the water with a fine turquoise color that set it apart from all others. The interior was sparsely furnished with a rudimentary cooking area, wicker chairs, and a wooden table. There was no running water and no electricity. Kerosene lanterns, blackened by long use, provided light. Sleeping was simple. Hammock hooks that were screwed into walls and pillars around the house provided us with private space. A separated bathroom structure was fifteen feet outside, along a narrow wooden plankway high above the ground and river. A simple hole cut in the wooden floor marked the spot. Over the next few days, squatting high on our perch above the muddy riverbank, we all had the same observation: it was the delay, those scant seconds when the evacuation ended and the sound of poop hitting mud resonated below—one Mississippi, two Mississippi, *splat*.

We set off to explore our little town. A wide concrete sidewalk led up a long flight of maybe a hundred steps well above the river to the central plaza. Small tiendas surrounded the square on two sides, a municipal building with a generator humming on a third, and a simple single-steeple church on the fourth. Dirt streets led out from the center with a mixture of small homes and shops. There were no cars, no post office, and no telephones. Electrical power, provided by the generator, only operated from dawn to dark. The four of us wandered through town until we found its sole open restaurant and settled in for lunch.

The staff told us we should head upstream for about an hour to a small settlement of Pucaurquillo. There were plenty of motor lanchas on the river and they'd help us negotiate a ride. Two native tribes, the Huitotos and the nomadic Bora people—once mortal enemies, they told us—now lived peaceably at either ends of the settlement. We'd see, they promised, the real traditional Amazon way of life.

The motor launch *Isa Quito* wound its way upstream. We passed two or three small settlements and then pushed farther along to the village. Curious children darted to the boat followed by the elderly *alcalde*, or local mayor, who introduced himself as Wanadi and his wife Pucu. Frits' furrowed brow relayed his disappointment. We expected traditional native dress, but everyone around us was somewhat westernized, dressed in the same clothing we'd seen at other villages and in town. Wanadi laughed, took Mary's hand, and led us up into the village. "Oh, we wear our traditional clothing on Fridays," he said, "and on the weekends, when the tourist boats drop by." He and Pucu walked us across the broken meadow of grass and trampled silt, through the village and introduced us to families and their children. The children never left our sides as we strolled amongst the modest homes. Strangers like us provided a wonderful diversion from chores. Two hours later we reconnected with the mayor and his wife to say goodbye. We caught a ride back on a local peque-peque loaded with passengers and bananas. "Come back soon," Wanadi yelled over the engine noise. "Come back and visit us again."

A rainstorm overtook us on the return to Pevas. The passengers watched as it closed in and then engulfed us in big splatters. We put in to shore for shelter and waited until it passed. I looked at the overhanging jungle and the warm, cotton-batting mist that hovered above the narrow, twisting river as morning sunlight filtered through. The landscape looked as if we'd ripped a page out of *National Geographic* and held it out at arm's length.

Arriving at Pevas we came in alongside a gunmetal gray Peruvian Navy river vessel. Its crew was off patrol and had moored their launch dockside, just below our house. We met them at the restaurant up in the town, and during supper bought them all a round of beer. They were from the *Caseta de Policía Militar* at Pituayal, which was just at the mouth of the Rio Ampiyacu—the River of Poisons—a kilometer or two downstream. Their job was to patrol the Amazon and the small rivers down to Leticia, protecting settlements and riverboats from smugglers, bandits, and *los narcotráficos* (drug traffickers). Between mouthfuls of beer, they assured us that lots of *botecitas*, as they called them, passed each day from Iquitos to Leticia. We should have no problems whatsoever finding passage.

That night, to keep the mosquitoes at bay, we lit candles, burned smoky green Chinese mosquito coils, and slathered on a cocktail of insect repellents from our packs. It felt good to be dry and safe in our little Pevas home so high above the jungle floor. The four of us lay in our hammocks under the sooty brightness of a kerosene lantern and reminisced about back home.

Thursday: Pevas

Encouraged by our conversation with the navy guys last night we
boated out to the Pituayal station. We were energetically welcomed
by our drinking buddies and encouraged to take a quick trip back
up to Pucaurquillo on navy business. They needed bananas. It was
a fast trip in the patrol boat. The launch sped up the river with
a large wake trailing behind and tied up at the village. Wanadi,
all smiles, recognized us amongst the crew and came running
down to visit. We helped load bananas and were back on the water
in minutes.

Once back at the *cuartel militar* (barracks), we sprawled out on the
high ground and made ourselves comfortable to wait for a passage
to Leticia. The river was unpredictable and so was its traffic. The
only thing that passed today was time, and even that passed slowly.
Always attentive to the long curve in the river in front of us, we
wiled away our time reading, chatting, and sleeping. Every river
craft was obliged to check in with the patrol at the Guardia. There
were scores of tiny dugouts and numerous wooden and aluminum
boats powered by small-capacity inboards or those two-cylinder,
long shaft peque-peque engines. They transported passengers and
freight to nearby villages and settlements. Most were local traders
who carried hardware, tools, canned foods, beverages, rice, or
beans. They traded for live animals, fresh fruits, vegetables, and
native crafts. None were headed as far as Leticia.

A brief rainstorm broke at sunset with two beautiful entwined
rainbows framed by a dark sky that arched across the river. The
gracious station commander invited us in to the officer's mess for
a delightful dinner and a bottle of wine.

Our backs ached from fourteen hours of waiting, and we gladly got into a boat to head back to Pevas for the evening. We turned back twice because of motor trouble, but finally the engine turned smoothly. A soldier in the bow guided the helmsman past danger-ous floating logs and small islands of foliage hidden in darkness. We resolved to try again tomorrow and forget about our disap-pointment today.

The generator had spluttered to a stop for the night and the little town of Pevas sat dark and silent. Frits and I decided it was a safe time for a personal cleanup in the river. We stripped down to our underwear, grabbed our soap, shampoo, and towel, climbed down the ladder from the house, and quietly headed over to the wharf. Apparently, somewhere along their journey, Frits had run out of his own underwear and had taken to borrowing from Wil. Two bearded guys cautiously snuck towards the dock, one in skiv-vies and one in skimpy red bikini panties. The moon was simply a sliver but our eyes swiftly accommodated and we made our way undetected out onto the wooden dock. We stood apprehensively at the end, neither wanting to be the first to jump in. There were too many scary stories about predators in the Amazon. Frits pointed to the little ripples in the water: fins. Occasionally fish would thrash about and then the surface would calm again. Something was feeding. We stood there screwing up courage. Suddenly it didn't seem like such a good idea to bathe in the Ampiyacu at night. We heard a muffled click and the village lighting blazed on. At the top of the stairway that led up into Pevas, a small knot of people, curious about unfamiliar movement dockside, had fired up the generator. They took in the scene. The two strangers they'd shared their village with for the past couple of days stood frozen, mostly naked in the spotlight. One wore women's panties. Frits and I shot into the dark waters amid laughter and catcalls. Fish or no fish, whatever dangers were in the river, it was less humiliating than standing there under the lights. In the record time it took to struggle ashore, we'd soaped, shampooed, and swallowed our pride. As we climbed the ladder back up into our house, Mary and Wil stood there smiling. They didn't say a word. They didn't need to.

Friday: Rio Amazonas

It was common knowledge in the village that four *extranjeros* were headed downriver to Leticia. It was also well known that we were down on our luck. Out of the blue the Loudspeaker's father loudly announced that he would personally chauffeur us in his boat all the way to Leticia for only twenty thousand soles each. There were audible gasps and the raspy sounds of air exhaled amongst the locals close enough to eavesdrop. That amounted to a small personal fortune of around two hundred dollars apiece. We just stood there with crossed arms and said nothing. Sensing our reticence, he blustered; he'd do it for fifteen thousand. No takers. From that point he was like an auctioneer in reverse, his price dropping with every utterance. By the time we left for the Guardia at Pituayal, he was down to five thousand soles, a modest forty-five dollars. If his daughter, the Loudspeaker, was coming, we figured he needed to pay us just to be captive in the same craft.

Back at Pituayal we watched from our perch on the high knoll as a boat rounded a distant bend in the river. She was bigger than most, and as she closed we recognized her. It was the fancy tourist boat *Adolfo* up from Iquitos. The *Adolfo* tied off and her captain, with his itinerary papers in hand, came ashore. He was met on the dock by the commander who put his arm around the captain's shoulder as they walked side-by-side back to the control building. A few minutes later they emerged and the commander beckoned us over. He had called in some favors. The *Adolfo* captain, he said, had somewhat reluctantly agreed to take us to Leticia. There were a few conditions. We would sleep in hammocks on the lower deck with the crew. We were welcome to any scraps from the meals prepared for the crew and passengers, but only if there were leftovers; *don't count on excess food, bring your own*. Finally, the upper two decks were strictly off limits. Those decks were for paying passengers only. Furthermore, the captain would take us back to Pevas and wait until we gathered our packs, said our goodbyes, and bought provisions for the trip. He smiled and informed us the fare he had negotiated with the *Adolfo* captain: it was a meager fifteen dollars, paid in full immediately.

THE ADOLFO, OUR RIVERBOAT FROM PEVAS TO LETICIA

As we loaded our packs and provisions on board the *Adolfo*, the well-heeled tourists ventured down to get a look at the four new passengers. Our unkempt appearance and traveling stories amused them. Instead of staterooms and beds we strung hammocks and lived a little wild. Before long we were invited, over the protestations of the captain, to join them up top. The captain finally relented. Better to bend his rules and have happy customers. He declared us welcome to mingle with the passengers and join them on their excursions as long as we ate and slept below.

The first excursion turned out to be the Huitoto and Bora villages of Pucaurquillo. The mayor Wanadi and a Bora welcoming party stood on the high ground above the dock. It was transformational. The western clothing we saw on our previous trips to the village was replaced with skirts and dresses made from pounded fibers of palm trees and painted with animal shapes and geometric designs. Strings of tiny shells jingled around their ankles. Wanadi and Pucu wore headbands crowned with scores of bright red and green macaw feathers. The villagers gathered behind them in chanting couples.

The *Adolfo* passengers, wide-eyed, filed off the boat with the four of us in the rear, followed by the captain and his crew. This was the Amazon. These were the fabled natives from the deep jungles, hidden for centuries, wild and untamed.

WANADI AND PUCU, MAYOR OF THE BORA/HUITOTO VILLAGE OF PUCAURQUILLO

"Jorge, Maria," Pucu cried as she rushed past the passengers and crew and threw her arms around Mary. I got a big handshake and smile from Wanadi. "You did come back." The passengers were perplexed. The captain was apoplectic. If laughter was the best medicine, he was definitely part of the placebo group. It was only after we explained our extended stay in Pevas, the trips up the Ampiyacu in search of bananas, and our visit at the village that a smile cracked again on the captain's lips—and only after we promised to keep the tribe's clothing transformation a secret. He just scowled and joked about throwing us off at the first isolated place—at least, I hoped he was joking

The old mayor, now clad only in a loincloth, carried a stout cane. He beckoned the group into the large thatched building where village members danced and sang to the beat of clapping hands and a wooden drum. The men, staves in hand, thumped rhythmically in the dirt, their shells chattering in time as the women hopped and skipped amongst them. Amid laughter and bantering they bade Frits and I to join them, simply ignoring our vigorous protestations. Soon other tourists, sweat glistening on their foreheads, eagerly wound their way in tempo around the enclosure.

The dancing was a pleasant diversion, but it seemed contrived and forced. Around us a people once free and nomadic now danced for strangers. A mere eighty years ago, now nearly at the outer edges of living memory, the rubber industry brought immense wealth and luxury to investors. To these people it brought mass enslavement and destruction. They were rounded up by the tens of thousands, taken from their distant jungle villages, shackled in chains, and forced to tap white latex from the rubber trees on the great plantations. While the plantation owners, mostly American and European, ate imported *pâté de foie gras*, the native rubber tappers lived in near-slavery and close to starvation. It was immoral, unethical, and unjust. Once proud nomads who lived comfortably between the physical and spiritual worlds, they now drummed and danced for strangers in a ritualistic parody of their ancestry. For the Bora it was their new world order.

Across the wide courtyard, the Huitoto of Pucaurquillo waited. While daily life differed little from their Bora neighbors, their traditional dress was markedly different. Women were bare-breasted and clad in short skirts of pounded paper bark painted with geometric designs. The men wore simple loincloths and woven head adornments symbolizing dugout canoes and fish.

Walking around a village full of bare breasts was a little unnerving; perhaps that's not the best word choice to express how I felt. As a young teenager I'd found a forgotten box of musty old *National Geographic* magazines in the basement. Under the glare of a bare sixty-watt light bulb I'd flipped through the pages to discover images described as "primitive" naked women from Africa or distant islands in Borneo. It was voyeuristic, a little exotic, and a touch erotic—well, maybe more than a *touch* erotic. It was my first real collision between bare breasts and a teenage libido. Perhaps now, at some deep, visceral level, I felt ashamed of my response. Was I embarrassed because of what I interpreted as a sense of moral or intellectual superiority over what at first blush appeared to be a primitive jungle existence? Was it simply a lack of clothing that caused such an intense reaction? To make matters worse, none of the village men or women cared. They just went about their business of entertaining us through dance, food, and idle chatter. We faced a whole village of nonchalant, bare-breasted women.

HUITOTO PEOPLES OF PUCAURQUILLO

The lives of jungle people described in those old mildewed mag-azines portrayed a sense of benign simplicity. It was romanticized, of course. The reality was completely different. In the Amazon there were rodents the size of pigs, snakes as thick as trees, and little green frogs so poisonous they could fell a man with a simple touch. If we walked a scant few miles out into the dense jungle that surrounded this village, the locals could almost certainly not only sustain and survive for days, but return. We, on the other hand, without the aid of maps, sextants, and compasses and lacking city streets, restaurants, and hotels, would be hopelessly lost. All our supposed superior education, loftier morality, and comfortable upbringing would be for naught. It was a strange duplicity.

We retraced our voyage down the Ampiyacu, past Pevas and back out on to the Amazon. Within a few hours we navigated to the small Yagua island settlement of Jessonia, built on the banks of the Chichita River, which was a small tributary that cut through the jungle. Jessonia was founded sixteen years ago as a native and nature preserve by Herman Jesson, an American adventurer–phi-lanthropist. Along with his Yagua wife Lila and daughter Jazmin, he still occasionally vacationed here. A young Indian boy and his dog waited for us on shore and we cast him the mooring line and then pushed the gangplank into the bank. The settlement was nothing more than a gathering of perhaps thirty natives in a group of raised thatched homes and a central communal structure.

The village men wore long grass-like skirts fashioned from the stringy fibers of aguaje palm. Blood-red dye of crushed achiote berries colored their faces and clothing. It gave them a fierce, hostile appearance, which was accentuated by the long *punaca* (blowguns) with curare-tipped darts they toted around. One shot from those darts and the prey was a goner, suffocating as its muscles paralyzed and lungs collapsed. We watched, fascinated, as the men demonstrated the uncanny accuracy of those weapons, hitting targets of small leaves pinned to a post a hundred feet away. The Yagua are hunters. They bring down wild pigs, tapirs, monkeys, birds, and small jungle rodents as well as fish along the river.

In fact, it was these same Yagua that inspired early Spanish explorers to give the Amazon its name. The Yagua men, hidden amongst the jungle vegetation, fired darts and threw spears at the Spaniards as they sailed upriver. The Spanish saw tall, dark, long-haired natives in grass breast coverings and skirts, assumed they were women, and decided the river was populated by the Amazon women warriors of Greek mythology. They christened the river "Amazonas."

As in every village we visited along the river, the children followed our every move, laughing and jostling beside us. Dressed in traditional aguaje palm clothing and faces streaked with achiote they mimicked their elders but, like children everywhere, they also dashed about amid the repeated admonitions of parents.

YAGUA CHILDREN FROM JESSONIA WERE AS CURIOUS
ABOUT US AS WE WERE OF THEM

Yet for all the activities, these people seemed to be quite shy and reticent towards visitors. Despite exuberant children, most elders seemed apprehensive towards our intrusion. Many stood awkwardly and stared expressionlessly at our group, uncertain as to what we wanted and what we were doing here amongst them. At times there seemed to be some mystical line between us, one not to be crossed, a space which we did not invade and they remained behind for sanctuary.

That evening our boat was moored downstream from Jessonia at another Yagua village. The sky was dark. The moon had waned to a sliver, the village kerosene lanterns cast subtle glows, and only a few deck lights burned on board. At night the jungle was still, but never silent. In fact, the nighttime orchestra got pretty loud. The tympanic clack of castanet frogs, the eerie trumpets of howler monkeys from somewhere deeper in the jungle, and a rich barrage of insect choruses surrounded us. At night the darkness brought a sense of security and a cloak of invisibility for many of the jungle creatures. It also brought out the predators in search of easy kills. Jaguars and leopards hunted now. So did the black caiman, the river's largest predator. Along the shallow edges we heard the rustles and splashes of caiman feeding on fish and unwary animals. The women had corralled all the loose chickens and carried them up the ladders and into the safety of their elevated homes. Some Yagua men came down to our boat and offered to take us out in their dugout canoes in search of caiman. The four of us climbed into a shallow wooden canoe and pushed off. Mary and Wil pointed flashlights shoreward, back towards our boat, and we found ourselves starring into the bright red reflected eyes of caiman.

We paddled up the small tributary. Each paddle stroke not only propelled us forward but also rolled the canoe disturbingly from side to side. Around us, amongst the overhanging vines and floating logs, scores of caiman rested and waited. Long, dark snouts lay vaguely visible just above the water's surface. As the flashlight beams caught wary eyes, crimson dots maliciously gleamed back at us. Each time we approached for a closer view we heard a snort or splash and reptiles slipped beneath the inky surface. Only rippling water illuminated by the flashlight arcs remained. It was a disquieting feeling, sensing these predators were around and under us, waiting to strike. I'm sure each one of us invoked a silent prayer that included an implicit request that we not tip over.

Saturday: Rio Amazonas

Deep into the early morning hours we experienced another heavy, driving rainstorm. It came in quickly and washed across the river before Frits and I could move from our hammock perimeter around the railings. Once we relocated out of the rain and dried off, I settled into a deep, sound sleep, oblivious to the damp and the jungle noises.

Today was what our captain confidently dubbed a day of relaxation. The tour group—that is, all of the paying passengers—wanted to hike inland through the nearby abandoned Tambo Piranha Lodge and along jungle pathways, into a wildlife preserve in search of exotic butterflies. The passengers had marveled at the framed exotic butterfly collection that hung down on our lower deck. They oohed and ahhed at the cerulean blue morphos, the robin egg swallowtails, the conspicuous birdwings with wingspans of over ten inches long, as well as the scores of smaller colorful butterflies pinned under the glass. They were eager to depart and get a glimpse at those real live specimens flitting by them in the wild.

Wil, Frits, Mary, and I, on the other hand, under captain's orders, were confined on board. The freeloaders, *los tacaños* as he called us, were to stay put. We were delighted. Without the captain, most of the crew, and all of the passengers, we had full run of the ship's amenities and we were determined to take advantage of them. First on our list was the shower. We drew lots, negotiated, and pleaded until we determined the order: Wil followed by George, then Mary with Frits taking up the anchor position. We dashed with towels and toiletries up to the main first-class showers. By the time we all finished there wasn't a drop of hot water left in the boiler. It was luxurious. Hot steamy water—and lots of it—cascaded over shampooed heads and soapy bodies. As we each finished it was down to the galley with its large sinks to wash and rinse our dirty and somewhat moldy clothes, then to the engine room to dry them on makeshift lines stung across the pipes and valves. A final push got us up to the beer fridge and deck chairs on the observation deck. That's where they found us; clean and well groomed, sipping cold beer and smugly sprawled out on the top deck in the noonday sun like we owned the place.

It was a dejected, mud-covered, and bug-bitten butterfly party that returned. They were clearly not a happy lot. They had seen no cerulean blue morphos, no swallowtails or birdwings, nor *any* exotic butterflies. The heavy rains early this morning had driven the insects to cover and turned the jungle pathway into a slippery mud bath. The returning group was soaked in perspiration, awash with jungle rain, and covered in congealed, fallow-brown mud from slips and slides. All in all, they were not in a very congenial mood as they tramped back up the gangplank. All they wanted was a hot shower and clean clothes. Apparently, for some unknown reason, perhaps a mechanical failure, there was no hot water.

During our semi-isolation on the lower deck we befriended all the crew. In some respects, the four of us held even a lower social standing than the crew in the ship's hierarchy. It was an odd situation. We were passengers—not full-fare passengers, but instead almost freeloaders in the eyes of the captain. We had been forced upon him. We could socialize with the well-heeled passengers, just not eat with them. We lived with the crew, but had the run of the ship with very few boundaries. Occasionally without asking, we helped the crew with dishes and general duties. Slowly, over the last couple of days, we all became friendly and accepting of each other.

When we originally boarded, the captain made clear that we needed to bring our own food on board. We could have any left-over food; we just shouldn't count on it routinely. The galley staff figured that issue out quickly. They simply cooked a little more for each meal. We ate with the crew after the meals up top were served. In fact, tomorrow the galley staff said they'd roast a pig if we bought one from the villagers. Even the captain smiled about roast pig and rubbed his hands together.

Later that afternoon, we traveled up another narrow tributary to fish and swim. While Mary baited hooks for tourists on one side of the boat, several others, including me, swam on the other side. The tourists caught the occasional red-bellied piranha, about the size of a big sunfish, while the spotter crewman on our side of the ship kept an eye out for caiman and river snakes.

Sunday, November 6, 1977: Leticia, Colombia

We woke up with our ankles infested with insect bites. We usually slept in our clothes, wrapped in blankets while green mosquito coils burned around us. Here on the open deck, the coils were not very effective so we slathered on bug spray. We weren't certain what insect caused the bites, but the crew was convinced they were fleas. I counted fifty-one bites on my left ankle and forty on my right. Although Mary had not counted hers, she assured me she had more. Frits and Wil were not spared either, as the four of us soaked our ankles in cold water and applied cortisone cream offered by the crew. We weren't surprised about the bites. We expected them. There are about thirty million different species of insects here in the jungle. Someone once said that if you spent an afternoon in the jungle you were sure to discover a new species of something. Whatever that new something was, they had bitten the crap out of us.

By early morning, an hour or so downstream, we reached Chimbote, a tiny river settlement and navy control post. While the captain and the commandant checked papers, passengers, and cargo, Frits, Mary, Wil, and I sprinted into the village to find a fat pig. We successfully negotiated a price for a small sow, looped a rope around its neck, and headed back to the boat. The pig wasn't keen on leaving familiar grounds to follow us and dug in its hoofs in dissent. We pulled harder and it reluctantly followed. Much to the local's amusement, it skidded and grunted and squealed, tugged, and protested right through the entire village. Even the crew teased us as we pulled and prodded our unwilling captive up the gangplank. No matter—we had the pig and roast pork beckoned.

Then the cook said, "I'll roast it—you kill it." We looked blankly at one other. Apparently, none of us had really thought this through. Somehow, we had envisioned the pig would go straight into a roasting pan, as if by some magic wave of a wand. Certainly we hadn't thought of ourselves as being a part of the pig's demise.

Heck, we only wanted to eat it. There was, however, one big step that separated us from dinner.

It wasn't really a matter of drawing lots for what lay ahead. I was the only one with a sharp knife looped on my belt. Mary, Wil, and Frits backed away a step or two, not wanting to be too close but still drawn by some irresistible force to watch the impending death. They were drawn like a car wreck; they didn't want to stare but they couldn't turn away. I pulled out the Ka-Bar my father-in-law had given me last November and flicked open the big blade. One of the crew knocked the pig off its feet and kneeled on the body to hold it down as the pig bawled and struggled to get upright. There was a terror in the pig's eyes as my free hand reached across its snout to force it down on the deck. I took a breath and then pushed the blade in deep and hard.

I had never killed an animal in my life. As a youngster I had used a magnifying glass to concentrate the sun's incoming rays on ants as they crisscrossed our sidewalk back in the small village of Arkell where I grew up. They smoked and sizzled under the focused power. Even then, I knew what I did wasn't right. I allowed myself to think of it as a science experiment, not cruelty. They were just ants. A few years later I shot a sparrow with my Red Ryder BB gun. The little bird was singing, idly perched in the cedar hedge that ran the length of our house. I shot it for target practice, instead of at the usual tin cans and bottles. Again, there was that instant remorse. I shot it for no reason other than I could. I took that bird's life because I wanted a target. One minute it was singing, the next it was dead. And of course I fished. But fish never seemed even remotely related to anything human-like. Fish were cold, scaly, and smelly. Mammals, on the other hand, were warm-blooded and sentient and often, like this pig, seemed to have feelings and maybe even emotions—like fear.

The blade went in deep and hard. The pig squealed in pain and terror and thrashed about. I wanted to find its heart, puncture it quickly, and end this. I jabbed again, then again, and again. I twisted the blade to sever an artery or cut into the heart. It was an agonizing death for that little pig. The cries slowly faded, the legs stopped flailing and twitched a few times, and then it just lay motionless. It had taken a couple of minutes—not simply seconds—to end that life. It was a clumsy attempt at best. Wil stood there shocked by the rather brutal end, her hand over her mouth and a real sense of sadness in her demeanor.

"I thought you were going to slit its throat. That would have been much faster and more humane," the cook mumbled as he pulled the carcass into the galley. Mary and Frits followed him in and watched a seasoned professional butcher the animal and prepare roast pig. The blood that lingered on the deck wasn't simply a sign of death; to a hungry crew, it was also an affirmation of life. At lunch, over plates full of roast pork, we revisited this morning's events. Every mouthful was a reminder of that poor pig's agonizing death. Every mouthful was delicious.

The final tourist stop for the *Adolfo* was at Isla de los Monos (Monkey Island), a small island purchased by an American entrepreneur who had a reputation for selling and shipping skins and animals out of the region. In the 1950s he captured and stocked the island with a hundred or so spider monkeys with thoughts to ship them home for a nice profit. The Colombia government with its new laws protecting fauna put the kibosh on that idea, and now, twenty-five years later, he had an island crawling with monkeys. Being a good businessman, he turned the island into a resort to attract a richer breed of monkey. Now over twenty-five thousand of the little showmen clambered through the trees screaming and playing and, well, monkeying around for tourists like us.

Back on the mainland we hiked inland along a jungle trail to a small oxbow lake. There, in the shallow waters, hundreds of Victoria lilies lay flat on the water's surface, their huge green leaves spanning six feet across. The leaves were delicate enough for a straw to pass through, but put a piece of cardboard or wood across them and they supported the weight of a human.

On the way back to the *Adolfo*, a green anaconda slithered down off a tree trunk and across our trail. It was only a small one, maybe ten feet long and ten inches thick. On the ground it was slow and lethargic. The green coloring and mottled black spots blended in well with the jungle around us. The four of us broke away from the group and followed it deeper into the jungle through the tangle of foliage. Sensing us, it moved faster through the swampy, shallow waters near the lake. We ran full force, splashing along behind, trying to flank it until the water deepened and the snake disappeared from view. There was nothing left but an undulating ripple along the water's surface. I don't know what we would have done had the snake decided to turn and face us. Even a small anaconda could strike back and in its defense have coiled around one of us. Even worse, what if it had called out to its momma, a full-grown, twenty-five-foot, three-hundred-pound, bone-crushing monster that decided to defend junior against these four intruding humans? It was exhilarating to chase through the jungle after our slithery friend. We were just lucky there were no other consequences than wet feet.

It was still daylight when we disembarked at Ramón Castilla on the island of Santa Rosa de Yavari. The air was taking on that odd cast that signaled the coming twilight. Ramón Castilla was the last of the Peruvian outposts on the Amazon. We bade the crew and passengers of the *Adolfo* farewell. The ship would reverse back upstream and return to Iquitos. Our destination was a mile or so across the river: the Colombian border town of Leticia.

With a bribe of a couple of beers and a few dollars slipped to a willing boatman, the four of us set off under the cover of an evening sun, across the river and through a narrow harbor channel that led up into the little Colombian town. With the confusion of the dockside melee, we snuck into town and bypassed the Federales and immigration control. None of us had Colombian visas or tourist cards and none of us wanted to pay bribes just to get into town. We settled into a comfortable little hotel, the Hotel Alemanas. It was pricey, but we needed a clean place to rid ourselves of these body fleas. The front desk manager demanded and kept our passports and then asked us to sign the police register. The passports, we were assured, would be returned when we checked out. The police would be around in the morning to check our permits and visas.

Monday: Benjamin Constant, Brazil

We gathered our passports at the front desk and checked out of the Alemanas early. We needed to clear Colombia before our names on the hotel registry were turned over to the security police. Frits thought we had a couple of hours, but I wasn't quite so confident. We wound our way down along the broken concrete and dirt of the main street, past the raucous spit-and-sawdust bars that lined the road. They were open for business even in the early morning.

Set in amongst the bars was an occasional big, colorful brothel, respectfully closed at this time of the morning. Leticia was a tough little Amazon frontier town and it made a comfortable hub for the drug dealers. Money and drugs changed hands in broad daylight here. It seemed like the entire town was engaged one way or the other in some illicit trade. Location was a big part of it. Leticia was the nexus where Peru, Colombia, and Brazil conjoined. River patrols from each of the three nations plied their respective country's waterways. But big money meant authorities frequently turned a blind eye to big-time smuggling operations. Instead, they often concentrated on the menial: the small-time drug dealers who didn't have the armed resources to fight back, locals caught in trivial acts, or those like us, travelers without the correct paper-work. Drug laws, it appeared, were more like suggestions, similar to good etiquette around the dinner table, such as chewing with your mouth closed and using the smallest fork for salad. However, federal soldiers were a constant armed presence here in town, a reminder to be cautious and keep moving. Just to be on the safe side we each traded our Peruvian money for Colombian pesos and Brazilian cruzeiros. At least our wallets would look like we belonged in the country.

Like most Amazon towns, Leticia stretched back up from the river along one main street. With a population of nearly nine thousand the town was pretty big by local standards. With money in hand we headed to the market. We met a group of Ticuna Indians, their faces painted grayish-indigo with pigment from the fruit of the huito trees, which were so common around here. It's funny; to us we saw a tall, crowned canopy tree, one of millions in the jungle. The Ticuna saw that same tree as fiber to make clothes, timber to build cabinets, medicine for antibiotics, and its fruit as beverages, dyes for utensils and clothing, inks for tattoos, and even insect repellent. Today they came in from local villages nearby to sell their colorful woven baskets, ornate carved masks, and bark paintings. We bought a few bark paintings, although we never learned the difference of quality primitive art from those simply knocked off for tourists. Just by the odds of probability we doubtlessly purchased the latter.

When we left the main road and headed down towards the docks at the edge of Leticia we wandered through a warrenlike hodge-podge of raised wooden houses. Narrow plank catwalks, some not much wider than a shoe size, wound over shallow, weedy canal ways lined with dugout canoes and up into the community. Wil led the way as we balanced, giggled, and worked our way up along the elevated walkways amongst the houses. We held our breath as the route took us into and through people's homes. Residents simply looked at us nonplussed, greeted us with a hello, and went back to whatever they were doing when we entered. I tried to think of what our response would be if a group of total strangers walked in our front door, exchanged greetings in some foreign tongue, smiled, strolled through the house, and exited out the back door without so much as a howdy-do. It just seemed incomprehensible, but here it was, just an everyday fact of community life on the river.

MARY, FRITS AND WIL ON THE PRECARIOUS BOARDWALKS IN LETICIA

We'd been hanging around town for a few hours and knew it was only a matter of time before Lady Luck caught up with us. We'd either end up paying bribes to some crooked Federales or worse, staring out of the wrong side of a jail cell on some trumped-up charge. It was time to skedaddle. We cautiously glanced over our shoulders for police and moved quickly, determined to keep one step ahead of trouble. The eleven-thirty ferry from the floating dock tied off to the riverbank got us over to the Brazilian side of the river and into the little town of Benjamin Constant. It was a short half-hour trip, but our whole travel experience changed when we disembarked.

The written word in Portuguese may look similar to Spanish, but the spoken language left us speechless—literally speechless. It sounded like Spanish spoken by the hearing impaired; you could almost understand it if you really concentrated, but after a while it was just too difficult to keep up the mental intensity. We were almost back at a communication square one, similar to when we were first introduced to the Spanish language in Mexico many years ago.

Before tracking down a boat to Manaus, we decided to grab a bite to eat. A local restaurant near the ferry dock looked inviting. There was a simple menu hanging over the door as we entered. Looking at the new Portuguese script it seemed the easiest thing to order was a hamburger. Hamburger was spelled *hamburguesa* in Spanish but an even more recognizable *hambúrger* in Portuguese. You'd think that people on the border of two Spanish-speaking countries would be bilingual and it would be a simple task to order one. I was wrong. I asked the waitress for a *hambúrger*. She looked perplexed. I asked for it louder. She looked positively terrified. I got up and pointed to the chalkboard menu sign above the door. "*Hambúrger, hamburguesa, hamburger*," I barked. Oh, for Christ's sake, just pick a language. One of them had to get through. "Here," I said, pointing directly at the letters of the word *hambúrger*.

"Ah—um am-boar-gear," she smiled, "vowsay keer um am-boar-gear?"

"Yup, um am-boar-gear," I repeated. Welcome to basic Portuguese.

The Javari River separated the frontier of Brazil from Peru on a sinuous course for over nine hundred miles inland through the jungle. Here at Benjamin Constant, the Javari provided a calm shelter for the riverboats from the fast-moving course of the

Amazon. That's where we found the *Lord Kelvin*, moored against the muddy embankment unloading cargo. The captain, to our delight, spoke a little Spanish—enough for us to negotiate our passage and understand we'd ship out on Friday. We grabbed our gear, tramped up the gangplank, and found space to string our hammocks amidships on the sheltered open space on the second deck. We weren't alone. We were greeted by seven other travelers, moving in the same direction, each with a different story and brought together by the promise of a journey. As it turned out, we would have lots of time to get acquainted. Right now, we considered ourselves lucky. We had free accommodation for the next few days and a solid ship under us as we headed for Manaus.

Tuesday: Tabatinga, Brazil

It was a lazy morning for introductions. The unloading was going slowly and the captain now declared we wouldn't head downstream until Saturday at the earliest. Waiting was a necessary evil we had all learned to cope with. *Lord Kelvin*'s group of travelers spanned eight different nationalities. We introduced ourselves to our new shipmates. Our group now comprised of Mary (an American), Wil, Frits, and a new traveler Henry (who were all Dutch), Sam, nicknamed "Shmulik" (an Israeli), Manfred and his female traveling companion (German), Michel (French), Paul (Australian), Ignacio (Mexican), and me, the lone Canadian. Spanish and English were our common languages, although we overheard conversations in every language.

Shmulik's adventures brought him from Luxemburg to Barbados, across Venezuela, and into Bogotá, Colombia. He flew the seven hundred miles south down to Leticia with Aeropesca, a small unscheduled cargo operation that winged anywhere the money took them. Dubious freight or paying passengers were stuffed into their C-46 Commando, a dual-piston engine aircraft designed by the Americans during the 1940s to transport troops and munitions. Aeropesca had a rocky safety record. With absent or unserviceable navigation equipment and always overloaded, the company had frequent mishaps. Just this August, wind had blown one flight off course and without working navigation it had crashed into a mountain, killing all seventeen on board. But it was one of the cheapest and easiest ways to get down to Leticia. With thirty dollars slipped to the pilot and perhaps a few silent prayers on board, Shmulik was on his way.

At about noon the group began to get a little stir-crazy and we edged off the boat towards town. The captain poked his head out of the wheelhouse and vigorously waved us back. We were leaving immediately upriver for Tabatinga. We complied, but after a couple of hours of inaction we stormed off the boat and despite the protestations walked into town for provisions and supplies. Moments after returning, the *Lord Kelvin*'s diesels fired up and the crew cast off. We were on our way two hours upstream to the opposite shore and the river port of Tabatinga that bordered Leticia. The captain nestled the *Lord Kelvin* along the banks under the overhanging trees at the base of a small street leading into town.

A knot of us headed up and along Avenida da Amizade, Tabatinga's main drag that led back into Leticia. These two little towns were an urban oasis sandwiched between endless jungle and the Amazon. There wasn't a soul at the customs shed at the border. A simple small, white cairn marked the frontier of the two countries. One minute we were walking on Avenida da Amizade in Brazil and the next on Avenida International in Colombia. We were surprised. Just yesterday, over in Colombia, the police had been looking for us. Now we crossed the border with impunity. With such a casual approach to border control, it was little wonder that drugs and contraband filtered so easily into these countries. If we could get through so simply, anyone or anything could.

Leticia was alive again today with the peppered sound of motorcycles, the hubbub of the riverside market, the movement of shady deals and dealers, and the presence of armed soldiers, most of whom seemed too young to shave let alone carry machine guns. It was ninety-three degrees in the shade. We sweated our way around town, dodging errant taxis that barreled aimlessly down the streets. We passed noisy pool halls, seeking out and spending time with fellow travelers in the local restaurants and bars. We drank beer with offbeat names like Brahma Chopp, Pony Malta, and Club Colombia. They went down fast and easy, and we imagined the ice-cold fluids replacing the beads of salty perspiration we were constantly brushing away.

Wednesday: Tabatinga

Enough sneaking around; Mary, Frits, Wil, and I desperately needed to formally enter Brazil before the *Lord Kelvin* sailed off on our nine-hundred-and-fifty mile trek downriver to Manaus. Mid-morning, documents in hand, we headed back to the customs shed on the frontier with Leticia. The officials were nowhere in sight but the door was unlocked. Office hours were obviously flexible. We patiently waited around outside for a while, but it was steamy hot again and the little shack offered shade, so we went inside and

made ourselves at home. The inside wasn't extravagantly decorated. There was a simple gray metal desk with a swivel armchair
and a couple of wooden benches. Taped to the wall between the
two open windows was a large street plan of the twin towns and
a map of Brazil. On the desk sat all the paraphernalia needed to
stamp our passports; rubber stampers hung neatly from a rotating
metal carousel, and an open ink pad along with a large, well-used
ledger book sat on a smudgy paper blotter. Frits wandered over
to the large Brazilian map and pointed at Marajó Island at the
mouth of the Amazon. He pointed out that the estuary island was
the same size as Holland. "In the number of square kilometers,"
he said with a big smile, "Holland is really insignificant, but in the
number of square heads it is very important."

Tempted as we were to help ourselves to an unofficial entrance
stamp, better sense prevailed. Instead, we wandered back into
Leticia where Wil called her sister and we helped our friends with
their limited Spanish to check airline schedules from Manaus to
Sao Paulo.

As we returned to Tabatinga, the Brazilian immigration officer
was closing up shop for the evening. We begged him to reopen the
door and stamp our passports. Grudgingly, he leafed through our
passports, frowned at the exit dates out of Peru, and then with an
officious air he smacked the rubber stamp down on the inkpad,
found a blank page in our passports, and carefully dated the new
issue. It was perfect timing; we wanted our passports stamped,
and he wanted to go home for dinner.

Thursday: Tabatinga

Drip! What the hell was that? One eye opened; then another drip.
It was pouring rain and I'd hung my hammock under the only
spot on the deck where the roof leaked. I stuffed wads of paper
and plastic up into the offending crack but only managed to turn
a slow drip into a deluge. I squished over to a drier spot and
restrung my hammock. Over the next hours the rain increased
in intensity. No matter where we stood the wind drove gusts of
water across the open deck. Even with the canvas curtains unrolled
over the railings there was little in the way of dry shelter, so we
all stripped down to the bare essentials and made the best of it. A
storm like this brought good news and bad news. The good news
was fresh water. Every container we could scrounge and steal was
out on the fantail, filling with potable rainwater. By the time the
storm passed over we'd have a few days' drinking water.

The bad news was the rainstorm provided perfect cover for the
crew to stop offloading the cargo and start drinking. Below us on
the crew deck we heard laughter and clinking bottles. The sacks of
flour, beer, biscuits, and bottled pop would remain in the hold
until the rain passed and the crew sobered up. One was going to
happen well in advance of the other.

The rain petered out mid-morning and our living quarters on the
upper deck of the *Lord Kelvin* returned to normal. Paying passengers,
along with the wheelhouse and captain's quarters, commanded the
upper deck. A slatted door facing the stern provided a smattering of
privacy to our small toilet. We shared a shower with the crew on the
lower deck. It was compact with barely enough space to bend over to
pick up the soap if you were unfortunate and dropped it. The shower
stall also served as a birdcage for the cook's noisy macaws. For basic

washing up, either personal or clothes, a small porcelain sink was anchored on the back wall behind us. A scratched and weatherworn mirror was fastened to the wall above it. There was a large wooden table and a few chairs and stools of assorted types and sizes. A gray metal kerosene lantern hung under the stern edge of the roof. That was the sum total of our amenities. Everything else we brought to the party.

During daylight most hammocks were looped out of the way into the crevasses between the roof support beams. A stalk of bananas, mostly eaten, was suspended in the corner by a piece of twine. Wet towels, clothing, and bedding hung from clotheslines, rigged like spider webs across the entire eighteen-foot span of deck. Several sticks of sugarcane rigged neatly together against the back railing of the fantail competed for space. As we moved around our cramped quarters we ducked underneath damp underwear and shirts, skirted past backpacks, and slipped around our mates. Amidst this, we and our traveling companions read, wrote, talked, daydreamed, and slept.

LIFE ON BOARD THE LORD KELVIN RIVERBOAT

Around noon the sun broke through, the sky brightened, and we watched the endless parade of river traffic float by below. A homespun wooden boat that was twenty feet long with a four-foot beam powered by a two-cylinder peque-peque engine passed by. It was loaded not with cargo but with fishermen, and they, along with their small dugout canoes, rode perpendicularly across the gunnels of the larger craft. We counted five hitchhikers, their catch covered with leaves and branches, like a kind of jungle refrigerator. The weight of the additional boats meant the larger canoe rode low and it was taking on water. One of the *pescadores* amidships bailed while the six others on board measured his progress with derision and laughter. What made the scene even more surreal was that the main boat also towed an additional six fishermen-laden canoes behind it.

We spent the next couple of hours engrossed in guessing the cargo of passing vessels. Bananas, fish, lumber, beer, and (of all things) mounds of sand sailed by us until we finally lost interest and headed into town.

A few of us walked down to the Federal police station and convinced them we needed a hot shower. Then we were off to a late-night Brazilian meal of rice, beans, manioc, beef, and beer.

Friday: Benjamin Constant

That morning, with the last of the payload dumped onshore, an empty *Lord Kelvin* moved a few miles downstream past Benjamin Constant. The cargo to be transported to Manaus was lumber. Our boat moored at the base of a muddy knoll. Twenty feet above us over the ridge and just beyond eyesight was a crude lumber mill.

Logging was the new replacement for the old rubber boom. A near inexhaustible supply of timber meant a near inexhaustible supply of money. The Trans-Amazonian Highway construction, which started only a few years ago, planned to bisect the rainforest from the Atlantic coast to the Peruvian border. At the time, it was only paved for two hundred miles, but during the dry season the road carved an easy route out for rainforest hardwood. Already this year lumber crews bulldozed hundreds of logging roads that radiated off the Trans-Amazon and deep into the jungle. The news was filled with conflict between lumber company crews and the natives. When companies illegally clear-cut in traditional native territory, the inhabitants often pushed back with primitive bows and arrows, spears, clubs, and blowguns. They were simple, effective, and lethal. Companies brutally retaliated with bullets and dynamite. Tribes right across the Amazon rainforest were being driven deeper and farther away. Up here, along the river frontier of the rainforest, logging roads stretched like tendrils up from the river. Local logging companies continued to push deep into native territory with social and moral indifference. Most loggers simply ignored federal laws that sought to preserve the sanctity of native territory and protect the forest. Here, the road out for timber was the river. The *Lord Kelvin* was part of that process.

Moored at the base of the rise we watched from our comfortable perch as an ungainly process unraveled below. A crude, wooden tray the width of a bundle of cut lumber was anchored with poles buried into the dirt. It ran thirty feet downhill towards us. It ended in the mud below us, stoppered by a couple of worn rubber tires laid down into the mushy quagmire. A second ramp, a sturdy four-by-twelve-inch board placed close to the ramp's end, was hoisted and lashed against the cargo entryway of the *Lord*

Kelvin. A second foot ramp plank was rested on the inner sidewall of a bumper tire. Nine men worked this bewildering contraption of lumber release, capture, and loading.

Two men lugged and shoved a stack of ten two-by-eight, five-foot lengths of sawn mahogany, banded them together with two tight metal straps on to the wooden tray, and pushed. While a few other men wet the tray with buckets of river water, the lumber sped down and crashed into the tire bumpers with a giant *sploosh.* If the banded stack held, another two men rushed over and pulled the wood out and slowly edged it up the big ramp onto the boat. Another group pulled it into the hold. Frequently, the bands broke as the stack hit the tires and the lumber scattered in every direction. The process stopped while the errant lumber was collected and hauled piece-by-piece up into the *Lord Kelvin.* For the next few hours as we watched, the air was laden with river smells and obscenities. The scene below us had degenerated into a muddy mess. Lumber was strewn everywhere. Workers dodged the banded lumber that cascaded errantly down the ramp way. The men had no protection; they worked barefooted in short pants and torn shirts, without the safety of steel-toed boots, gloves, or hooks. It was simply brute, manual labor. We watched the older men, the ones that had done this all their lives. Their legs were scarred, their faces worn and expressionless. They were resigned to forever push lumber up a crude gangplank. There were lots of workers who had very few alternatives here on the river. Eventually, darkness overtook their labors. They would start again tomorrow.

Tonight, isolated a few miles downriver from Benjamin Constant, we were treated to a preview of coming meals aboard ship. Our cook brought up plates of cold gritty rice, cold pasta, black beans, and a lukewarm fish soup, with fish parts none of us recognized. She called it *moqueca*. An English translation was "smelly pot of inedible fish bile." Most of the meals remained untouched, the rest thrown overboard. It was a harbinger of things to come.

Saturday: Rio Amazonas

At dawn they were at it again, cursing and shoving stacks of boards down the chute and then up into the hold. It all moved at a snail's pace. What might have been loaded in minutes at a modern port took the rest of the morning. We heard the resonant booms as lumber tumbled into the hold and the slap of boards thrown into random corners. Instead of neat stacks for wood below, we visualized haphazard piles of wood. Unloading would be a logistical nightmare. We prayed it didn't happen until after we disembarked in Manaus.

The rain swept in around noontime just as the loading finished. As soon as the laborers stopped loading they started drinking. Something or someone was going to get loaded, come rain or shine. We, on the other hand, raced to refill our potable water. Like in a choreographed dance we moved around the upper deck and out on the fantail with cups, plates, and bowls, eager to catch even drops of fresh clean water.

Around sunset, even the captain apparently had had enough of the lumber-loading charade and announced we'd head back to Benjamin Constant to offload a drunken sailor, pick up a replacement crewmember, and be on our way. We were elated. What we didn't foresee was a big celebration in town; one that no one should miss. We heard the captain say we'd leave as soon as he found new crew. Our lack of Portuguese tethered us to the boat as surely as leg irons, and we waited on board. After another of our new cook's infamously inedible meals we were close to mutiny. It was nearly 10:00 p.m. and we still hadn't cast off. Wils, Mary, Shmulik, and I, along with a mob of other angry passengers, stormed up to the captain's quarters to complain. Mary and Wils pounded on the door. There was vengeance in their eyes and a threatening commentary from most of our fellow shipmates on what we ought to do to the captain. Walking the plank was an option. Quite frankly, I feared for the captain's safety. I needn't have worried. He wasn't there. He had slipped undetected off the ship and was now safety ensconced at the party in town, getting drunk.

We heard raucous laughter and loud drunken voices at about three in the morning. Shortly after the engine fired up, the lines cast off, and we turned downriver. From our hammocks, none of us had the energy for a confrontation. We just hoped there was someone sober at the helm.

Sunday, November 13, 1977: Rio Amazonas

I was naked in the shower with the cook's two red-plumed macaws who nervously eyeballed me. They had separated; each one retreated to a different corner of the enclosure and balanced on small upturned oilcans. They stared unblinking into the corner, ignoring as best they could this giant intruder. It was like pulling the covers over your head to hide from the monster under the bed. It might give you a little sense of security and control, but did little to counter the actual boogeyman.

Outside the screen window the Amazon was washed in the gold and purples of dawn. The river was wide again, almost two miles across. The shower water warmed me. It was pumped up from the river to the sun-warmed tanks topside on the roof. Inside the shower, the water sprayed out from a makeshift showerhead mounted on the ceiling. It drenched me and splashed out to the perimeter, causing the parrots to squawk in protest. The galley cook hammered on the shower door. "Stop teasing my birds," she screamed. "Get out of the shower right now, you bully." Cookie was a truculent, miserable person. And worst of all, she was a rotten cook! It was revenge time. I rattled the door back at her and doused her parrots with as much water as I could. It was a cruel tactic for the birds. They fluttered and screeched in disapproval, but it felt good to get back at Cookie.

By nine this morning, sixty miles downstream from Benjamin Constant, we stopped at the little nondescript river settlement of Belém to pick up more passengers. There had to be some signal, some mysterious cues we missed, for the captain to bring the boat about and head into the little town for a passenger or two.

Another hundred miles brought us to the outflow of the dark-watered Camatiã River and the bordering town of São Paulo de Olivença. The town was the origin of all the mounds of sand we saw on the river barges back in Tabatinga. São Paulo sand was the best in the area for cement production. More passengers boarded. They and their crates of cargo remained below. Our little vessel was officially packed to the rafters.

The *Lord Kelvin* moved along, aided by the current, at a leisurely fifteen knots. The constant rhythmic drumming of the engine and propeller wash were the gods that never slept. The hypnotic, continuous green of the jungle soothed out the ache of the last few days of stasis. Occasional tributaries flowed into the river. Plumes of dark outflow washed downstream with us as they folded and disappeared into the massive Amazon. It was a day of reading and reflection.

Monday: Rio Amazonas

Last night the *Lord Kelvin* navigated to the town of Amatura and tied up against another riverboat. Early this morning a few of us disembarked in search of anything edible. We crested the small rise above the docks and stilted houses and headed for the old church in the town square. It was all in vain. The small riverfront vendors were closed and no amount of bartering dislodged any fruits or vegetables from the locals. Dejectedly, we returned to face the mess cook's breakfast of cold rice, pasta, and beans. The meals on board have not changed one iota. Breakfast, lunch, and dinner all included cold rice, plain spaghetti noodles, and a scoop of black beans. The soup at dinner, her specialty, was getting progressively worse. A day or so ago we were pretty confident there was some type of fish floating in the broth. Now all we got was fish heads and tails bobbing in the swill she served. We threw more slop overboard than we ate. I was surprised the Brazilian Federales hadn't stopped us for polluting the waterway. We complained to the captain who assured us we'd get better. We were skeptical. Not that we didn't believe him; just that we were becoming wise to the ways and false promises of our nefarious river captain. We strongly suspected the next good meal we'd eat was in a restaurant in Manaus.

Dark storm clouds swirled above us, a harbinger to the driving rain. Thunder boomed around us and lighting slashed down.

The captain put in a few times, seeking shelter under the jungle overhang while the rain swept in hard across the decks. The deck coverings, lashed to the railings, flapped and protested against the downpour. At times visibility was only a few hundred yards. The jungle appeared and vanished in the heavy rain. It was just too treacherous to be out on the water. The twin dangers of lightning strikes and submerged logs brought the captain to his senses.

Having passengers meant occasional stops in out of the way places. Today we navigated up the small, dark Jutai River to the hilltop settlement Porto do Jutai. Mist from the recent storm wafted up from the river like a white veil as we slowly wound our way upstream. Dugout canoes moved like silent apparitions through the mist.

Just as the hammocks came down, the rain began again. In the darkness I looked over at Mary, snuggled in her hammock asleep, wrapped in Wils' borrowed raincoat.

The crew was tired and convinced the captain to pull into shore to rest. The boat brushed against the shoreline foliage as we tied off. Giant wasps, angered at the intrusion, swarmed around our lantern. Down below, the tired crew found a little energy and a bottle of *cachaça*, a potent distilled sugarcane alcohol. They serenaded us deep into the evening.

Tuesday: Rio Amazonas

Late last night we were visited. Every evening the hammocks came down and hung across the open deck. Most of us slept with our heads to the outside railing so that we caught the river breezes along the shore. The water was at least eight feet below us, well beyond the height a hungry caiman could leap. Sleeping on the open deck we felt secure, but always a little exposed. In mid-sleep last night we heard something unworldly directly below us. There were wheezing and whooshing sounds of expunged air, long sucking sounds of deep, inhaled breaths, and the splash of roiling water. In the darkness we could make out movement on the surface beneath us. Shmulik lit the stern lantern and held it out over the railing. There below, feeding beside the boat was a herd of dark gray river manatee. We watched as they surfaced and sank, feeding off the plants on the river bottom. They were huge, maybe ten feet long each and weighing hundreds of pounds, with broad, dark bodies and flattened heads. Even with the knowledge that the source of the noise was harmless, the sounds from the darkness below were eerie and unsettling.

In the early morning hours we passed the town of Fonte Boa on the portside. The day was cloudy but pleasant. Afternoon showers were a constant companion, but this morning was lovely. Another passenger exited at the native settlement of Tamaniqu on the edge of the Jurná River. As a gauge of our remoteness, the Jurná meandered southwest for over fifteen hundred miles inland, across the deepest rainforests of Brazil to its source at the very edges of Peru, a mere two hundred miles from our starting point in Pucallpa.

We disembarked at the settlement and raced around, intent on finding any food that our cook hadn't yet touched. Our only reward was a few bananas and several doughy buns. We returned dejected, girded to face another of Cookie's abominations. Tonight even the crew recoiled at the sight of the slop she served. They led a gastronomic mutiny and threw the food overboard. We heard the raised voices, recriminations, and taunts below deck. Dishes and pots slammed around the galley, followed by the captain's pleas for calm. An hour later, Cookie appeared with our dinner. Nonplussed, she set the bowls down and left. It was a miracle. The food was hot! It was still the same recurring nightmare of rice, pasta, beans, and unpalatable fish soup, but it was hot.

We overnighted at Alvarães at the mouth of the Caiçara River. We moored under the shelter of thick trees behind a small island that hugged the shoreline. Unlike most settlements we visited along the river, this little municipality had a modern feel to it. Cement sidewalks paralleled trimmed, grass-lined streets. A tapir calmly grazed in an open field, its long nose rooting and snuffling through organic goodies and periodically curling to pop a tasty leaf into its mouth. We spent the evening in a pool hall, the only retail building that was open. Amid the crack of billiard balls and thumping baselines of ear-splitting music, we drank beer to wash away the lingering aftertaste of Cookie's latest meal.

Wednesday: Rio Amazonas

We're still alive. Those three simple, isolated words at the top of Mary's otherwise empty journal page gave testament to our survival skills over the past ten days aboard the *Lord Kelvin*. The rest of the page was blank, as if those words and those words alone expressed the cerebral space where she found herself today. But surely things were looking up. The fleabites still itched but faded daily. Manaus was getting closer by the hour and Cookie's culinary adulterations now shortened by the same degree. Our living arrangements were confined, but we liked our fellow travelers. We'd grown ever closer to our companions Wils, Frits, Manfred, and Shmulik. The rain that drenched us each afternoon or evening brought fresh drinking water. The newly repatriated box of forgotten, moldy, bug-infested biscuits, long hidden beneath unwashed clothes at the bottom of her backpack, could be discarded and replaced. The slow, long uneventful days were passing, lost in conversation, writing, and reading. Each day ticked off the calendar was one day closer to a journey's end. And as Mary proclaimed—we were still alive.

We proceeded downstream at a rhythmic fifteen knots, watching as hour after hour the endless green jungle drifted by. Frits had a hypothesis as to why the crew and locals ashore seemed so lethargic and slow. "It's not their fault," he opined in broken English. "They're surrounded by green jungle, and green is a calming color. All in all," he offered, "there's just too much calm-down around here." He was right—there was a hallucinating quality to endless flow of green jungle that slipped by us.

Paul, our Australian companion, determined to lighten his pack, ripped pages as he read them out of his pocket novel and let them flutter into the wind to wash away along the water. Obviously, we each wiled away the time in our own little space with our own little eccentricities.

We weren't sure if it was outright deception or simply an ugly coincidence, but just a mere half hour after Cookie carted up dinner and we forced tonight's concoction down, the *Lord Kelvin*'s engines slowed. She turned starboard on to the deep, coal-colored waters of Lake Coari and moored at a modern floating dock a few hundred feet from shore. In front of us were the lights of the modern, well-laid-out town of Coari. We saw illumination from the restaurants that lined the wharf area. Restaurants that were open. Restaurants that had food—real food—just out of reach across the open stretch of water.

Another herd of manatee milled around the boat tonight, foraging along the overhanging banks and shallow shore waters for those succulent plants and river grasses. We fell asleep listening to a lullaby of wheezes and snorts.

Thursday: Manaus, Brazil

Our captain promised we would reach Manaus today, although it would be a long day. We still had almost three hundred miles ahead of us, over eighteen hours provided the stops were short and the crew stayed sober. By the time Cookie cleared away the breakfast dishes, we had threaded our way from Coari to Codjás, ninety miles downriver.

The storms that broke over the region the past few days had swollen the lower reaches of the tributaries, and now fast-moving water rushed down towards the Amazon and the alluvial basins along the river. Chunks of waterlogged jungle shoreline broke free, were swept out by current, and floated downstream. Most of these floating islands were merely slowly-sinking masses of grassy embankments. They were of little consequence to either ships or navigation. However, around noon, as the *Lord Kelvin* squeezed between two islands that lay nestled in a bend of the river near the town of Anamã, we spotted a floater over twenty feet across. A thirty-foot acai palm stood resolutely at attention in the center, as if saluting back to us, as it floated majestically erect along with the current.

It was late, nearly nine in the evening, when we first saw the soft white halo of city lights against the dark silhouette of the jungle canopy. A young moon hung low in the northern sky and four bright stars of the Southern Cross guided us from the southern heavens. The dim, glowing band of Milky Way stars arched overhead. We all stood around the wheelhouse, leaning on the railing and watching as the halo slowly grew brighter. Cookie, always quick to catch the obvious, pointed at the glow ahead and squeaked "Manaus," and then turned to us and said with an optimistic grin, "This was adventure." She couldn't have been more spot-on. The *Lord Kelvin* had been an adventure.

Two hours later we passed the outer edges of the Catalao Peninsula, where the Rio Negro joined the Amazon. Across the river lay the city of Manaus. We broke through into the black waters of the Negro, and within the hour the crew threw mooring lines along a small precarious dock deep inside the Irarapé de Educandos harbor.

With permission granted to sleep on board that night, our little group scrambled down over a series of makeshift wooden gangplanks and headed shoreward in search of food and beer. At this hour the streetlights mostly illuminated empty thoroughfares and shuttered shops. The majority of the city's legitimate residents were at home, tucked in bed. The waterfront bars and brothels, on the other hand, were in full swing, bright seedy oases in a sea of darkness. We were drawn like moths to the lights, the noise, and the promise of beer and real food. We ended up in a small bar-come-brothel, the kind of place where you sat with your back against a wall or constantly checked over your shoulder. It was full of rough river crew and easy women—or maybe it was rough women and easy river crews. Who knew? But we were smart enough to keep our heads down and refrain from pointing it out to any of the bar's patrons. In a haze of cigarette smoke and loud music we drank beer and ate plates of *batatas fritas*. Then we sat back and watched the night unfold.

Friday: Manaus

We awoke this morning to yelping dogs. Not on shore, but in the water beside us. It was, to be sure, one of our more unusual alarm clocks. Our three wet, howling, furry friends were driven into the water by a larger pack of dogs on shore. They barked and yelped as they swam together, tails erect, trying to find a safe haven. They were none-too-happy the ship didn't provide refuge and headed for safer territory, wailing their displeasure.

Our gang of seven loaded up belongings and said goodbye to the captain and crew. Even Cookie, now that she no longer controlled our dietary destiny, got a hug as we left the *Lord Kelvin* behind. That she was absolutely useless in the galley no longer distressed us. From this point on, she was someone else's problem.

We searched out the tourist office over on Avenida Epaminondas. A young, attractive woman in accented English explained the city, its sights, and most importantly, some inexpensive hotels close to the center of Manaus. She recommended a hotel frequently used by travelers like ourselves. It was nearby on Avenida Joaquim Nabuco 495, just a short walk north.

Pensao Formosa was a simple, one-storied, flat-roofed stucco building. It was an open concept hotel. In front, facing the sidewalk, a clerk behind a small reception desk screened people entering the hotel. "Paying clientele only, no guests," read the sign above the key hooks. Adjacent to the reception area a spacious homespun restaurant served basic meals. Behind all that, a courtyard led out to two rows of small, basic rooms, each with a padlocked door, a single screened window, and a ceiling fan for ventilation. It was central, convenient, and inexpensive.

Manaus was a vibrant, bustling, modern city. The downtown was full of traffic that roared along under the shadows of twenty-story buildings. The city's gentle rolling hills were crowded with clean and colorful houses. Born centuries ago as a Portuguese fortress and modest supply base for exploration, the rubber boom of 1800s transformed it into a city of rich cultural and architectural wonders. Then a hundred years ago the main source of revenue, the natural rubber industry, collapsed. A Brit smuggled seeds from the rainforest and planted saplings in the rich soils of Malaysian plantations. That duplicity coupled with the innovation of synthetic latex was a one-two punch from which the town faltered down to one knee. When production soared in Asia and rubber prices dropped, Manaus went into a spiraling decline. Without the economic driver of rubber, industry moved out, shantytowns around the port areas migrated towards the city, and neglected buildings fell into disrepair. The art, culture, and architecture—so much an enterprise of the wealthy, educated rubber barons—faded with them. Out of desperation, Brazil declared Manaus a duty-free port. Now the city was flourishing again, with manufacturing and gas refineries around the edges while the streets bustled with retail shops and street vendors selling jewelry, cameras, clothing, and precious stones. The wealth returned. All around us, the city was rebuilding and rebranding to find its spirit again. Manaus and the new wealth from the jungle would not be isolated for long; a road six hundred miles south to Porto Velho, which already connected to Brasilia, was virtually complete.

We caught a glimpse of the past grandeur of Manaus as we stood in Plaça São Sebastão with *Teatro Amazonas*, the imposing Opera House, framed behind the colossal fountain of the Four Continents. Rubber barons, flush with money, tried to recreate the lavish lifestyles of Europe right here in the middle of the jungle. The entire plaza of inlaid black-and-white tiles undulated beneath us as an illusion of waves from the two massive rivers that dominated the city's history.

Back rooms and dark alleys may not seem like the ideal spots to exchange money, but it's where we usually got the best rates. A currency black market flourished throughout every country here in South America. Right now in Manaus the official rate was around twelve cruzeiros to the dollar, but we could generally count on finding someone with a roll of money and a yearning for US currency. There was always elasticity in currencies. If we negotiated well, we got at least ten—and sometimes twenty—percent more than the official rate. For the vendor the exchange was a dodge against ever-present inflation, which in Brazil was over thirty-five percent. For us it was a ten to twenty percent discount coupon on everything we bought along the way. There were really only three concerns: getting ripped off with counterfeit bills, getting robbed right on the spot, or getting caught unofficially exchanging money by the police or military. After a while you got a feel for the game. We picked our black marketeers with a discriminating eye, we tried to never get ourselves too far out of the way for the transactions, and we relied on the fear of the guy with the roll of money to keep an eye out for the police. It had worked so far. That day we managed nearly seventeen cruzeiros for traveler's checks and a tad less for US greenbacks.

Saturday: Manaus

Oh wow, it was hot today. It was only ten in the morning and the temperature, even in precious bits of shade, was already above ninety-five sweaty degrees and climbing. Activities take on a speed of their own when it gets that hot. We often kidded amongst ourselves about the lethargic nature of the locals, but now as we walked towards the massive floating docks at the edge of the city our gait slowed to a crawl. In today's heat it was a complete role reversal. This morning the locals knowingly smiled and glanced back over their shoulders at us as they passed by. The docks were less than an hour walk from our hotel, but we spent as much time drinking sodas in convenient watering holes along the way as we did walking. To our dismay, the docks were closed this morning, but the captain of a Greek tramp steamer leaned over the railing and hollered at us to come back on Sunday. His name was Petros. "Ask for Captain Petros," he called. He promised the gates would be open, and he proudly pointed towards the ship's name on the bow: the *Aegis*. He invited us to tour aboard if we returned tomorrow.

Not all was lost this morning. As we turned to leave, a German sailor exited the dock and suggested we join him. He shipped out tomorrow and one of his mates recommended he head up to a shop called *Casa Beija-flor*, the Hummingbird, on Rua Quintino Bociauva for the best selection of Amazon souvenirs. This was Wil and Frits' last day in the Amazon and they were eager to find mementos of their trip as well. As it turned out, the shop was a collector's bonanza. Thousands of Indian crafts, pottery, and artifacts from all reaches of the river hung from rafter hooks, were displayed along tables and in bins, and stuffed into every nook and cranny of the shop. Woven mats from the Baré Indians hung along the wall. Intricate Ticuna baskets and colorful masks crowded for space among Xingu blowguns, curare darts, and primitive long-bows with long, slender arrows fletched with macaw feathers. Pottery decorated with geometric and animal designs sat beside bins of stuffed, gaping-mouthed piranhas, pirarucu scales, and odd assortments of weird river creatures, both real and imagined. Hammocks of woven chambira fiber formed graceful arches over-head. We were surrounded by the machinations of daily indig-enous life reduced to curiosities to be sold to the highest bidder. Still, it was fascinating. We'd seen so many of these things along our journey. The four of us smiled and retold river stories as we worked our way through the shop.

I picked up a blowgun. What better a souvenir than a ten-foot-long blowgun and a handful of curare-tipped darts; perfect for shooting all those errant monkeys in our backyard in Guelph—or perhaps even one well-placed dart in my brothers' backsides if they mouthed off to me again. Alas, it was perhaps a tad cumber-some for our backpacks.

Mary was more circumspect. She selected a few of the enormous pirarucu scales. The monstrous fish was common enough along the Amazon, but the scales were still a curiosity to us. We'd seen fishermen lug a two-hundred-pound pirarucu out of their dugout at the Bellavista market back in Iquitos, but we knew some of these river catfish weighed in at double that. As fish scales go, they were gigantic; three inches long and over an inch wide. Dried, the surface was as raspy and rough as sandpaper. Manicurists used them to finish the rough edges of client fingernails.

That afternoon, despite the heat, we bused out to the zoo. It was on the military's operational Jungle Operations Center and Action Command (COSAC) training grounds. In fact COSAC was the home turf to train the Brazilian military in jungle warfare tactics and survival. Over three hundred species of mammals and reptiles were captured and caged to make sure trainees understood the dangers they faced out in the rainforest. Wild cats, monkeys, caiman, turtles, snakes, tapirs, and wild birds were dangerous to the uninitiated, but food to the knowledgeable. The zoo was simply an afterthought. We spent a sweat-soaked afternoon amongst the animals and reptiles, sometimes eyeball-to-eyeball with the big cats, the black jaguar and its spotted twin. Even the smaller ocelots looked menacing. Numerous snakes coiled and wrapped around branches in their enclosures. They all looked venomous and evil, just waiting for a chance to strike. By the time we finished with the capybaras, monkeys, tapirs, sloths, tarantulas, poisonous frogs, vampire bats, and the crying bush babies, we were pretty confident we weren't trekking into the jungle alone anytime soon.

Tonight was Wil and Frits' last night with us. In the wee hours of the morning, they'd fly out to Recife to meet up with Wil's sister. Together, they planned to tour around central Brazil for another two months and then head back home to Amsterdam. We'd miss them. They had been adventurous, easy-going, and patient traveling companions, adding a unique perspective to our adventure.

Sunday, November 20, 1977: Manaus

Mary and I returned back down to the floating docks. The city of Manaus sat a hundred feet above sea level and nearly a thousand miles from the Atlantic. The city sprawled over gently sloping hills, separated by creeks and bays and anchored by the swift black waters of the Rio Negro. The floating dock, built at the turn of the century by a Scottish engineer, coped with the annual forty-five-foot rise and fall in river depth between the rainy and dry seasons. The dock was connected to street level by a five-hundred-foot floating bridge way. Marks on the shoreward stone retaining wall ticked off the high water levels for each year since the dock was built. In 1953, it reached a record of just over twenty-nine meters or ninety-seven feet, a mere child's height from overflowing the levee and catastrophe. We walked along the dock and over to the freighter *Aegis*. True to his word, captain Petros beckoned us on board, welcoming us with a slap on the back and a hearty handshake. The *Aegis* was a twelve thousand tonner with its hold full of bags of cement from the Górazdze factory in southwest Poland. We climbed down steel ladders below deck into the massive engine room. The enclosure smelled of bunker fuel used to power the nine-cylinder engine. The captain said the bulk of the engine ran another deck deeper. He took us up through the kitchen, galley, and crews' quarters that felt so confined we could barely maneuver past each other. Then, up topside again and while we sat on deck chairs near the bridge and sipped grape raki, the captain offered to take us to Belém, his next port of call. Of course, the departure date was up in the air right now, he explained. It all depended on offloading here and arranging the load of hardwood in Belém destined for a customer in the French port city of Lorient. If we weren't in a hurry, we were welcome. We had heard this story before. Mary and I were patient people, but another month in Manaus was not in the cards.

The afternoon was hot and humid. We tried to sleep it away in our hotel room. Even with the ceiling fan on full power, the air seemed on fire around us. It was just a prelude to a hot, stuffy, suffocating night.

Monday: Manaus

We had slipped into Manaus under a waxing crescent moon. In the darkness we had missed the dramatic confluence of the yellow-brown Amazon floodway and blue-black water of the Rio Negro. Both rivers had such force the waters ran parallel and straight-edged for about five miles downstream. The *South American Handbook* suggested two possibilities to view this natural phenomenon. Tourist agencies ran scheduled but pricey sightseeing boats. Or, for those on tight budgets, another option was to get up at three-thirty in the morning, hike down to the lower shanty wharf, and catch one of the milk boats that departed at four. Nobody in his or her right mind, if they didn't have to, woke up that early and walked the docks. However, the tight budget option won out with our frugal new gang. Mary the American, Manfred the German, and Michel from France, Shmulik the Israeli, and I, the lone Canadian, gathered outside the hotel in darkness. We wound our way down wharf-side, through the hardened people who made the riverfront edges of Manaus their home, and boarded the little milk boat *Inhmum* tied off at the margins of the mud and water. Empty milk cans were lashed atop the roof above the wheelhouse. Around us, life on the docks was stirring, stretching, and slowly awakening. Vendors bantered with neighbors from tiny colorful wooden stands that were now opening and crammed with sacks of rice and *farinha* flours. The air was heavy with the smell of exposed drying fish, uncovered meat, and the remains of discarded rotting fruit.

INHMUM, THE MILK BOAT IN MANAUS THAT TOOK US

OUT TO THE MEETING OF THE WATERS

We cast off straightaway and slipped out into the channel, dodging through a maze of incoming fishing boats returning to sell their catch. Our captain and his son had a busy day ahead. His first stop was at the river base at the old Frigelo ice factory near the channel entrance. Blocks of ice, from the factory sixty feet above us, slid down an old wooden chute and were pushed and prodded into the hold. We spent the rest of the day on the milk run around the inlets, tiny streams, and islands of Careiro. The exhaust from the *Inhmum*'s diesel engine pounded relentlessly through a rusty hole in the muffler stack. Within the hour we all had hammering headaches and daylight was just breaking. We faced another ten hours on board. The *Inhmum* stopped countless times, the routine always the same. A farmer stood on his makeshift dock with small tin containers of fresh raw milk. The raw milk containers varied from standard metal milk cans to five-gallon Shell Oil tins to glass bottles. The farmer handed his milk to the son who poured it into a container on board and weighed it. Then cruzeiros passed hands and our little craft pushed off in search of the next farmer. After twenty or thirty stops, our curiosity turned into mild interest, mild interest morphed into observation, and observation mutated into dull routine and, finally, just plain boredom. We still had another six hours on board and so we settled into what we did best: snoozing, talking and staring at the interminable green jungle. Finally, around two in the afternoon, we rounded the east end of Careiro Island and into the convergence of the Rio Negro and the Amazon River. We ploughed into the middle and straddled the convergence, the bow following the demarcation of licorice-colored water on one side and toffee-brown on the other. We were homeward bound, heads throbbing, tired, and listless from the tight confines of the small boat. The final stop was a milk processing plant adjacent to the ice factory to offload nearly a hundred and fifty gallons of raw milk.

As we approached the harbor the captain made a pronouncement. The original agreed-upon fare of fifteen cruzeiros was null and void. The new fare was forty cruzeiros. The bickering began and got louder and more expletive-laced the closer we got to shore. By the time we tied off it was an outright verbal slugfest.

What the milk boat captain didn't quite grasp was that he had taken on an entire vessel full of cheapskates. We were on his boat, for heaven's sake, to save every single cruzeiro we possibly could. Bargaining with skinflints was never a winning proposition. Bargaining with five tired tightwads with pounding headaches was even less productive. "The price is now forty cruzeiros," he demanded, "forty cruzeiros or nothing." Nothing was an offer we couldn't refuse, and we all walked away to a loud torrent of colorful Portuguese directed at our backsides.

Our gracious manager at the Hotel Formosa had stored our backpacks while we adventured out on the milk boat. Now he allowed us a quick cleanup and shower. Refreshed, we headed to the docks and our rendezvous with our transportation to Santarem.

The *Sobral Santos* was a beautiful ship. Compared to the barges, dugouts, and weatherworn boats we'd shipped out on upriver, she was absolutely elegant. As we boarded we smugly held up our first-class tickets we purchased Sunday at the Onze Maio shipping office a couple of blocks away. Our fare cost us three hundred cruzeiros apiece—a whopping nineteen dollars each for passage to Santarem. Captain Ferreira greeted us as we embarked and proudly toured his ship with us. She was a turn of the century iron-hulled rubber freighter, converted only twenty years ago to carry passengers and freight. At a hundred and forty feet with a beam of twenty feet, the *Sobral Santos* looked long and sleek. Her engine room was silent, but a big six hundred horsepower diesel sat waiting for the crew to fire it up.

SOBRAL SANTOS WAS RENAMED THE *Cisne Branco* AFTER SHE
SANK IN OBIDOS. PHOTO BY ARNOLDO RIKER

Amidships, near the big circular gold Onze Maio logo painted on the hull, dockhands loaded crates of vegetables and fruit, nuts, aromatic plants and herbs, and endless cases of beer and soft drinks from trucks and wagons parked on the wharf. Propane and acetylene cylinders clanked as they were rolled and secured into the hold in anticipation of departure. The second-class passengers and deck crew would sleep around and atop the freight. By tomorrow the ship should be full of goods and passengers heading downriver.

The first-class deck stood twelve feet above the waterline. Up front, two sets of five cabins ran down either side. The sleeping cabins were hot and stuffy and only a modest improvement over slinging a hammock aft on the expansive open air deck. Tucked in the port stern corner was a single air-conditioned first-class cabin. Adjacent to it a metal ladder ran up to the top deck and a large open-air recreation area with a bar and kitchen. Fore were the captain's quarters and ultimately the bridge. Faded, red-canvas-sheathed cork lifeboats were lashed to the railings on either side.

The five tired foreign *companheiros de viagem* had permission to sleep on board that night. We slung our hammocks in the spacious first-class deck behind the cabins and snuggled in under our blankets. It would be our last comfortable night aboard the *Sobral Santos.*

Tuesday: Rio Amazonas

This morning we stowed our packs under our folded hammocks and headed back into Manaus to eat and explore. Captain Ferreira suggested we return early, as the *Sobral Santos* would be underway by mid-afternoon. We were learning to take departure schedules with a grain of salt, but this time we heeded his warning and returned just after lunch.

STACKED HAMMOCKS AND CROWDED QUARTERS ON
BOARD THE RIVERBOAT SOBRAL SANTOS

Passengers were already streaming on to the *Sobral Santos*. Just as we settled in one spot, another twenty people jostled around, shifting luggage and hanging hammocks. First class was filling to capacity. Second class was literally overflowing out of the section and onto the stairways. The maximum capacity was three hundred passengers and two hundred tons of cargo. We'd reached that by late afternoon, and still more freight edged around empty spaces and more passengers embarked, finding the barest of spaces to settle. Delays added to the confusion. As mid-afternoon slipped by and the sun set behind us, there was a mass of hammocks across the deck, hanging railing-to-railing and two deep like bunk beds. Mixed through that melee were passengers who sat or sprawled in any empty space they found. When we finally departed under the light of a bright moon, I reckon there were over five hundred passengers, and lord knows how many tons of excess cargo as we edged out of the harbor and on to the river.

All told we were a curious group of passengers. There were foreigners drawn together by familiar languages and manners, as well as locals from villages nearby who shopped in Manaus' duty free stores and now returned, loaded down with parcels of household items and gifts that were too expensive to buy back home and too good a bargain to pass by. There were businessmen and their wives headed back down to Santarem, the hold stuffed with their cheap goods they planned to sell at immense profit. Within that mass of people were some that simply stood out.

A bulbous, balding man dressed in a wrinkled, white linen suit with a young girl on his arm jauntily disappeared into the exclusive air-conditioned cabin. Crew carried in several brown cardboard boxes securely wrapped with rows of yellow binder twine. The couple closed the door, clicked the lock, and never resurfaced.

Carlos was a miner with brick-rough hands and a crooked smile who claimed he had struck it rich on a vein of gold along a tributary deep inside the jungle. He proudly showed Mary and I two leather pokes full of dust and nuggets although he kept them hidden from other passengers. Carlos broke out in song when the mood struck and his rich tenor voice resonated from time to time throughout the evening.

In amongst the passengers were some with their heads down, eyes diverted, never making contact with those surrounding them. They were the schemers, the smugglers, the drug mules, and the pickpockets. A crowded ship, we had been warned, was fertile ground for thievery and good cover for nefarious activities.

Some of life's most enduring memories begin with the words "Oh, shit!" The ship had settled in to a sleeping routine when a burst of automatic gunfire rattled up near the bow. The big diesel cut and then reversed and then cut again. We heard the metallic rasp of the anchor chain sliding down the hull. Passengers spilled out of their hammocks to the railings amid cries of surprise and dismay. It was the Federales—the federal river police. It was a midstream midnight raid. The *Sobral Santos*, it turned out, was a favorite boat for smugglers. Passengers sprang into action. Treasures retrieved from suitcases and bags were stuffed into crevasses and crannies, hidden, or in panic, simply thrown overboard. Radios, watches, little plastic bags of stash and drugs disappeared over the side and into the dark water below. Our newfound friend Carlos actually lifted the plant out of a large ochre-colored clay pot at his feet, hid his gold stash inside, and dropped the plant back down. It was like a parody of a cheap spy movie. He turned and smiled at me, and with a head gesture motioned that I stand in front of the pot as a diversion. Seconds later, a few feet away, a grappling hook rang off the railing. Within minutes, armed Federales boarded below and were followed by six others over the railings of the first-class deck. They looked nothing like police. Most were casually dressed in worn blue jeans, T-shirts, and running shoes. But the authority they commanded and badges clipped in their belts were real. The guns they cradled over their chests were *definitely* real. Confused cries and terse commands resonated below. Moments later they controlled the main deck, shouting orders as they separated men and women on either side of the ship. The screams reduced to whimpers and then to whispers when automatic weapons were raised and pointed. All the foreign passengers were rounded together and directed over to the railing where our group stood. The Federales wanted us out of the way and safe.

The police pulled down the labyrinth of hammocks to give them an unobstructed view and started interrogating passengers and removing contraband. Two officers broke away and banged at the locked door of the aft air-conditioned cabin. When there was no response they used their rifle butts to reinforce the urgency. Finally they took a step back, reversed their weapons, clicked off the safeties, and upped the ante. "Get out now," they yelled "or we'll open fire." There was a pause. Over at the railing we held our breath, expecting a burst of gunfire and the wooden structure to disintegrate before our eyes. A moment later, a muffled plea from inside and then a sheepish woman and the white-suited guy emerged with their hands in the air. He was immediately handcuffed and led away out of sight towards the bow.

During the confusion a woman collapsed onto the deck. Her young daughter ran to her prone body, anxiously shook her, listened for a moment, and screamed. "She's stopped breathing," she shrieked. "My mother's stopped breathing. Help us. Please help us!" The Federales ordered everyone to stay put. The woman was dead or dying, and she was of no concern. Mary's quiet curses directed at them simply elicited smirks. "Stay back and leave her be," they ordered.

We couldn't. Shmulik and I broke ranks from our little group and moved across the deck. The gun barrels followed us. "Get back," one soldier demanded. We mimed we didn't understand Portuguese and kept going. Shmulik and I both agreed to continue to help until the safeties clicked off or the bolts on the machine guns pulled back. If we heard either we would stop in our tracks.

Perhaps the daughter's tears, the growing murmurs of anger from the passengers, or our brazen disregard for their authority gave the Federales pause. They relented and I carried the young woman over to my hammock. We pried her tongue back out of her throat and Shmulik gave her mouth-to-mouth CPR while I alternately applied chest compressions. The little girl hovered over us and watched as we worked to resuscitate her mom. An apprehensive silence fell over the passengers. It felt like a theater production; all eyes locked on the roles played by the two foreigners and the woman in the hammock with her anguished daughter. The subtle differences here were that this was a real life-or-death situation, and a few members of the viewing audience held machine guns chambered with live rounds.

There was a cough followed by a quick, deep sucking of air and more coughing. The woman's eyes opened and she weakly smiled up at us. Her daughter hugged her, then us, and then her mom again. A cheer went up from the passengers. Even the Federales seemed relieved and allowed us to stay with her. Shmulik cornered the captain and convinced him to give her one of the private cabins and then went off in search of the ship's first aid supplies. Over the next half hour, Shmulik monitored her blood pressure and her steadily improving heart rate.

The Federales departed at two-thirty in the morning with several handcuffed passengers in tow and a second launch full of contraband. Our white-suited gentleman turned out to be a pornographic movie producer and the cardboard boxes so carefully wrapped with twine were full of his latest creations. The other prisoners were a mix of overzealous free-trade zone entrepreneurs and drug runners.

The remaining passengers watched the police depart and set to salvaging the stuff they'd hidden in the nooks and crannies, recesses, and corners of the ship. Carlos patted me on the back, smiled, and retrieved his gold. Not only had I stood guard in front of his flowerpot, I'd created a giant diversion that he assured me had saved his bacon. Slowly the passengers regained a sense of decorum, restrung, and settled back into their hammocks. We tried to reclaim the night. The deck lights went out and we settled into our tight maze of hammocks and recaptured what sleep was left to us.

From time to time during the night, as I turned to find a more comfortable position, I heard Carlos as he stood by the railing, his hand cupped to his mouth like an impromptu microphone, joyfully singing into the darkness.

Wednesday: Rio Amazonas

The *Sobral Santos* may not have departed on schedule yesterday, but by golly, the crew was determined this morning to serve breakfast on time. Despite our late night episode with the Federales, the crew awoke us just before first light, insisted the hammocks come down, and then removed the folded tables from the storage racks above us and set up for breakfast. We sat, the five of us, and listened to the conversations and laughter of friends and strangers from the tables that surrounded us. The little girl of the woman we resuscitated early this morning drifted back and forth between her mother and our table with little handfuls of fruits or nuts and candies. In fact, for the entire day and throughout the evening, until we reached the town of Obidos where the woman and her daughter disembarked, we were treated like heroes with smiles and handshakes and little gifts.

A passenger conversant in both Portuguese and English sat with us and translated the mother's story. Her name was Luciana. A month ago she and her husband were involved in a terrible car accident. Her husband died in the seat beside her. Luciana survived with no internal injuries but badly bruised and with lingering bouts of hypotension. She had gone upriver to Manaus to collect her fourteen-year-old daughter who had stayed with relatives while her mom recovered. She inadvertently left her medication behind when they packed for the return journey. Without proper medication and with excitement on board she had chest pains, felt weak, and collapsed. The young daughter was still mourning the loss of her dad. Luciana was all she had. To watch her mom collapse on the deck must have been heartrending and the joy of her revival an overwhelming relief.

During the night we had traveled midstream and let the strong currents carry us along. By ten this morning we put into the agricultural river town of Itacoatiara on the north shore, just past the mouth of the Madeira River. We offloaded a few passengers but many more boarded. Crates of cassava, passion fruit, papaya, and string nets of watermelon were pushed up wooden ramps and loaded on board. By noon we were off again.

We spent the rest of the day writing letters, reading, lost in thought, and dodging around the almost incomprehensible thicket of passengers. The *Sobral Santos* was definitely overcrowded. While we jostled for every free space, missteps were always followed with cordial, pleasant banter of intrusion and apologies. It's just how it was, and the locals accepted and adapted to the diminishing deck space.

There were new house rules for sleeping tonight: the women on the portside half of the deck, and men over on the starboard half. Men would have to wear shirts at all times—no exceptions. Husbands and wives, fiancées, and simply friends were separated by gender. We understood why, of course. This was machismo central—South America and in the middle of Amazon. Virility, masculine pride, and dominance over women were common traits along the river, but here with people so tightly packed together it was an invitation for trouble. I suspected the crew had seen it all before—the groping, the sexual innuendos, the squabbles, and the fights. Separation was a pre-emptive strike. Mary and I foiled the system. She slept at the middle outer edge of the women and I strung my hammock at the adjacent edge of the group of men. Mary thought the new sleeping arrangements were a great idea and relished the thought of only women sharing the portside bathrooms. No wet toilet seats or puddles from errant streams of pee. Sometimes it was the little things that brought the most happiness.

Around midnight we edged into the port of Parintins and the deck lights burned on. No one stirred. We heard freight offloaded and new cargo pushed into the hold and the shuffling of passengers disembarking. We were all-too-comfortably wedged into our hammocks to even get up and have a look at the town. As we lay there half dreaming and half awake, the engine throttled up and we were back out on the river.

Thursday: Santarem

Just as breakfast was being served, the ship threaded its way through a group of islands midstream, around a sharp bend in the river, and into the port town of Obidos. The river narrowed there. The deep water and powerful current forced the captain to maneuver his way dockside under full engine. The crew tied off the hawsers, lowered the tire bumpers against the wharf, and pushed down the gangplank. The fast water swirled around the ship and the rubber bumpers pinched and buffeted against the dock. Luciana and her daughter bade us goodbye with hugs and kisses and then walked away and vanished into the town.

Amazon riverboats frequently flirted with risks. Overweight with cargo and passengers and the maximum load lines submerged, they were often operated for profit without much concern for safety. Our boat was one such vessel and its luck would run out soon. In just under four years hence, in the early morning hours of September 19, 1981, moored to this very dock, the *Sobral Santos* would become the worst maritime disaster every recorded on the Amazon.

She would arrive up from Santarem just after midnight, overloaded with passengers and cargo. The official passenger manifest put the number at three hundred, although witnesses—including the dock master, Manoel de Souza, and the crew—later pegged that number at 530. Like us, passengers were wedged in amongst and on top of freight and cargo skids on the main second-class deck, and massively packed in together on the first-class and bridge decks. Skids of beer and soft drinks weren't secured, and as the passengers all moved starboard to the railings in anticipation of docking, the load gave way and shifted violently towards them. Witnesses on shore said the boat suddenly listed and the *Sobral Santos* keeled over, half submerged. She hung there precariously for a few minutes and then just disappeared. The ship sank 130 feet to the bottom within seconds. A local merchant named Maurice watched from shore in horror. "When the boat went down there was just silence. Those people died without being able to call for help or able to scream," he said. Of the over five hundred passengers, only 187 survived that morning. Scores of those that did clear the ship alive were swept away by the strong current, their bodies forever lost in the silt of the Amazon.

Most simply couldn't escape. It happened too fast to respond. They drowned inside in panic. The chaos, noise, and blood brought the river predators in to feed. Over the next several days, two hundred unidentified souls, so badly stripped of flesh, were buried in a common grave in the little town cemetery at the edge of Obidos. Only a few bodies were ever identified. On that future morning in Obidos four years hence, 350 people would perish on this very ship at this very spot where we now casually drank coffee, pushed back our empty breakfast plates, and laughed.

The *Sobral Santos*, nevertheless, would survive. The navy would bring in a floating lift crane after the accident and salvage the ship. It would be refloated, refitted, refurbished, and renamed. She would fly the Brazilian flag again and sail the Amazon as the *Cisne Branco*—the *White Swan*. The boat would have both a new owner and new conditions for cargo and people. She was mandated to carry no more than 230 passengers and 160 tons of freight. However, no matter what they named her, the *White Swan* would forever carry the ghosts of hundreds of silent souls.

We reached the sleepy port town of Santarem at the mouth of the Tapajos River in the early afternoon. The yellow Amazon water was mottled with greenish patches from the Tapajos as the *Sobral Santos* slid into the docks. As we disembarked our little group walked along a red dirt road, past lines of trucks waiting to pick up cargo. The five of us were all headed downriver and we decided to travel onward together.

The manager behind the desk of the Hotel Morologo looked puzzled with our request to share one big room. "There are only two beds and hooks for two hammocks," he appealed, "and there are five of you." We insisted it wasn't a problem, and indeed it wasn't. You'd think after all those days on crowded boats we'd love some space and privacy when we had the chance, but we were in a frugal phase. Shmulik and Michel each took a bed, Mary and I strung our hammocks, and Manfred rummaged in his pack, pulled out a tiny pup tent with poles and set it up in the corner. There we were, packs strewn around the edges of the room with two full beds, two hammocks hanging across the room, and Manfred's head sticking out of a tiny tent with its thin little cords tied off on adjacent chairs and bed legs. The ceiling fan whirled and clicked in our comfortable and full little room. That we didn't find our situation in the least way unremarkable was testament to how far our standards had fallen.

Mar and I walked down to Plaza Tiradentes and sat under the shade of some towering ficus trees. The air was blistering hot. As we licked fresh passion fruit ice cream, translucent white blotches ran down our hands and dripped onto the red dirt. Stretched out along Avenida Tapajos, which ran parallel to the harbor, thatched-roof stalls were being constructed in anticipation of the big fair here on Sunday. We strolled around, nosing into shops and walking the retaining wall along the sand. To be honest, it was nice just to be together, hand in hand. No strangers, just the two of us.

Tonight, as the sun cast long shadows, the whole group sat idly on the retaining wall overlooking the riverboats on the Tapajos.

In the distance, along the deep channel, an oceangoing freighter maneuvered upstream to Manaus, pushing cautiously against the current. Around the river edge little batelãos and lanchas of all sizes carried cargo and passengers in a never-ending parade. Fishing boats rigged with brightly-colored triangular canvas sails skimmed past on their way out for the evening's catch.

SANTAREM DOCKSIDE WAS TYPICAL OF THE MANY PORT SCENES ALONG THE AMAZON

Friday: Santarem

We tackled the harbor methodically today and broke into three scouting parties, each one assigned a section of the docks to reconnoiter. Even then we hedged our bets. Anywhere downstream that brought us closer to Belém would do. We would meet back at the plaza in two hours to compare notes.

Michel found her: the *São Francisco do Paulo,* a fifty-ton barco motor that was headed that very afternoon for the town of Macapá in the estuary of the Amazon. Single-decked, she ran sixty-five feet from stem to stern with a long, graceful roofline that followed the contour of the boat. The open-windowed wheelhouse sat up front with the captain's quarters. Behind that was a large open deck space laced with hammock hooks. The tiny galley and head were spaced near the rear fantail. We walked back to the boat and introduced ourselves to Captain Almir Paulo de Oliveira, paid our three hundred cruzeiros for passage, and headed back into town to wash some laundry, pack, and grab a little lunch.

Humor can be a local thing, often wrapped in narrow prejudice, sometimes ill-conceived, and every so often just plain offensive. Today's noontime special at a nearby lunch counter was a *Sanduiche Bauru,* a crusty, hollowed-out stick of French bread loaded with deep layers of corned beef and mozzarella cheese. Mary, Shmulik, Manfred, and I ordered and retired to a little table in the crowded space. We were excited to be on our way again and the *São Francisco* seemed sturdy and safe. As we ate a local man in his fifties pushed away from the bar and wandered over to our table. He pointed at Shmulik's sandwich. "I wouldn't eat that," he said mischievously, "don't you know where corned beef comes from?" We shook our heads and waited for the warning. "Jews," he said, "ground up Jews from the war."

Manfred's chair legs scraped backwards as he pushed away angrily from the table. His face was etched with rage. Shmulik raised his hand towards Manfred, a gesture to be calm, and then with a civility and determination that carried so many undertones, he turned and smiled at the jokester. "I'm Israeli, and my good friend here is German," he quietly intoned. "Perhaps you'd like to reconsider that statement." The man turned crimson, apologized, backed away, and then turned and fled.

There were limits—barriers—to the mockery of human tragedy that could never be crossed, regardless of our detachment or the passage of time. I've often wondered if our jokester ever spoke of that restaurant encounter with his friends or family. Did he say he met some bitter, crazy gringos who had no sense of humor, or did he recognize the implications of the boundaries he had crossed?

Mary and I had never known the closeness of war. Our fathers had. Mary's dad Eddie, attached to the 34th bomb group, ferried Martin B-26 Marauder bombers down through South America, over to Africa, and up into Europe. My dad Hugh was a member of the Canadian Army Corp of Engineers and, like tens of thousands of other Allied soldiers, fought his way eastward from Juno Beach.

William Shirer's *The Rise and Fall of the Third Reich*, published in 1960, was the thickest book I had ever read. I would come home from high school, head to my bedroom in the basement, and lose myself in history. A thousand pages of strategies, battles, and intrigues, the misery and pain of wounded and dying men reduced to words. And there, somewhere in the entrails of that book, was the madness of the Holocaust. I read about the unspeakable inhumanity and unimaginable terror of crowded boxcars, the camps with those infamous names, separation, desperation, and a final walk towards those buildings and ditches from which there was no return. How do you even begin to contemplate doing that to another human being, let alone millions?

Manfred, I'm sure, looked at the war from a different perspective. He was a little older than us and would have been a young child towards the end of that madness. His country was broken and occupied. All the bluster and bravado of the Thousand-Year

Reich was in ruins, replaced with guilt and hopelessness. He would have been old enough to understand the Nuremberg trials and the implications of those convicted. As in all great tragedies, he would have felt denial, anger, and guilt. And now, confronted with such insensitivity, so far away and so isolated from those barbaric acts, it left him numb and speechless. No matter how acutely he felt about his country's history, he was powerless to change it. His legacy was to live with the deeds of his parent's generation.

Shmulik was enigmatic. He really said nothing about his past or that of his parents. His expression was hidden beneath that thick black beard. Yet I suspect there was a closeness of that errant comment, a reminder that the Holocaust would never fade, and should never fade. The dark years of the Shoah were still a haunting memory of so many family histories. He reached for his *Sanduiche Bauru* and began to eat again.

As usual there was a combination of inactivity and mayhem at the docks. We were scheduled to depart at six that night but the afternoon ticked by without a hint of action. Ox cart wagons and mud-mired trucks full of burlap sacks of corn stood idle nearby. With five minutes to go, the crew decided now was a good time to start loading cargo. Schedules, it seemed, were something you spoke highly about but were rarely worth the effort to actually follow. We got underway at ten o'clock.

Our little craft, like every other along the waterway, was crowded and loaded to capacity. Two dozen hammocks stretched across the deck and ran the length of the ship. The Amazon was wide here, and the water rough and choppy. The bow pounded through waves, rising and falling back onto the river with thumps that shuddered along the entire structure. Hammocks swayed with the motion, but never at the same frequency, or even always in the same direction. I'm sure it had something to do with the laws of physics. You know—those inclined planes, fulcrums, and periodicity. The entire night we bumped and chaffed against neighboring hammocks, too tired to complain, and even if we did, unable to do anything about it.

OUR BOAT FROM SANTAREM TO MACAPÁ, THE SAO FRANCISCO DE PAULA

Saturday: Rio Amazonas

We awoke this morning at the little river settlement of Monte
Alegre, a short fifty-five-mile run northeast of Santarem. Adobe
and stucco houses sat high on a hill that rose up through the rainforest. Like most settlements along this stretch of the river, it had
strong historical ties to the rubber industry. We edged towards
the docks behind a motor launch, its roof laden with hundreds
of tawny-colored clay water jars that were lashed down with ropes
looped through their handles. A young boy sat on the roof, his
legs dangling off the edge as he smoked a cigarette and traded
taunts with kids on the dock. Our captain pointed at long, dark
demarcation lines that rippled in the sand along the shore. "Low
tide," he said and then pointed and laughed at the boat ahead. It
had loaded at high tide and now struggled to free itself as its keel
scraped against the river bottom. On our captain's order, Manfred
threw the bowline over to the stranded boat and the *São Francisco*
reversed and tugged her off the bottom and into deeper water.

Manfred was a sailor, and with a seaman's curiosity of ships he
ended up in the wheelhouse along with me in tow. The captain,
glad for the company, explained the workings of the ship in a
combination of Portuguese, Spanish, mangled English, broken
German, and hand gestures. Manfred nodded his head with a *sim,
eu entendo* (sure, I get it). When the captain turned to me for that
same acknowledgement, I just smiled back.

"Take the wheel," he said, and Manfred leapt at the chance.
Stay this distance from shore, he motioned. "Watch out for floating
and submerged trees, don't hit other boats, and stay on the main
river way," he said as he counted the rules down on his fingertips. Manfred nodded again with a full comprehension of the

gauges before him and rules of navigation. I just smiled back. We expected Almir Paulo de Oliveira to stand there, allow us to play captain for a few minutes, and then retake command. Instead, he abruptly turned, told us he was tired and needed a nap, headed into his quarters behind us, and closed the door. That was it. Manfred and I were alone in the wheelhouse of a fifty-ton motor barco, heading down the Amazon at fifteen knots. One of us knew what he was doing.

It went smoothly for the first half hour while Manfred navigated and I spotted for submerged and floating logs in the water. River traffic was light. We passed a few tramp steamers headed upriver and small fishing boats that hugged the shoreline. Even Mary enjoyed the experience. She spread out a towel on the bow in front of the wheelhouse and was busy reading and catching the heat from the midday sun. Then it was my turn at the wheel.

I am not a sailor. I'm not really very good at anything even related to water. I was pretty decent at showering, but my sailing experience was confined to paddling canoes and futzing around in a small motorboat under the watchful eyes of my father-in-law. Now I was navigating a fifty-ton boat down the Amazon. A westward wind picked up. The water got choppy and our ship cut through, lifting and falling in protest. Cascades of spray splashed over the bow. Everything worked just fine as long as I headed in a straight line. *Easy*, I thought.

"Logs dead ahead," bellowed Manfred pointing at distant branches in the water directly ahead. I spun the wheel to port. My first mental connection was this ship doesn't turn like a car. I turned the big wheel and nothing seemed to happen. The *São Francisco do Paulo* was still headed for the logs. My biggest fear was in grafting the side of the ship and the log together like some horribly miscalculated botany experiment. I turned the wheel harder, then even more again. Suddenly, she responded. She headed, not in some graceful curve around the logs, but directly at the portside shore. In desperation I overcorrected, spinning the wheel back starboard with the same results. Then port again.

The captain's cabin door behind us flew open and a sleepy head poked out. The violent turns had awoken him out of his reverie. "What the hell are you doing?" he grilled. "Are you trying to write your name in the water?" I just smiled back. "*Direto, direto*," he roared, pointing the way with open-handed chops to the expanse of river ahead. I nodded my head and continued to smile. Then he turned, slammed the door, and went back to sleep.

I must admit I got better as time went by. By the time the captain decided to reclaim his ship, Manfred and I had three hours at the wheel and had worked our way nearly fifty miles down the Amazon without a single mishap or any more indecipherable signatures in the water.

Just outside of the village of Almerin we cut along small narrow river channels, the banks thirty feet on either side of the ship. Working boats with their triangular sails beating with the wind slid past. Towards evening, the lingering rays of sunset transformed the faded brown bamboo-thatched homes along the river into shades of subtle aurulent. Macaws darted in and out of the overhanging trees with momentary flashes of blue and scarlet. Fishermen in small dugout canoes hugged the shoreline and threw weighted nets into schools of small fish.

That night, we sailed in deeper, rougher waters. To escape the battering we experienced the night previous, Manfred lowered his hammock and slept on the deck, Mary lashed herself to a post, and I hung my hammock near the bow beside the wheelhouse. Now with water from the bow occasionally spraying over me, the idea didn't seem so clever. Chilled, I pulled the wool blanket in tighter. At least I wasn't in the tangle of hammocks behind me.

Sunday, November 27, 1977: Macapá, Brazil

This would not be my best day. I awoke to the beginnings of a good cold. My raspy throat burned and I picked something shaped like an escargot out of my nose. Later in the morning, as the sun rose in a cloudless sky, I climbed up to the roof to sunbathe with the others. I should have remembered I don't suntan. I skipped all the intermediary steps of brown, dark, tawny, and god-like bronze and went directly from pasty white to burning red. Lunch today was another gastronomical delight of rice soup with pieces of leathery dried fish that floated and bobbed somewhere near the oily surface. This time, eating came at a price, and I got the runs. *Great*—I would arrive in Macapá with a perfect trifecta of river maladies.

MARY AND OUR RIVER COMPANION SHMULIK GOOFING AROUND IN MACAPÁ

The *São Francisco do Paulo* wouldn't make it all the way to Macapá. Instead, she put in at Porto Santana at two o'clock in the afternoon and tied up beside a dirty manganese pellet plant that belched dark plumes overhead from the coke furnaces of the ore-sintering process. We bused the last thirty kilometers to Macapá and found a hotel suited to the five of us on Rua Tirendes. While Shmulik, Manfred, and Mary went out in search of a boat to Belém, our ultimate river destination, I stayed back at the Hotel Amazonas parked on the toilet. Thank goodness for Lomotil, the anti-diarrheal potion of choice here in the local *farmacias*. It was at least slowing things down. "Excuse me, I gotta run." And I mean that on so many different levels.

Monday: Macapá

By five in the morning the temperature was blazing hot. We could feel rivulets of sweat through our clothes and the heat clawed at us as we worked our way back toward the port lands. Over in Santana we found a motor barco headed for Belém. She was the *Principe do Mar*, the *Prince of the Sea*—an optimistic appellation for the small, frumpy, paint-peeled, wooden two-deck boat. We purchased a first-class passage, realistically aware of what "first class" really implied on these riverboats. Our final river journey would take us to Breves, Curralinho, and into Belém. As we parted, one of the crew winked and slipped us tickets for first-class meals during our voyage over to the mainland. I think he was taken with Manfred's long dark sideburns and macho mustache. Or maybe it was the battered straw hat. With the ticket purchase behind us, we explored the town.

Back in 1953, high-grade manganese was discovered in the heartland of the Serra do Navio region, about 120 miles north of where we stood. The Brazilian government signed a fifty-year agreement with Indústria de Comércio de Minérios, a conglomerate of Bethlehem Steel and the state. The easiest and quickest way to extract and deliver the steel was by rail down to Santana and by freighter along the Amazon River. The massive manganese pellet sintering plant dominated the skyline and the port. The gate was open and we wandered in and stopped at the guardhouse. Surprisingly, our request for a tour was quickly arranged and a young guide took us through the plant, explaining the process from raw manganese ore to the smooth round pellets bound on freighters for America.

As we passed the northern perimeter of the plant, our guide pointed to the adjacent fenced model community. It looked displaced—a kind of Mayberry in the jungle, the mythic ideal of small-town America, surrounded by typical weathered Amazon buildings. Inside the wire, low white adobe homes with manicured lawns and flowerbeds lined wide paved streets. People ambled down the street, chatting as they darted in and out of an expansive supermarket. Children yelled and frolicked in the playground of their modern elementary school. A new two-story, red-bricked hospital anchored the subdivision. Our guide proudly bragged that this section of town was the only part of Santana with functioning sewage treatment. It was a company town, developed by the manganese consortium for workers and their families. Then he frowned as he told of reports of diminishing manganese deposits up north at the mines. Those deposits would peter out within the next two decades, he explained, and the plant and town would expire along with those very resources that created them.

GEORGE STRADDLING THE EQUATOR LINE ON THE OUTSKIRTS OF MACAPÁ

On our return to Macapá, we climbed out of the bus at the equator line near the southern edge of town. It was a simple eight-inch-high concrete barrier that stretched a hundred feet through the middle of a modest dirt-filled roundabout. Tiny square black tiles spelled out "LINHA DO EQUADOR—MACAPÁ BRAZIL—LATITUDE 00 00 00" in bold block letters. Two small green obelisks marked the east and west directions of the line. The four of us straddled and reclined along the narrow barrier, one foot in the northern hemisphere, one foot in the southern.

By late afternoon we found our way out to the Fortaleza de São José de Macapá. It was built on the high ground of the Amazon by the original Portuguese explorers and soldiers in defense against the French incursions from the Guianas. The Portuguese and the French didn't play well together and hundreds of ships sailed from Portugal in defense of their colony. The ships carried ballast bricks in their holds and those bricks became the fill between the thick stone pentagon walls of the fortress. The military police was in the process of turning the fort over to the city, and while the citadel and their living quarters in the center were well trimmed and painted, the fortification's walls were badly in need of repair and grooming. We walked the bulwarks along compacted dirt with tall dying weeds and pretended to fire the hulks of rusty cannons at the French fleet below. The colony was saved.

Tuesday: Rio Amazonas

We were the first to string our hammocks on the *Principe do Mar*. Shmulik, Mary, and I found a place out of the wind adjacent to a bulkhead on the upper deck near the bow. In our minds we measured out our private space, that comfortable envelope of seclusion we hoped might surround us on the journey. We imagined a space where our hammocks might swing unobstructed with the pitch and roll of the ship. The *Principe* was twin-decked and we yearned in some vain, foolish way for a reasonable number of passengers joining us on this last leg of our journey. We were crushed, both literally and figuratively. Over the course of the morning and then afternoon, passengers streamed on board. Spaces filled and then refilled. People edged into tiny gaps between luggage and passengers. Hammocks edged closer together until we overlapped head-to-head, foot-to-foot, and bum-to-bum. To move meant stepping over and around fellow passengers, which was no mean feat out on the choppy, wide, and windblown waters of the estuary. Washrooms filled with the caustic fragrance of urine and fresh excrement. Like everywhere else on the river, used toilet paper didn't go into the bowl, but rather got scrunched and thrown into a basket. That's when the aim is good; mostly it went on the floor to mix with urine, creating fetid, mushy cellulose that stuck to the bottom of our boots. Mary and I huddled together near the bulkhead, gathering some comfort and emotional strength from each other.

Ninety percent of the inhabitants in this region of Brazil were illiterate. It was surprising then to see how many passengers, brows furrowed and lips silently mouthing words, were so deeply engrossed in magazines. As it turned out, the most significant bit of literature on board were comic books replete with photographs from movies rather than animated drawings. *Tarantula: Fantasy Monster Horror Thriller,* the splashy title of one bragged. It featured a monstrous, crawling spider over a hundred feet tall.

We traveled across buffeting open water, down a maze of narrowing channels, and through the estuary on the northern edges of the Island of Marajó. Perhaps navigational charts would be useful here, but with the rise and fall of the river we suspected our captain navigated by touch and feel and years of experience. The full moon rose higher as we entered open water yet again. The waves picked up and once more our night was spent in the midst of pendulums swinging wildly in every direction. Mary and I were spared the worst of it that night; we were at the end of the hammock line and able to lash ourselves up against the bulkhead mostly out of reach.

Wednesday: Rio Amazonas

We awoke as the *Principe do Mar* navigated down a narrow thread of river, through mangrove-lined backwaters. Maybe a hundred feet on either side of us, the banks were green, lush, and overgrown with wild trees and tall grasses. The river twisted like a giant tree root, its feeder systems branching in all directions in an incomprehensible maze of waterways and channels.

Hammocks came down as the crew set up tables and prepared the tiny aft first-class eating area for breakfast. It would seat a dozen of us. With the gifted food tickets in hand, we sat down to a surprisingly pleasant breakfast of eggs, rice, and beans, along with steamy mugs of coffee and idle conversation. Over our shoulders fellow passengers sat contentedly, munching on fruit and *pão de queijo*, a kind of chewy Brazilian cheese bread common along the coast. The *Principe* slowed to ten knots or so, its engine near idle, generating a soft propeller wash that lay out behind us. The new morning light had clarity to it and we watched the river bend and curve behind us. The never-ending shoreline, that constant green of the jungle, wrapped around the river edges and followed us forever. Fishermen slid by in small wooden dugout canoes that carried wicker traps and woven baskets. Occasionally, another motor barco maneuvered by, headed back out to the estuary. Our captain engaged it with long blasts from the air horn and special intricate nautical hand waves and gestures known only to men of the sea.

It was a day to be optimistic, with a deep blue, cloudless sky and bright sunshine. The wind of last night died and the little *Principe* plowed ahead with a rhythmic rocking motion. It was hard to maneuver in and around the mass of passengers, but we pushed our way forward and were rewarded as we rounded a sweep in the river with the sight of the little town Breves off to the portside. It was a colorful town perched safely on high banks above the river. A large, whitewashed, single-spired church, set back a block from the waterfront, dominated the skyline. Working boats with sharp, pitched bows and large, colorful, triangular sails and duck-tailed cabins bobbed lightly in the water. As we headed out from town, the narrow river Praxaci widened out into the Straits of Breves and open rougher water. A large cargo ship, deep in the water, headed out to the Atlantic while smaller sailing boats darted around the hull and crashed through the rolling wake. The modern and the ancient sailed the waters in harmony.

On board, the night air was harsh again. Perhaps on land it was in the mid-sixties, but here, out on open water and in the wind, it was chilling. Mary wrapped herself in our wool blanket and I layered virtually every bit of clothing from my backpack. Blue jeans, T-shirts, and sweaters all overlapped as we tried to stay warm in our hammocks.

Thursday, December 1, 1977: Belém

The *Principe* was stuck on a sandbar. Early that morning, before the sun was up, we put into the Curralinho harbor on the most southerly shore of Marajó Island. We had one last push toward Belém, out into the wide waters of the Bay of Guajará. Our captain guaranteed we would reach Belém by mid-morning. He had his favorite shortcut in mind. He maneuvered the *Principe* into the *Furo do Arrozal*, a shallow, canal-like waterway that cut a path between the mainland on starboard and the island of Trambioca off the portside. It would take hours off our journey, he boasted. During low tide, the water level in the channel dropped about fifteen feet and altered the entire navigational pattern. We neared low tide as we entered the *Furo*, and within the hour, in a moment of inattention, we slammed into a sandbar at fifteen knots. Passengers were propelled forward with the impact, crashing into hammocks and over luggage. We heard angry shouts of recrimination from the wheelhouse. The engines reversed and drove forward, again and then again. River mud ripped up from the propellers and swirled around the boat, surrounding us in a gray-gold aura. Then, miraculously, the *Principe* sluggishly pulled free, reversing slowly, and finally, with increased power, backed away from the bottom and into the middle of the channel.

Within two hours we cleared the *Furo* and rounded Marajó Island, the giant that guarded Belém's front sea gate. There, across the bay, lay Belém. God, it looked beautiful; I could see the tall spires of the cathedral and the ochre-red tiles that topped clean, whitewashed buildings. We pulled into the wharf close to the Ver-o-Peso market at the base of Plaza Relogio. Awaiting higher tide, fishing boats of all shapes rested with their keels in the mud, the tillers and propellers exposed and their rigging canted precariously. It was colorful and chaotic with the smell of the sea and the noise of the dockside. Passengers streamed off, pushing to get forward, to be the first to disembark, dragging luggage and trunks and bundles along with them. We stood back and watched the frenzied parade. We were simply too drained to fight our way out with the crowd.

I took a deep breath of Belém's air into my lungs, let out a long sigh, and looked at Mary. Neither of us spoke. Not because we had nothing to say, but because the last forty days had pushed us to our maximum. We were physically and emotionally exhausted. Mary and I silently reflected on the long days of our Amazon journey. Nearly three thousand miles along the rivers and their tributaries and into the estuaries were behind us. Since leaving Leticia, Manfred, Shmulik, Mary, and I had been on overcrowded barcos and lanchas, our patience driven to the outer limits by the mind-numbing attitudes of river mentality, bouts of diarrhea, unending insect bites, overloaded boats, rough river justice, and just plain crappy food. But we had never given up. We had never faltered and we had persevered. A journey to be remembered was finished, but another awaited us on shore. I reached over and touched her hand. It was time to leave the Amazon behind.

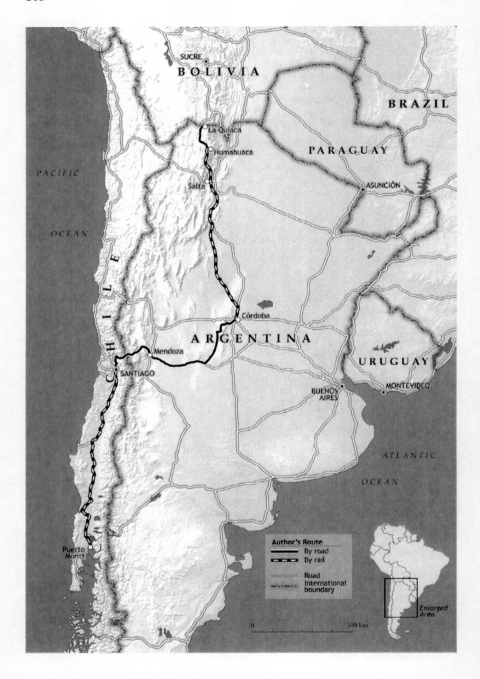

CHILE

Sunday, March 12, 1978: Puerto Montt to Santiago

The Ferrocarriles del Estado train yard up in the north end of Puerto Montt was black and gritty. It matched the cloudy, dull weather and surrounding wooden houses up on the hills above us. We sat transfixed, pressed up against the window while we watched the activity of the yard from the relative comfort of the first-class section of our car. Old steam locomotives, each piston stroke emitting a hiss of steam, shunted dirty gray boxcars and flatbacks from track to track in a seemingly endless parade. We had no idea their destination or purpose. But the process continued so long that I decided to get out and photograph some of the action. Mary waited inside and readied her writing paper and envelopes.

I climbed down the metal steps outside at the end of our car and walked up the burnished tracks to a locomotive that waited patiently on a side rail. It was a big steam engine configured with two front wheels, eight big, five-foot coupled drive wheels, and two bogie wheels under the cab. On the side of the engine cab, in faded paint stenciled long ago, was the engine designation 750. Its bent-iron latticed cowcatcher and stoic single carbon arc headlight mounted atop the old engine's smoke box looked forlorn. She was made in the 1920s by Baldwin Locomotive Works out of Philadelphia, Pennsylvania. Once a proud champion of the rails, she was relegated to mostly shunting excess freight out of the yards and only the occasional long-distance journey. I took a couple of photographs and headed back. It was almost departure time, and Mary would be worried.

As I passed by the cab, the fireman leaned out of the cab, jerked his head back, and yelled over to me: "*¿Quieres ver el interior?*" (Hey, want to see inside?) He didn't need to ask twice, and I veered off over the tracks and climbed up the ladder and into the cab. Both he and the engineer smiled back at the shocked look on my face. Front and center before us were the controls and firebox of the big locomotive. The engineer proudly pointed out some of the gauges and levers. The air brakes on the locomotive and tender were in the fully applied position to keep things from rolling away. The sight feed lubricator was set to the off position so as not to waste oil. The Johnson Bar was centered, the cylinder cocks open, and the throttle cracked just enough to add a bit of steam to the cylinders to keep them warm while we waited.

"Want to shovel some coal into the firebox?" the fireman asked. What steam aficionado wouldn't jump at the chance?

"Sure would," I said.

"Fine—here's how it's done." He handed me the shovel and explained a task more complex than I imagined. "Never put in more than three or four scoops at a time. Each scoop is going to weigh about fifteen pounds, so make sure you don't just pile each scoop on the last or you'll create clinkers. Wait about twenty seconds between scoops," he cautioned. Then he opened the heavy firebox door. The heat filled the cab and he set me to work, all the while keeping a close eye on my technique, timing, and sweat.

Meanwhile, as I concentrated on my imagined career in steam locomotion, a newer diesel engine backed up and coupled with the passenger and freight cars heading for Santiago. Mary felt the impact and heard the metal couplings lock together. She was sitting alone with no husband, and the train was ready to leave. The diesel throttled to full power and then just stopped. We never found out if it was a mechanical or electrical problem, but the diesel was decoupled and then ignominiously towed out of the yard by a second steam locomotive. That diesel failure saved my bacon and gave us a chance to have one last moment of steam rail history.

THE OLD STEAM LOCOMOTIVE 750 AT THE PUERTO MONTT RAIL YARD

The failure meant I was able to get safely back into the passenger car and seated beside a rather unhappy—but relieved—woman. My side trip to the engine cab apparently didn't impress her as much as it had me. The diesel malfunction also meant that the crew of Engine 750 had a major journey in front of them. They backed up, coupled with the train car, and with whistles, fanfare, and a lot of black, sooty smoke, pulled us out of the station and

on to our journey northward. I fantasized I was in the train cab
stoking the firebox. Mary fantasized I was in the doghouse.

Shortly after leaving Puerto Montt we skirted the edges of Lago
Llanquihue, with the snowcapped peak of the Osomo Volcano
visible on the eastern shores. The trip was flat all the way up to
Frutillar, a small town some hundred kilometers up the tracks at
the northern edge of the lake. Passengers came and went at the
tiny stations along the route. In fact, in the thousand kilometers
to Santiago there were over forty stops, most at towns and villages,
some at only crossroads where locals waited to board. We rolled
along for over twenty hours with a slow, secure pace, surrounded
by that old majestic railway atmosphere. But with a steady stream
of vendors, we were never without food. Vendors hopped on and
walked between cars during station stops, hawking delicious meat
filled empanadas, greasy sopaipillas dripping in *chancaca* sauce,
and *completos* (a kind of hotdog with everything on it), bags of hot
peanuts still in the shell, steamy corn, and for the health-con-
scious, a never-ending variety of fruits that tasted like they were
just picked from the garden.

For hours we rolled by endless farm fields and gently sloped
hills. Together we passed the time chatting, daydreaming, reading,
and playing rummy with a tattered deck of cards. Eventually we
pulled out writing paper for thoughts and memories to send
back home.

Mary tried to summarize her litany of recent travel emotions
and wrote:

> Guess I haven't made the trip real pleasant for George. During
> the past few weeks I've become so eager to get back home to
> North America. The Latino attitude has worn my patience thin.

Two of the most irritating things are the subservience of women and the attempts of so many locals to take you for a fast buck— although here it's pennies rather than bucks.

When you get off the bus or train, the hawkers move in and attack en masse. They pressure us for taxis, hotels, and tours while vendors constantly attempt to shortchange us because they don't have the correct denominations of coins or bills in the register. Meals in restaurants are rounded up to the highest bill or coin or simply just misrepresented on the chalkboard sign at the entrance.

Men of all ages ogle me on the street and the relationships between young men and women are frequently all swoony and syrupy. It feels hollow, like a throwback to early times back home.

Spanish is a very emotional and loud language. Even the poorest vendors appear to yell at one another and their customers. They never seem to discuss things quietly and casually. I feel espe-cially irritated here in Chile, and in Argentina where people, by and large, have lifestyles similar to my own. I guess since we travel on a modest budget we interact mostly with the lower, poorer classes.

I don't think this fully describes the frustration I feel, but it should give you some idea of why I'm looking forward to getting back. Groan—all this complaining has put me in a sour mood.

As warm as the day had been, the night was bitterly cold. We pulled sweaters, jackets, and vests out of our packs and put them on and still couldn't shake the chill.

By the time we crossed the high railway bridge of the Melleco Viaduct and reached the outskirts of the Araucania town of Collipulli, the sun had about given up for the day. The rest of the journey would be in darkness, through towns with soft lights from house windows and harsh streetlights that guided us to unnamed stations. I clicked off the overhead illumination, folded up the table, and we snuggled together for warmth. The only sound was the resonant clack of steel wheels on steel rails and the muted cry of the steam whistle when we crossed occasional roadways. As Mary pushed in closer I could smell the pleasant fragrance of her hair. It felt like home in her arms.

Somewhere in the night they took our engine from us. At some unnamed town while we dozed in and out of sleep, they decoupled the 750, the old steam engine, and replaced her with a diesel. We didn't know it then, but this would be the last of the great steam locomotives on which we would ever journey.

Through the cold dawn, the Andean Cordillera poked up into view. The high snowfields of the Tupungato volcano rose up above the mist and overlooked the valley. We were close to Santiago now. The engineer throttled back and the train slowed as we came in through the industrial bands of seedy factories, unkempt maintenance yards, and tire heaps that seemed to surround big cities.

Monday: Santiago

We pulled into Estación Alameda, the central rail station in Santiago, at mid-morning. The train shuddered to a stop as the coupling knuckles between the cars screeched and banged in protest as the diesel engine slowed. The station was a huge, cavernous, iron building designed by Alexandre Gustave Eiffel, the architect and builder of the Eiffel Tower in Paris. The station was finished in 1897 by the French company Schneider-Creusot. The graceful steel braces arched overhead and supported rows of glass windows along the rooflines that projected sharp-edged bright rectangles of sunlight amongst the shadows of the concrete platform. It had been a cold night on board, in the mid-forties, along the rails from Puerto Montt. We had spent it slouched on the hard seats in the unheated first-class passenger cabin. Now, we pulled off the extra layers of sweaters, vests, and jackets we used to brace off the cold, climbed out of the rail car, and slipped on our packs. We walked past the great dark mass of the new engine as we headed out into Santiago's morning sunshine. We took one last look back the station's exterior and the flowing roof structure with an ornate clock perched at its pinnacle. The air was warming already and the day would be a scorcher, but we were tired and worn down with the intermittent sleep of endless stops and starts throughout the night.

Mary and I walked west down the wide boulevard of Liber Bernardo O'Higgins and were struck with the normalcy of the city. Car horns, diesel fumes, and the sounds of accelerating buses mixed with pedestrian chatter. Shops were open, crowded, and prosperous.

It had been a little over seven years ago in October of 1970 when Salvador Allende became Chile's first democratically elected socialist president—not by an overwhelming popular vote, but by a runoff presided over by Chile's Congress, between the two candidates with the most votes. The problem was that he became president at a time when the world was polarized into Marxist and capitalist camps at the height of the Cold War. Both the American CIA and Russian KGB took strong positions. During the run-up to the election the Americans sponsored anti-Allende, anti-Russian propaganda and the Russians openly funded Allende's campaign.

Allende certainly didn't look dangerous. He was a jowl-cheeked, bespectacled, and somewhat overweight little man, a former medical doctor. The problem was that he was a declared Marxist who believed in democracy. To the American psyche, Marxism was incompatible with democracy. The Nixon presidency began an immediate campaign of economic and military coercion. Henry Kissinger, Nixon's Secretary of State, said of this new government: "I don't see why we should have to stand by and let a country go Communist due to the irresponsibility of its own people." That was the American position right from the start. It would all go downhill from there.

It was an hour-long walk with heavy packs along Liber Bernardo O'Higgins and then north along the smaller, more sedate Avenue San Martin to our little Hotel Caribe. Since we were close, we dropped into the American Express office and were pleasantly surprised with a pile of mail from friends and family, neatly wrapped with string. We were able to stock up on an additional five hundred dollars in traveler's checks and some local pesos. We tried to keep as much money in traveler's checks, as so far this year, the inflation rate here was just under fifty percent. The twenty-eight pesos to the dollar we were offered now would change daily over the next week. Compared to the catastrophic inflation by the end of the Allende government and the post-coup chaos, this was nothing. Just a couple of years ago inflation ran over eight hundred percent. Now at least it was on its way down, perhaps even manageable.

We were sweating in the noonday sun as we pushed open the little wrought-iron gate of Hotel Caribe. There, in the tiny courtyard, half hidden by shrubbery, our intermittent traveling companion Raymond was deeply engaged in conversation. We heard his British accent before we actually saw him. Tired as we might be, within minutes we were reinvigorated. While I negotiated a room price of seventy pesos a night, Mary and Ray continued in conversation. By the time I arrived back at the patio it was decided we'd all head down to the *Palacio de la Moneda*, the National Palace and the centerpiece of Chile's government. Mary and I threw our backpacks into the room, padlocked our door, and headed out with Ray.

The three of us caught a local bus back down San Martin. Along the short route back to our stop at Avenida Moneda, we all marveled at the activity on the street. It seemed everything was working and everyone was employed or engaged in some activity. It all seemed so normal, and yet we knew the country's desperate story.

Within months of Allende's ascent to the presidency he and his party nationalized the copper mines, banks, and large industries. The miners immediately struck for higher wages. Others from the growing pool of now nationalized employee roles did the same, demanding unprecedented wage hikes. At the same time, to prevent inflation, the government froze prices. For about a year everything seemed to work. Then industry came to a grinding halt. The nation faced an unprecedented sixteen hundred strikes with over two million lost workdays. Under the pressures of unrealistic wages and the artificially low prices for goods and the lack of any industrial entrepreneurship, the country spiraled into economic chaos. America's control over the international banking made loans that might have had a short-term impact on the economy nearly impossible. Inflation ramped up to over three hundred percent, shop shelves were empty, and the middle class fumed.

The conditions were already explosive in the late summer of 1973 when the government decided to nationalize transport and form a state-owned trucking company. Chile's independent truckers reacted en masse to Allende's threat to socialize their industry. They blocked and paralyzed Chile's thin north-south ribbon of roadways. Doctors, engineers, small business owners, and people from all walks of middle-class life joined in protest. A few weeks later, frustrated, a hundred thousand Chilean women jammed the Plaza de la Constitución, noisily banging spoons and lids on metal cooking pots to vent their rage against the insanely rising costs and food shortages. The national currency was virtually worthless. They were roughly dispersed from the square with wooden batons and tear gas. Chile was on the verge of collapse. The middle class, small business owners, the congress, and the army were turning against him. In three short years, Allende once the savior of the country, was now its leading villain.

We walked the four blocks from our stop over to Plaza de la Constitución and stood in the now quiet and orderly square of grass and concrete that fronted the Moneda. The violence of the coup was still evident in the pock-marked façade. Cannon fire from tanks and fighter jets chipped pieces from the front wall and left gaping holes. Through a half-opened door locked with heavy chains we glimpsed a gutted dark interior still shorn up with heavy boards nailed over damaged walls.

The three of us strolled over to the Carrera-Sheraton Hotel, across the street diagonally from the presidential palace. It was an unremarkable, fourteen-story brown building described in our guidebook as a "deluxe hotel with tastefully decorated rooms having a popular night club and a roof-top swimming pool." But it was from here we got our first full glimpse of the Moneda and a true sense of the chaos and cruelty that followed. An elevator took us to the roof and a view of Santiago. The presidential palace lay almost directly below.

THE COUP-DAMAGED MONEDA FROM HOTEL CARRERA
SHERATON ROOFTOP VANTAGE POINT

On Tuesday, September 11, 1973, Santiago awoke to a new reality. In the mists of early morning the navy seized the port city of Valparaiso and began the coup. Allende rushed to the Moneda with a group of supporters and presidential guards. Within minutes the national paramilitary police, the Carabineros, surrounded the Moneda. Allende tried desperately to contact his military generals for assistance, but he couldn't reach even one of them. "No one is answering. I think that this time all of them are involved," he remarked to his aides. He was right.

Shortly before nine, the coup plotters showed their hand and announced their intentions in a radio broadcast. Their leader was

Augusto Pinochet Ugarte, Commander-in-Chief of the Chilean Army. He would head the new ruling junta.

Desperate, Allende made one final broadcast from the Moneda through a pro-government station that had not been silenced:

> This will be my last opportunity to address you. I am not going
> to resign. I address the youth who gave us their joy and spirit of
> the struggle. I address the man of Chile, the worker, the farmer,
> the intellectual, those who will be prosecuted. They were com-
> mitted. I have faith in Chile and its destiny. Long live Chile.
> Long live the people. Long live the workers! These are my last
> words and I am certain that my sacrifice will not be in vain, I
> am certain that, at the very least, it will be a moral lesson that
> will punish felony, cowardice, and treason.

Over his voice, the sound of gunfire and the explosion of tank shells could be heard in the background.

By nine-thirty in the morning, the first of the air force's Hawker Hunter swept-wing strike fighters screamed in low over the city from their southern base of Talcahuano. Their targets were the city's pro-Allende radio stations. Bursts of cannon fire and under-wing rockets destroyed the stations in minutes. This would deny his supporters news of resistance, restrict communication, and ensure broadcasts were filtered through the one remaining station already in military control. Just as Allende ended his final transmission, another wave of planes taxied, rotated up, and headed for the Moneda. Junta soldiers fired tank shells and machine guns, shattering windows and destroying entire walls of the Moneda. Helicopters circled, taking out Allende sharpshooters stationed in surrounding buildings. During a late-morning lull in fighting, most of Allende's aides and loyalists surrendered.

By noon the fighter-bombers streaked and strafed and rocketed the building, blowing doors off hinges and leaving gaping holes in the roof. Just as the army stormed the building, helicopters fired canisters of tear gas into the melee.

Under fire, Allende, armed with an AK-47 rifle gifted to him by Fidel Castro, retreated deeper into the Moneda and up to the second floor along with a small group of loyalists. Just before two in the afternoon as the junta soldiers closed in and with the palace gutted and in flames, Allende told those last few supporters that they would surrender together. They would go down the stairs unarmed and he would take the rear as they filed out. Instead of following behind, the president slipped off alone to the palace's red room—Independence Hall. He sat down in a chair facing a window, alone and defeated. The noise of the battle was deafening, the smell of cordite everywhere, and the acrid tear gas clogged his throat. With one last gesture he placed the muzzle of the AK-47 under his chin and the stock between his feet, reached down and snicked the selector to full automatic, clicked off the safety, sighed, and pulled the trigger. It was a fast, brutal, and disfiguring death. In that instant, with that short burst of gunfire, democracy died in Chile. It was the last flickering moment of freedom for seventeen years.

Below us now, as we stood leaning silently against the retaining walls of the Sheraton Hotel's rooftop, was the country's new reality.

Tuesday: Santiago

Our little hotel was central to everything. This morning Ray, Mary, and I walked over to the Natural History Museum in Parque

Quinta Normal. Mary insisted we go after she read in our *South American Handbook* about a mummified Incan child found on the summit of El Polomo, one of the highest mountains of the Andes Cordillera, a mere forty kilometers outside Santiago. We walked back down the now-familiar Avenue San Martin and then west on Catedral. Half an hour later we crossed Avenida Matacuna and into the park.

As luck would have it, the Natural History Museum was closed for repairs. We pleaded with the guards stationed outside the front entrance door. We came all the way from Canada just to see this exhibit. Couldn't he make just one exception? Foreign tourists just never took a straight *"no"* for an answer. Finally, one of the guards relented and took us upstairs. We left footprints on the steps from the fine, white chalk dust of plaster repair as we climbed to the second floor. There, in the center of the dimly-lit room, was the little refrigerated display case in which a small boy, offered as a sacrifice some five hundred years ago, sat silently. Found frozen and perfectly preserved in the Andes in 1954, he has sat there in the freezer ever since. Unfortunately, there were no lights on due to the repairs, so we struck matches, held them up to the glass, and peered inside.

He sat with his knees pulled in to his chest and his arms resting gently upon them. He looked as if he'd just serenely and peace-fully fallen asleep. His clothes were vicuna and alpaca cloth with a coarse, gray shawl wrapped around his shoulders. The little boy's face was painted yellow and red and dark, braided hair fell across his forehead. He still wore his moccasins. In preparation for his sacrificial entombment, he was probably drugged and given alcohol until he started his long sleep that led to his death in the freezing cold cave and his perfect preservation for five hundred years. I'm sure each of us wanted to turn away for a moment, but couldn't. We were transfixed. It was eerie to stand there as observers and just look in the flickering light of our matches at this little boy still cold and sleeping after all these years.

Cerro Santa Lucia is a lovely part of the city. We climbed up along the winding roadway and sauntered through the parks and fountains. It was one of those days when life felt good as Mary and I walked hand-in-hand up the ornate winding stairways that led past crenulated castle walls to a marvelous view of the city. Santiago lay below in a flat, bowl-shaped valley with the snow-covered Andes behind us and the spurs of the Chilean Coastal Mountains across the city. It was early evening before we returned back down and headed home to our hotel.

We went out to a brothel that night! We didn't mean to. Okay— maybe we meant to, but we didn't plan to. Our hotel just happened to be at the edges of Santiago's red light district. Little bars and restaurants were scattered amongst the unmarked bordellos. During the daylight hours the doors were closed and the shutters latched. We planned to go out to eat but Mary felt a little queasy and begged off from dinner. Ray and I and a couple of fellow travelers from the hotel headed out and stopped in at a nearby bar for dinner and beer. One beer led to another as we told and retold spirited travel stories. As the night drew on we noticed three armed security police hovering over at the bar, talking and nodding our way. We knew the *toque de queda*, or curfew, was still enforced, but it started at eleven at night. We still had an hour and a half. Chileans knew well enough to be off the streets by curfew or they faced whatever sanctions the junta's police felt like meting out. Being stopped could mean a warning, a beating, arrest, or worse: simply disappearing. We were only a few minutes from the hotel, so as the appointed hour approached we planned to leave.

The bar was dimly-lit and smelled like beer as the three of them got up from the long wooden counter and wandered over to see what the laughter was all about. They greeted us in accented English, asked if they could join us, and without waiting for a response pulled chairs over to our table. It turns out they were just passing time until the curfew kicked in and wanted to know if we wanted to see another side of Santiago: the local brothels. We still had an hour before curfew and besides, they said, nothing would happen as long as we were with them. Maybe it was the beer that prompted us to agree, but agree we did. We paid the tab, including the beers for our new friends, and headed outside with our police escort.

In the time we had spent inside the bar, the neighborhood had changed. The shuttered brothels were now open for business. Illuminated by the harsh streetlights, women lounged seductively in doorways and leaned out open windows to call for us to come in. The boys needed very little encouragement, and we entered a house apparently favored by our police pals.

I must admit to being a little naïve. I had never been in a real brothel before. I'd seen them in the movies and this place fit right into my expectations. Women lounged around in the main living room in various states of undress, smiling at anyone who smiled at them. We were invited to sit, relax with a cup of tea, and enjoy the atmosphere. One by one the guys filed out and vanished to unseen rooms upstairs until just Ray and I remained. The scantily-clad girls who lingered behind sat snuggled up on our laps, their hands straying provocatively along our bare legs as they leaned revealingly in to coax us to join our comrades in the evening delights.

I never sensed anger or frustration from the women as we sat unconvinced, only curiosity and confusion. They never stopped being anything but polite and flirtatious.

Slowly, our friends reemerged from hidden rooms and just before the curfew hour we all nonchalantly headed back through empty streets to our little hotel. Our newfound police friends headed out to enforce Pinochet's curfew. As we returned along the quiet sidewalk, there was an unsettling discomfort to the evening's encounter.

Wednesday: Santiago

Typical of our declining energy, we arose quite late in the morning and made our way over to one of Santiago's most famous landmarks. We were off to Cerro San Cristobal with a small diversion to the Central market for a late breakfast where Ray and Trevor, a hotel friend from last night's adventure, promised us a fabulous meal at reasonable prices. We wove between the aisles of fishmongers cutting, gutting, weighing, and wrapping all species of waterborne creatures. During the morning, it took a brave stomach to eat there amongst the stench and the guts. While we guys sat down for a plate of fish and chips, Mary wandered off and bought a couple of empanadas, a local meat-filled pastry. Our chubby waitress had told us it would be a few minutes, but over an hour later we were still waiting. Mary, patience stretched to the limit by our inactivity and the nonchalance of the cooks, let fly with a colorful tirade of Spanish epithets. The stream of off-colored appellations out of a foreign woman's mouth in a strange accented Spanish only added to the amusement of the kitchen staff. I made a serious judgment error and rattled Mary's increasingly fragile spirit with a public rebuke of her behavior. With a raised voice I told her to cool it the next time she was upset at Latino incompetence. She broke down in tears. Tears came more easily now for some reason. Her emotions over the past few weeks seemed closer to the surface, more easily aroused, and more easily expressed. Then the crowning insult and a vindication of Mary's outburst: our meals finally arrived, stone-cold. Our waitress served them deadpan, without even looking us in the eye. We left in disgust for greener pastures and bought a roasted chicken lunch at a nearby stall.

An hour later, tummies full and emotions in check, we crossed the gritty-brown Mapocho River and headed northeast along Calle Santa Filomena. We stopped in the limestone funicular railway terminal at the base of Cerro San Cristobal, paid our fare of ten cents, and waited in the shade alongside a Chilean couple for the little cable-driven railway cars to come down.

Our new acquaintances introduced themselves. Diego, in his late thirties, was visiting from their hometown Quilpue near Valparaiso. His younger sister Catalina studied medicine at the university here in Santiago. Like many educated locals, they spoke faultless but accented English to us but conversed between themselves in a fast-clipped Chilean Spanish. They were curious about our travels and Mary and I spent the next several minutes reliving our adventures with them.

The line of little, green, open-windowed wooden cars arrived and the six of us piled in the lead car and started our ascent up the hill. The train groaned and shuddered as the cable pulled us over the driving wheels between the rails. The cars rose steeply and, although we may have held our collective breath more than once, the view was fantastic. We ascended up to the Terraza Bellavista station some thousand feet up the hill and above the city. The city of Santiago lay below us. The mountains to the west disappeared in a gentle haze, but the city was clear. We could see back towards our hotel and pick out the market and the Moneda.

We climbed the outdoor stairs up another few hundred feet to the summit and the gardens of the Sanctuary of the Immaculate Conception. We stood sweating at the base of the Virgin Mary statue, under the protection of her outstretched arms, and gazed once more over the city below us.

As Mary and I stood there at the railing above the rocky out-crops, Diego came over, stopped beside us, and leaned in closer. He didn't point, but rather motioned with his head. In Chile, even today, he couldn't be too cautious. The secret police were everywhere and watched everything. "Over there," he said quietly, nodding and not pointing at the distant soccer stadium. "Over there is where they killed Jara."

Back in June 1973, months before the *coup d'état*, the gener-als finalized their lists of those who might oppose them. Those registers included names of people suspected of being in radical leftist parties, members of Allende's Unidad Popular party, politi-cal leaders, Marxist journalists, leftist professors, and everyone that participated in neighborhood, communal, national, or union activities. There were thousands of names on those lists. Chile needed to rid itself of this communist infestation within its population. The secret police were everywhere. They had dossiers on tens of thousands of leftists, intellectuals, and Allende party members. It was never a long step from being a name on a dossier to disappearing without a trace.

Minutes after Allende's death, in the early afternoon of September 11, 1973, the army gained control of the palace. Even before the smell of cordite cleared, the roundups and the executions began.

Victor Jara, according to our friend Diego, was a pacifist songwriter, singer, and university professor. On Wednesday, the day after the coup, he was arrested along with over four thousand other political prisoners and taken to Santiago's soccer stadium. He was tortured for days, his hands crushed with the butt of a revolver handle by junta thugs. To add humiliation, his captors threw his guitar on his beaten body and taunted him to play and sing for them. They shot him dead on September 16 and then machine-gunned his body. Jara's bullet-riddled corpse was dumped on the street near a cemetery three days later. He was to be an example of what happened if you opposed the junta.

VICTOR JARA, POET, SOCIAL ACTIVIST AND ONE OF THE
FIRST CAUSALITIES OF THE PINOCHET COUP

Jara's last song, written in the stadium, knowing that he and many others would probably die there, was a tome for freedom and the tragedy of those imprisoned with him:

> *How hard it is to sing when I must sing of horror*
> *The horror in which I'm living*

The horror in which I'm dying
Silence and screams is the end of my song.
What I now see, I have never seen,
What I now feel, I have never felt.

It was no wonder Diego whispered his opposition. Perhaps
someday he would be able to express these truths out loud and hon-
estly. Not now. The endless brutality of this regime brought order.
But it also brought a simmering anger, sadness, and uncertainty.

By the time we had arrived in Santiago two days before, four and
a half years had passed since the *coup d'état*. By the time we arrived
at the railway station and slung on our backpacks, over forty thousand people had been arrested, thousands tortured and executed,
and many more thousands had simply disappeared. Families of
those *desaparecidos* never knew what happened. A father, a mother,
a son, or daughter was picked up on the way to work or school or
in the dark of night and never heard from again. They were not
in the jails, the prisons, the hospitals, or the morgues. They were
just gone. The arrests and murders would continue during our
stay in Chile. They would go on long after our departure.

Yet there were many who praised this government. There were
many who approved the ruthlessness because it brought order and
prosperity. Copper mines were back in private control, industry
and businesses that once were shuttered or feared nationaliza-
tion grew and expanded, and the giant middle class felt the wealth
returning and the money stabilizing. That's what we saw and experienced on the streets of Santiago when we arrived and walked
around. And still, beneath the surface, somewhere at a visceral
level, we knew the curfew was in effect, the dissonant voices spoke
only in whispers, and there was a stoic silence about the violence

lest it be visited upon them. The old economic burdens had been replaced with political bondage. Those deep wounds continued to haunt the people of Chile.

Thursday: Santiago

We simply walked about the streets today looking at buildings and people. It was a great way to get a feeling for the area. The supply of consumer goods here is quite remarkable. The stores are well stocked with a great variety and good quality. Even more remarkable is that five years ago, according to some of the locals, there were bread lines in the streets and chronic shortages and extreme inflation. By and large, the people appeared to accept the government with few complaints. The world press was not so kind. In fact, it was hostile and condemned Chile's civil rights. Many Chileans took it as a direct criticism of their country, a personal attack if you will, rather than a criticism of Pinochet's regime.

In the afternoon Mary and I, along with a group of travelers from the hotel, took a bus down Avenida Central out to O'Higgins Park with its wide, terraced, open grass fields. We slouched down on the grass and watched the locals picnicking in the shade while children, perhaps playing hooky from school, flew colorful paper kites above us. We wandered along the edges of the park where kite vendors in kiosks competed with food stalls. It was a lazy day to browse through the artisan shops. Mary purchased a lump of deep blue lapis lazuli, a local semi-precious stone. Ray bought new sneakers and has been sneaking around ever since. He told us he planned to stay here in Santiago awhile, perhaps finding work as an English teacher.

That evening Mary and I strolled down the crowded, recently-opened pedestrian street of the Paseo Ahumada a few short blocks east of the Palacio de la Moneda. We walked along under the belfry of the Santiago Cathedral and past signs for Gucci and the Chilean textile giant Oveja Tome. Slatted wooden benches, full of restful people nibbling ice cream, reading, or like us, simply watching the passing crowd, lined the edges of the Paseo. Santiago was calm as we wound our way northward through the streets and back to the hotel.

Friday: Santiago to Mendoza Argentina

It was five-thirty in the morning. Last night's curfew was over. As soon as the curfew lifted, Mary and I made our way over the central market for a quick breakfast and then over to the nearby bus company stop. Our trip began in a smallish minivan filled to capacity with Chileans, two gringos, and a lot of luggage. Our packs were lashed on the roof rack under a torn and weatherworn tarpaulin. The drive took us across the rich agricultural flatlands and fruit farming communities north of Santiago. Two hours later, at the town of Santa Rosa de Los Andes, we turned east and headed into the low morning sun and in amongst the foothills of the Andes. We had crossed these mountains six times, and each time we were surprised with their variety of scenery and incredible beauty. Today was no exception.

The road followed the river and the railway line towards the summit through the Uspallata Pass. Our bus wound back and forth for half an hour, crossing and re-crossing the river as it climbed up along the valley. The dark gray rock of the Andes crowded in towards us, towering above, blocking the sun. The rock faces were sharp and exposed and we had to slouch down in the seats to see the ridges above us. Beyond the tiny outpost town of El Peñon our little van struggled with the altitude. I counted seventeen switchbacks in just a few miles. We climbed along the valley floor. The roadway seemed to twist and turn in impossible directions like a maze in front of us. Our driver concentrated as the van engine growled and then, alternately, the brakes squealed as we approached hairpin curves. The steep grade continued as we climbed toward Portillo, the gateway pass at the Chilean–Argentine border. We were now at 13,000 feet above sea level. Beyond the border customs shed, in the distance, we saw Aconcagua, the highest peak in the Americas, with its snow-covered peak still two miles above us. There were few formalities at the frontier beyond stamping our passports and we entered Argentina for our fourth and final time. All along our left side was a striking mountain ridge. Bereft of snow but rich in subtle hues of reds, greens, and earthy browns, the jagged rock seemed entertained by the blue sky around it. The powerful, solid rock void of vegetation made it all the more impressive. Harsh weather had not changed its sharp features. Only the occasional landslides of gray rock indicated weaknesses in its steely face.

The hour-long descent to the northern Argentine town of Uspallata on the wide alluvial plain was easier. The massive mountain cordilleras gave way to a widening valley. It was a gentler descent still surrounded by distant, snowcapped peaks. Out of Uspallata we followed the Mendoza River through the cordilleras and along the valley until suddenly it ended and we found ourselves in farmland once again. As we drove on the Mendoza we passed vast vineyards and bodegas with anticipations of good evenings to come.

Seasoned travelers quickly learned to be leery of free help. Help, it turns out, was rarely a free commodity. At bus and train stations throughout the journey help appeared from nowhere, especially for *extranjeros* like us. Someone was always willing to provide information about the cheapest hotel, the best restaurant, and the quickest route. But it all came with a catch, and in the end, a hand extended palm side up. Mendoza was different. Our great skepticism about all the help we received at the bus station turned out to be ill-founded. Here in the Argentine northland, assistance, such as a free ride in a taxi to find an inexpensive hotel, turned out to be just plain good people helping out.

We settled into our little Hotel Richmond. It was another one of those low-priced gems. The charge of $2.85 included a room with a real honest-to-goodness private bathroom and a walkout to an arbor-covered patio. We threw our packs on the floor and plopped down on our bed together. The bed squeaked and the mattress sagged. Squeaking and sagging were common features of the cheap rooms allowed on our modest budget. Mary boiled some water with our immersion heater and on the patio we shared a packet of herbal tea grown in the nearby town of Oberá. Shaded by the broad leaves of the gnarled grape vines overhead, we sat on two metal folding chairs painted rust-red a generation earlier and relaxed in idle chatter.

Saturday: Mendoza

Like a hormonal imbalance, our emotional levels were in turmoil. Time, once our friend, was turning against us as our energy and enthusiasm waxed and waned, grew and then flitted away just as quickly. Missing the excitement of our early travel adventures, we reminisced about Mexico and Central America, our escapades through the Amazon and across Peru. Mendoza, the city, seemed far too urban and urbane for our tastes. It may have been the epicenter of Argentina's wine region, but the city itself sprawled out around us like every other large city anywhere in the world, a tangle of commercial buildings, noisy thoroughfares, retail shops, and plazas. Both of us longed for more diverse experiences and cultures. Every moment we spent anchored here meant less time we'd have in other more interesting locales. So, determined to move on, we wandered over towards the train station to buy a fare out for tomorrow. While momentarily stopped at the intersection just a block away from the station we recognized a familiar red backpack perched on the roof rack of an approaching taxi. It was Ray, our English traveler and friend who obviously had changed his mind about working in Santiago and was now moving in more or less the same line as we were northward. We did our best windmill imitation, arms flailing as we shouted out his name. The taxi stopped and out popped Ray, with contagious hugs all round. Suddenly, under Ray's sunny disposition, the city seemed less dull. In fact, we turned on the spot and headed back to our hotel and then deeper into town, determined to explore the city and taste its celebrated wines.

Together, starting at the city's heart, the Plaza Independencia, the three of us walked the central grid of Mendoza. The fountain

Fuente de la Bandera anchored the plaza, but today it was surrounded by little food and craft stalls. We munched on street food as we wound our way slowly outwards towards the edges, where there were larger bars and outdoor restaurants. We relaxed and sipped wine at seven cents a glass and passed time watching people wandering by. This afternoon the dusty Zonda wind, warmed by its descent from the adjacent peak of Mount Aconcagua, blew down along the foothills of the Andes and into the plaza, ruffling the fronds of the tall caranday palms surrounding us. We covered our wine glasses with our hands and waited patiently until the gusts subsided. Another toast followed another round of laughter. Perhaps an extra day with good company wasn't so bad.

Sunday, March 19, 1978: Mendoza

Our hotel manager left for a morning coffee with friends and foolishly put me in charge. Just outside our room, out of reach in the wooden ceiling lattice, grape bunches dangled tantalizingly. It was all just too tempting. Besides, we could always rationalize a little minor thievery when huge clusters of deep purple and green grapes beckoned us from overhead. Ray and I found an abandoned mop and taped my knife to the pole end. While Ray precariously balanced between a chair back and the table and struggled to cut the vines high above him, I ranged out below like some national league outfielder under a high fly ball, ready to make the catch of the century before the grapes splattered on the concrete patio. Breakfast of tea and grapes right off the vine tasted pretty good.

It was a delightful sunny day and we spent it walking through Mendoza, all the way out past the zoo to *Cerro de la Gloria*, a steep hill located in San Martin Park at the fringes of the city. On top was an impressive monument to the Army of the Andes, a group of several thousand patriots under General San Martin who, in the early 1800s, massed here in Mendoza before they marched for twenty-five days across the Andes in a successful effort to free Chile from the Spanish Empire. Above the memorial's stone outcropping, which mirrored the naked rocky slopes of the high mountains of Mendoza, was a frieze of the cavalry attack. A condor soared at its edges, and above, an allegorical winged Liberty wrapped in the flag of Argentina stood with her arms resolutely outstretched and holding the broken chains of tyranny. The irony wasn't lost on us. Last March as the army deposed President Isabel Peron and initiated its reign of terror on the Argentine people, one of the generals optimistically declared, "We have finally broken the chains of tyranny." Now, liberty was simply oxidized patina that formed on the surface of a bronzed historical monument, just a memory, a mocking inscription on rock and iron from a bygone dream.

CERRO DE LA GLORIA MONUMENT TO THE ARMY OF THE ANDES IN MENDOZA

Monday: Mendoza

We were in the heart of wine country and were encouraged to tour a local bodega. The Bodega de Arizú, one of the region's most well known, family-owned wine producers, was only a short ten-minute bus ride south into the suburbs. We were treated to an hour-long tour (with the musty odor of fermenting wine) by one of the current family members. He showed us the workings of the bodega pretty much backwards, starting with the immense kegs made from oak imported from France, each holding up to thirty-five thousand liters of wood-aged wine. As we toured it was evident this was a modern manufacturing facility and, with the exception of the wine taster's nose and palette, run with precision and mechanization. There was a labyrinth of tunnels and hallways crowded with stacked, fifty-five-gallon oak barrels of wine. One was identified as *Comun*, lightly aged for six months and the wine typical of those inexpensive glasses we'd been belting back since we arrived in town; *Reservado*, which was aged to at least one year; and *Fino*, a fine wine aged at least three years, probably more. Mary and I were *Comun* folk, with the occasional splurge on *Reservado*. For a treat we bypassed the proffered glasses of cheap wine and indulged ourselves to complimentary glasses of *Fino*. What a remarkable difference. It was deep and rich and smelled of exotic spices and fruit. Henceforth our taste buds would demand to be treated to these new delicious flavors. Our wallet would continue to demand *Comun*.

After meeting up with more of his traveling friends, Ray was out showing them the town and together they had decided to stay another day in Mendoza. Mary and I were ticketed to take the late night local bus to Cordoba and were back in our hotel room packing and preparing to check out when we heard the knock on the door. Mary cracked it open and peered out at two strangers standing in the hallway. "Police, show me your documents," they commanded as one intolerantly held out his hand. Neither was in uniform nor showed us any identification. Maybe it was simply a long, tiring day, or anticipation of moving on, but we balked, not intimidated by their arrogance, but rather angered by it. We'd seen it so many times before and this time, fed up, we demanded they show us their identification before we handed over ours. There was a discussion, voices elevating. "Our badges," one said, "are back at the police station, and if you want to see them, we'll take you down to the station."

"Okay, fine, let's do it." We were tired of all the intimidation. In anger we picked up our passports, locked the room, and followed them out to their unmarked VW beetle, wedged ourselves in the back seat, and sat there with arms crossed and in silence as we wound our way through city streets. It only took a couple of minutes for anger to change to a sense of unease. All four occupants of the car knew what the secret police were capable of doing. This was a country where people simply disappeared and we had just provoked the very people who were responsible for those actions. We had no idea whether our destination was the police station or one of those secret detention centers we had heard spoken about in whispers. Suddenly our resistance seemed like a really bad idea. When the car braked to a stop to our relief we noticed marked police cars parked around the building. We actually were at the *estación de policía municipal*, the local police station. I let out a sigh of relief. Perhaps, just to let us know the possibilities, we were escorted to a desk in front of the holding area. In rapid Spanish our two police acquaintances explained the situation to the other cops in the room. Heads turned our way with laughter, but the most ribbing seemed directed at the two cops who brought us in. The whole situation obviously tickled them and one wandered over and offered us a couple of bottles of soft drinks. Our two erstwhile cops dug out their identification and waved it at us as if to say "we showed you ours, now you show us yours." We did.

It took us over an hour to walk back to the hotel. Along the way, we decided not to poke the bear again.

Tuesday: Cordoba

We were tired and hungry from the overnight milk run bus trip from Mendoza. We'd either acclimatized to our continual travel-ing or were simply too exhausted, and we slept through the con-stantly jolting ride and the endless stops under the aurora-like glow of small-town streetlights along the way. The newly built *Terminal de Omnibus* here in Cordoba was clean and modern and, most importantly, had a spacious restaurant up on the second floor. We hustled off the bus, grabbed our packs, headed upstairs, plunked down by the bay of windows that overlooked a side street below us, and ordered breakfast amid the clatter of dishes and loud, disjointed conversations.

Minutes later, two dark green Ford Falcons braked to a halt, tires screeching against the pavement below us. The Falcons were immediately reinforced by olive- and brown-camouflaged utility trucks full of seated soldiers, their guns pointed skyward. The troops dispersed with one contingent spreading out to cover every escape route from the station, the secondary exits, the bus plat-forms, and the roadways in. Another squad of soldiers, weapons at the ready, surrounded the plain-clothed officers in blue jeans and white shirts who had casually exited the Falcons and were headed inside through the main entrance.

By the time the soldiers had secured the exits, the entire bus station had gone silent, save for the soft, resonant stuttering of a lone diesel bus engine idling below us in the yard. Upstairs in the cafeteria, no one spoke, but chairs scraped across the tiled floor as people pushed back from their meals while heads craned nervously, glancing at fellow patrons. There was a palpable sense of unease. Everyone knew what the arrival of the Ford Falcons meant. Everyone lived in horror of the occupants of those cars and the heartbreaks that so often followed.

The Falcons were the cars of choice for Argentina's secret police and death squads. Those sleek, dark cars with the heavy, menacing, horizontal grillwork and quad headlights were already synonymous for torture, despair, and death. The newly formed *Secretaría de Inteligencia de Estado (SIDE)*, Argentina's security apparatus, had morphed into the Secret Police, whose mandate was to root out, by any means available, the Marxist extremists, union leaders, intellectuals, and troublemakers. No method was too extreme to achieve that outcome. Here around Cordoba, the notorious *Campo de la Ribera* detention camp, one of over three hundred such clandestine camps across the country, was home to the secret police. Many picked up off the streets or in raids like this one were prodded with electric shocks within hours of arrival. Not as a punishment in and of itself, but as a cruel way of welcoming their new guest. Part of the torture was the knowing and not knowing what would come next. The detention centers soon became simply a way station for torture—or worse.

Down below us, past the staircase and in the cavernous waiting room, a line of people, suitcases at their feet, shuffled their way towards the only available exit. A soldier gestured to Mary and me, broke the queue, and motioned us in. Those we joined said nothing at our intrusion. At the head of the column the secret police interrogated and checked documents. Helmeted soldiers, grenades strapped to their chests and automatic weapons at the ready, stood mutely by, carefully inspecting the line and demand-ing absolute quiet as we slowly inched our way forward. We watched as we lumbered forward. Everyone was silent and gazed vacantly ahead. No one in front of us had been singled out. That meant that whomever they were searching for was behind us, maybe standing in line and knowing the ultimate outcome, maybe still safe and hiding in some dark recess of the station. Finally, it was our turn at the front. A tall, solidly-built soldier with lifeless, unblinking eyes held a short-barreled, twelve-gauge, tactical pump-action shotgun pointed directly at me, its ominous dull, matte-black finish just inches from my chest. My eyes were drawn irresistibly to the large, black bore of the muzzle. I forced my focus back to his face. We made eye contact and he smirked with an arrogant, goony grin. My discomfort obviously amused him. One of the plain-clothed police from the Falcon stepped closer and impatiently held out his hand. The muzzle never left my chest. My backpack was taken and handed off to a group that rummaged through it on a makeshift table. There were no smiles as the interrogation started.

"Passport," he commanded and flipped through the pages. "You're Canadian. What are you doing here? Where did you come from today? Where have you traveled in Argentina? Why did you come by bus? How long will you be in Cordova? Who do you know here? Do you have friends in Cordova? Where are you staying? What were you doing in Chile? Who are you traveling with?" I answered each question in Spanish with simple answers, using the fewest words possible. The vagaries of translation might lead to confusion. He turned towards the table for confirmation that the contents of my pack were innocuous—no subversive books or detailed maps, nothing that would link us with seditious deeds. Finally, he thrust my passport back into my hands and abruptly dismissed me, motioning me out of line. The cordon of soldiers shuffled aside to let me pass, but I stopped short and turned back towards Mary. The shotgun swiveled over to her.

Mary had always been a private woman. She did a good job of keeping her emotions checked tightly behind a rigid demeanor, locked away from others. Traveling together over the past two years, we had passed through countless military checkpoints with so many demands for documents and property searches. We'd even weathered a Federal police raid in the dark of night on our boat deep in the Amazon jungle. But these past weeks had profoundly shaken her. After yesterday's trip to the police station and now standing here at the head of the line, a shotgun pointed inches from her throat, and surrounded by armed men and a menacing secret police interrogator, she looked frail and afraid. Her face was pallid, her lips tightly pursed together, and her hand visibly trembled as she passed her passport to the outstretched hand. She glanced over at me, just momentarily, perhaps gathering some reassurance from my proximity. They took her pack and then after a lingering, silent pause as the interrogator thumbed back and forth through the pages without taking his eyes off the document he sneered, "You're American." It wasn't really a question directed at her—it was an indictment. "*Usted es americana, ¿por qué tu esposo tienen un pasaporte canadiense?*" (You're American, why does your husband have a Canadian passport?) In awkward and stumbling Spanish, she tried to explain the story of our meeting, she being Minnesota-born and me a Canadian who had studied in America and sought work in the Midwest, that we had lived in the same apartment complex, met, courted, and got married. It was difficult. The words came slowly, jumbled through a whirl of translation into a rudimentary Spanish full of grammatical and

contextual errors. I think the guy was bemused by the mangled
Spanish and amused by his obvious power to humble us foreigners.
He held her there before he waved her through, just long enough
to demonstrate that he and he alone was in complete control of
our destiny today. We would leave only because he allowed it.
Together we walked out of the station, squinting into the glare of
a low morning sun and past the empty dark Ford Falcons. Beyond
the emotional revulsion there was a physical reaction to our latest
encounter. Our breathing was still tight and our legs felt spongy.
For the first time in our entire journey we truly sensed the helplessness and fear that others living in these dictatorships must feel
on a constant basis. At the best of times, death was always in close
proximity to life. But here, for the past several weeks, we had lived
and traveled in countries where hate and unimaginable violence
was visited on their citizens. As we walked along the sidewalk Mary
turned to me, her eyes just short of tears and her voice barely
audible, betraying the panic of the past hour.

"I want to go home," she whispered.

Wednesday: Cordoba

Our little hotel room in Hotel Florida in the heart of Cordoba was
a study in kitsch run amok. Yesterday morning the hotel manager,
a friendly but strange man with black hair so matted with grease
that it actually reflected the light, galumphed down the hallway to
our room, opened our door with aplomb, flicked on the light, and
motioned us inside. We found ourselves standing in the doorway
of a room that appeared to be transported from some alien planet.
A riot of rich, deep hues, every wall claiming its own exotic color,

jolted our senses. A brilliant lime-green shag rug even managed to outdo the wall colors. Old faded prints of the nearby central sierras—the undulating hills with their pinkish-gray ridges and jagged outcrops—hung on the walls, fastened with roofing nails pounded through the centers of the drawings. Plastic pails with primitively drawn images of the cathedral and city estancias balanced on a single shelf over the bed.

The bathroom danced in a mosaic-like mix of ceramic tiles in indigo, aqua, and yellow that extended across the floor and partway up the walls where they collided with bright, pink-patterned wallpaper. The mirror, a remnant broken from a much larger piece, the sharp edges smooth and rounded, hung precariously over a cracked green porcelain sink. The floral shower curtain barely covered the raised concrete rectangle that outlined the floor drain and makeshift shower. The colors and décor were nicely set off by a single forty-watt light that dangled from the ceiling on a long, frayed, and plaited electrical cord.

We slid off our packs and showered, trying to wash off the last disturbing vestiges of the morning's encounter with the police at the bus station. Mary and I dealt with our anger the way thousands of others around here did—we muttered under our breath.

There was a strange dichotomy in these countries, governed as they were by military or quasi-military dictatorships: an intuitive disconnect between daily living and the constant fear of repression. We had experienced this on the periphery as simple travelers, as we moved southward after our Amazon adventure through Brazil, Paraguay, Argentina, Chile, and now here once more transiting northern Argentina. On the surface everything seemed calm, often prosperous, just like life back home. I imagined it like looking out at the smooth, inviting waters of a crowded coastal beach. People enjoyed the sunshine and sand and frolicked in the breakers along the shore, but somewhere out there, amongst the waves, a strong, malevolent undertow was ready to sweep the unknowing or unlucky away. That's the way it was here in Cordoba. The shops were open and well stocked with goods, the people helpful and friendly, and the streets noisy with the engines of cars and buses. The military brought something missing only a few years ago: order, order, and more order. It also brought terror. In this town there were more silences around us than truth.

We toured Cordoba, an architecturally elegant city anchored by the central Plaza San Martin and the rich stone façade of the Cathedral of Cordoba. In the peaceful presence of the evening sun we crossed the plaza, silent save for the sound of chirping birds that sheltered in the nearby carob trees. The great church façade was bathed in a soft valedictory sunlight that cast faded shadows across the pillars and carvings. We sat and watched them slowly arcing across the delicate stone filigree, forming ever-changing silhouettes as the sun swept lower.

Wednesday: Cordoba

This morning we cleaned out our rucksacks and washed and aired every scrap of clothing. We were gypsies now, with no permanent address and all our worldly contents on our backs, never anchored, traveling from pillar to post through the continent in our caravan of boats, buses, trains, and the odd rides from strangers. The tricky thing with rucksacks is that everything eventually migrates to the bottom of the pack. When unused clothing or once precious treasures are not in daily use, they sit forgotten, sinking into the depths and collecting mold or becoming havens for odd, creepy-crawly bugs or insects. So once in a while, just for our peace of mind, we scoured our packs from top to bottom. I had several rolls of Kodachrome slide film I wanted to send home for processing and Mary added a few souvenirs to the pile. So while the clothes dried on a line strung across our room, she and I headed out to the main post office to send a package home.

Back home everyone put a premium on efficiency. Our public services should serve us, not the staff that operates them. Whether it's the post office, license bureau, or city hall, get in and get on your way. That's our maxim. *Norte Americanos*, me included, were frustrated with any inconveniences, especially long lines. We expected a well-lubricated and functioning system or we complained to the manager.

Correos Argentina, the central post office in Cordoba, on the other hand, was run by a cumbrous, Kafkaesque bureaucracy crossed with Shakespeare's *Comedy of Errors* whose sole goal in life seemed to be "how can we make this experience more irksome for you?"

We stepped inside the building and started the clock ticking at 10:05 a.m. We inquired of the clerk at the entrance as to the procedure to send a parcel to America. "Simple," she says. "Just head down the hallway on your right to the *Aduana*, the customs agent. The cage is marked with a big brass nameplate. You won't miss it." She was correct, we didn't; it was the cage with the longest line-up. We waited in line, encouraged that it was at least moving. The speed was glacial, but moving. Finally, it was our turn. We explained what we wanted to do and he told us we'd have to open the box so he could actually see and count each of the items we described. Everything met with his approval, and as we repacked it he weighed it, recorded the date and weight on an official slip with his rubber stamp, added his signature, and tucked one copy into a drawer.

"You need to take this signed form and the box to the packers just over there," he clarified. We wandered over to the packers and into another line. They accepted the official slip and the package, and with the *Aduana*'s nod we were allowed to re-wrap the package. When it was finished it had to be overwrapped in a special cloth— *funda de tela*. We handed the package back to the packers so the cloth could be sewn and then snuggly secured with a heavy cord. A worker appeared with a stick of wax and sealed all the knots. Then we were off to another section to fill out a declaration form in triplicate.

"Oops," she ripped up our form. "Please fill it out again." We used an Argentine address—our hotel—as our home address. "Foreigners are not allowed to use Argentine addresses as their home address," the clerk softly scolded. Another assistant painstakingly copied the information on the declaration form into a ledger and then onto a second triplicate form, asked to see our passports as proof of our identities, and finally weighed the package again. Now with validated, stamped, and signed forms and a properly-wrapped package in hand, we were off to see the postal clerk, the one with the postage stamps. The postage line was lengthy and I asked Mary to hold our place in the queue while I dashed to the men's room. As I finished my business I realized I hadn't brought any *papel higienico* to this dance and there wasn't a sheet of toilet paper—or any other scrap of paper—in sight. It was a rookie mistake and I had to sacrifice a crisp, new, Argentine fifty-peso note for my blunder. I speculated what the secret police would have thought of that heretical action. Back at the line Mary was approaching the cage. Our officious clerk smiled, took our package, looked at the forms, and thumbed through his drawer for just the right number and value of stamps, some of which he added to the forms and the remainder on the package. Then with great aplomb he rubber-stamped both sets of postage with sequential numbers and signed each one. After showing the clerk our passport to verify our names matched that on the return address, we signed yet another form allowing the post office to abandon delivery if the package went unclaimed back home. For that entire two and a half hour process we paid thirty-two pesos, eighteen pesos fewer than my erstwhile sheet of toilet paper. Our package was on its way.

Thursday: Cordoba to Salta

This morning I sat alone in exile, scrunched across the seat with my head braced against the dirt-stained window of an old second-class railway car, absentmindedly listening to the clicking of the wheels on the track and idly watching monotonous fields of sugarcane slip by.

The journey started innocently enough. Last night Ray, Mary, and I purchased economy-class tickets for an overnight train originally christened the *Cinta de Plata*—the *Silver Ribbon*, that ran northward along the high tablelands bordering the eastern edges of the sierras to the city of Salta, our next destination. We found our facing bench seats in a big, decades-old, silver- and blue-colored passenger carriage. The seats were cozy enough, just not terribly spacious. The train wasn't full and Ray sprawled out across his empty seat while Mary and I fidgeted around in ours, trying to get comfortable. I playfully splashed a few drops of water on her from our canteen as she tried to find some resting position against the window frame. Apparently she didn't find it as amusing as I did and lashed out, banishing me from our seat and ordering me to find my own somewhere else. She complained she wanted to be more comfortable. While she and Ray settled in I relocated to an open seat up at the front of the car, and amongst strangers settled in for the night. Alone I flirted with mental scenarios of Mary's behavior, producing fanciful, exotic schemes and conspiracies that toyed with my insecure psyche. My mind filtered through the uncertainties of Mary's sudden departure last year in Mexico and our two-month separation. Over the past several weeks I've watched her behavior grow more unpredictable more irritable and her demands sometimes more trying. I wondered if the cause was my behavior or her way of expressing some lapse in our relationship or simply the pressures of our extended travels. It was confusing.

In the morning, amidst all those conflicting, thoughts, and emotions, I wandered back to rejoin Mary and Ray. Under a negotiated truce we all traipsed back to the dining car for breakfast, where Mary and I mostly drank coffee in measured silence and ate breakfast rolls while staring absently at everything but each other. Ray looked like a deer caught in the headlights of a marital squabble. He encouraged, conversed, gestured, and joked, all to no avail. Mary was stubbornly obstinate. I was stubbornly adamant. Neither of us was going to bend one iota. Finally, Mar demanded I buzz off for a while; the atmosphere was just too toxic. That did it. I made some stupid—probably hurtful—retort that after all these years I can't even remember, and I stomped out of the dining car, angry at Mary and jealous of her friendship with Ray. I just couldn't let go of that sense of anger and was feeding it with doubts and imagination. In reality, Ray had nothing to do with it. Sure, our nomadic traveling companion was tall and handsome, well spoken with a smooth, engaging English accent, but he had never shown anything but friendship and real concern towards both of us. Jealousy is such an ugly state of mind. It poisons relationships and friendships alike. I was in a toxic place, acting out and saying things that might never be taken back. So, two cars back from Mary and Ray, I spent the entire day stewing in hormonal juices of pretty much my own creation.

The day was hot, the air heavy and humid from last night's rain, the trip only made bearable by frequent stops at small pueblos with the inevitable hoard of vendors and the comings and goings of passengers. To make matters worse our train had electrical problems with the emergency braking system, occasional shorts causing abrupt stops and the inevitable delays while the engineers tried to find the cause. Between reading and journaling all day I brooded away, often perplexed by a high sense of anxiety as I questioned the emotional distance from Mary in which I found myself. There were so many things I loved about her—the way she reached for my hand, her joy at new discoveries, her sense of independence and determination, her moments of unexpected laughter, and of course her beauty—she was a dazzler with an engaging smile and a remarkable figure. Over the course of my eviction I'd examined and wrung out enough insecurity from this old, emotional washcloth. As the afternoon wore on and we waited along a siding outside of Metán, I knew it was time to own up, return to Mary and Ray, and face headlong all the inevitable self-inflicted consequences.

I kind of tiptoed back to our seat, not knowing what to expect or what I should say other than I'm sorry. I needn't have worried.

Mary must have gone through the same agonizing mental arguments and so instead of words, there were hugs, smiles, and tears. I think Ray felt so relieved to be freed from the stilted atmosphere of the past twenty-some-odd hours that he invited us to join him in the dining car for beers. Mary and I joined him, walking hand-in-hand as best we could with the swaying motion of the train. It was such a comfort to find release from that terrible frame of mind I had found myself in all day.

Friday: Salta

Karma has a way of evening things out. Yesterday's boorish, juvenile behavior on board our train caught up with me in spades. As Mary scrubbed clothes in the washbasin in the hotel courtyard, I did a little detective work on a problem that surfaced last evening—a peculiar, nasty, and intense itching in the nether-regions. By "nether," I mean down there! Stripped naked in the bathroom I started exploring for the cause. It didn't take too long to figure it out. A sudden movement amongst the hair, and *voilà*—a little creature exposed itself to the light of day. I pulled out my trusty Swiss Army knife and opened the magnifying glass. A tiny pubic louse, not much bigger than a smudgy speck, sat gaping back at me. I was staring at what looked like a miniature version of a sea crab, with a small head, wiggling legs, and a big fat body. I called out to Mary and showed her my catch of the day. She held her laughter in check pretty well—then equally as well her annoyance. Finally, she offered some advice. The next time I headed for a brothel, don't. The brothel adventure could be the only reasonable explanation. Maybe it was the girls wriggling around in scanty underwear on our exposed and hairy legs. Ray and I both wore short pants that evening, but he never suggested he had any similar problems. Karma! With Mary in tow I headed for the *farmacia*, determined to explain my problem and get something to kill off the critters before they spread.

We picked our way over towards one of the main plazas with its statuary depicting the defeat of the invading Spanish loyalists back in 1813. There was a *farmacia* a block from the square. An older man, the owner and pharmacist, balding but dignified with his crisp, white half-coat and newly knotted tie, broke away from a conversation with someone in the stockroom and faced us across the counter. I tackled the issue head on.

"*Buenos dias. Necesito su ayudo, por favor. Tengo un caso de pequeños langostas*" (Good morning. I need your help, please. I have a case of . . .). In my defense, I really didn't know the words for crabs. We hadn't learned that particular expression back at our Spanish lessons in Mexico when we started our adventures fourteen months ago. We hadn't encountered the word "crab" in any of our travel conversations, we hadn't once ordered crabs from a menu, and we certainly hadn't consulted any medical dictionaries. So I blurted out what I thought was the closest fit: "*pequeños langostas.*" At the time it was the best I could do. "I've got a case of little lobsters," I pleaded. The pharmacist looked at me for a moment, then over to Mary, and then with a most amused incredulity slowly returned his gaze back at me. During those brief arcs his expression changed from one of astonishment to outright merriment. Amidst his laughter and snickering from the stockroom, he waved his hand at me.

"Just a minute, just a minute," he said as he unsuccessfully tried to regain his composure, "I've got just the thing in the back." During a rapid-fire conversation with his colleague in the back and amid more laughter, he assured us he was looking for just the right medication. A few moments later he returned smiling, holding a tube of ointment. He explained how it worked and how to apply it, and then he clapped me on the back and ushered us out the front door with one final humiliation of *"buena suerte con esas langostas"* (good luck with those lobsters, kid).

It was Good Friday today, although why the word "good" was associated with the crucifixion of Christ for the sins of the world was a little confusing. You'd think it would be a day of mourning and sorrow over sacrificial death. But here, throughout the square across from the old Cathedral, Christians gathered in the streets to see a dramatic reenactment of the last hours of Christ, shown entering Jerusalem, being judged by the Roman procurator, and wearing a crown of thorns while he dragged his heavy cross through the streets to the final crucifixion. The Passion reminded believers of how much Christ suffered for their sins. On Sunday the festivities would begin again with the resurrection.

That evening we dined *al fresco* amongst the revelers, wandering through lines of empanada vendors and sampling the little doughy pastries filled with beef, chicken, cheese, and our personal favorite, *charqui*, a kind of gaucho jerky filling. Under the gaslight glow we convinced ourselves that just one more would satiate our appetites for these little treats. We were caught up in the delightful aromas, the noise, the excitement of the crowd, and those tasty little endless mouthfuls. By the end of the evening we were on empanada overload, with our good sense stretched as much as our tummies.

Saturday: Humahuaca

The Saturday-morning local Central Northern Railway train to Humahuaca left before sunrise. The old creaky carriage had elegance about it. The seats were well-worn velour, the car spotlessly clean with faint odors of disinfectant mixed with creosote from the rail ties. Seated across from us an old gaucho dressed in baggy, black-and-white checked pants, a rough wool poncho, and a wide-brimmed hat sat stiffly upright and stared ahead, glancing neither left or right. A few groups of women wearing the traditional Andean full skirt and heavy blouses topped with felt hats chatted together. We had missed this part of the cultural mix. Lately we'd traveled in a kind of westernized, big-city bubble.

We headed east into a breaking dawn, along the Mojo Toro river valley and then northward through tobacco fields and farm-lands, stopping at the tiny pueblo stations of Guemes and Perico. At the clapboard railway station of Jujuy our train reentered the Andean highland culture that was so absent from lowland Chilean and Argentine society. When the carriages filled to seating capacity people crowded into the aisles, their colorful cloth bundles wedged into the overflowing overhead racks and their well-used cardboard boxes placed under the seats or on laps. In amongst the legs of those standing, children giggled and played, lurching with the train as we pulled out of the station and headed north into the Andean foothills once again. Along with our new passengers, we'd taken aboard a forgotten friend: the smell of layers of unwashed clothing and urine. *Campesinos*—the peasant farmers—worked. They labored hard and long hours up in the high altitude pla-teaus, sweating under bright sun and cloudless skies, where water was cold and electricity sparse. Up there, bathing wasn't a daily activity and clothing took on those pungent country odors. Now, here we were all stacked together as the smells concentrated in our carriage for the next few hours. There was no blame, no cursory looks. It was just a fact of life here in the Andean outback.

The track pushed northward through the *Quebrada of Humahuaca*, the spectacular narrow rift valley of the Rio Grande, a traditional north–south trade route used by muleteers and caravans for thousands of years. Scattered along the valley were the remnants of settlements and farming communities and towns that had remained over the centuries. The valley villages of Yala, Volcan, Tumbaya Ticara, and even our destination of Humahuaca were all once part of vital trade and commerce links from the high Andean mountains through these hardscrabble valleys to the southern temperate plains. As we gained altitude, the valley narrowed and the west wall of the rugged mountains burst into spectacular hues and alternating horizontal lines of earthy reds and ochres that blended with scrub and tall saguaro cacti.

Each stop at outlying villages brought out the vendors scurrying after our train, their baskets swinging wildly as they cried "*compra mi, compra mi*" while holding aloft oranges, apples, grapes, empanadas, and even full home-cooked meals. We were traveling on a mobile buffet cart.

By the time we arrived at Humahuaca station the train was overflowing. Mary, seated on the inside seat, managed to grab our backpacks off the racks, handed mine to me, and then pushed her way through the crowd of embarking and disembarking passengers and squeezed off the train. I couldn't move. The aisles were completely blocked with new passengers and luggage. I did the only sensible thing. Through the open window I eased my pack outside to Mary and then climbed out myself and dropped onto the platform. The conductor smiled and shrugged his shoulders as if to say, "good job, kid." Back in the carriage people were scrambling for my seat. A cagey old lady outmaneuvered everyone, settled into my vacated seat, and with a big toothless grin, bade me goodbye.

Humahuaca was a small settlement of cobblestone streets lined with old colonial streetlamps, whitewashed adobe homes, and populated by a people who clung to ancient traditions. We walked over from the small train station, avoiding packs of scavenging dogs to our Hotel Humahuaca, one of the more basic hotels in which we had the pleasure to squat. Later that night we ran afoul of our landlady when she caught us swapping out the feeble twenty-five watt bulb in our room with a larger wattage one in the hallway. From the fuss she made, you'd think we were trying to steal the silverware. We only wanted to see more than vague outlines in our room when we switched on the ceiling light.

After dinner in the main square near the church, we climbed a small rise west of the plaza to the Monument of the Independence and the remnants of an old Jesuit church. Below us, past the town and across the darkening Rio Grande Valley, the sun was slipping behind the distant cordilleras of the Andes Oriental. There are moments to savor life. Surrounded by tall cacti, we sat there on the upper steps, leaning shoulder-to-shoulder and looking across the valley.

Sunday, March 26, 1978: La Quiaca and Villazon, Bolivia

In the light of morning, we understood our proprietor's reluctance to exchange light bulbs last night. Long cracks in the plaster wall exposed the crumbly, raw adobe foundation. An old tremor had shaken the town and the hotel management, rather than looking for structural damage, had simply plastered over the crack. As the plaster dried it contracted and flaked away from the brick, re-exposing the damage. The low wattage bulb solved two problems: it reduced the hotel's electric bill and hid the evidence.

Our Pan Americano bus up to the Argentine border town of La Quiaca was a cattle car. Well, maybe that's being a little unfair to cattle cars. We had been on crowded buses before, riding up top with the luggage, squeezed three to a seat, or sitting on bare boards laid across the aisles down the entire length of the bus, but this line was taking the old college prank of "how many people can you stuff in a Volkswagen" to unforgiving levels. There was absolutely no room. Every seat was full, people sat on other's laps, the overhead racks were solid, bundles were wedged under seats, and even then twenty-five of us stood belly-to-belly and back-to-back the entire length of the bus. It was easy to spot the gringos; we stood head and shoulder above our *campesino* counterparts.

We'd learned by experience that in rural Latin America things worked just well enough to give you hope, but never quite well enough to give you faith. Sure enough, a half hour out of town at a narrow rusty iron bridge over the shallow Rio Grande the bus engine coughed a few times, backfired in protest, and then went silent as we coasted to a stop. The driver and his *cobrador* stood on the front bumper, peered into the engine compartment, animatedly discussed the problem, and then gave up. They flagged down an oncoming truck and the sent word back to Humahuaca: gummed injectors. While we waited, most of us piled outside and lounged on the railings of the bridge or simply squatted at the side of the road. The *Quebrada* valley was a beautiful place to be stranded. Across the shallow riverbed, saguaro cacti wound up through fluvial rock to the rich hues of sedimentary strata, the red ochres, soft umbers, and ethereal greens all twisted by primeval tectonic upheavals into visual fantasies.

The sound of an approaching empty replacement bus brought us back to the reality of travel. There was a madhouse rush to exchange buses. The locals knew the system well enough to throw their baggage onto empty seats through the open windows and then scramble on to claim the seats inside. The foolhardy few who formed a queue found themselves standing in the aisles once again. Mary and I were the last ones on board and stood in the door well for the next hour. It wasn't a bad place to stand if you didn't mind the inconvenience of passengers pushing by you at every stop and were willing to ignore the driver's tiresome pleas of "*mas atrás*" (move back). We found if we stooped low enough we could watch the passing landscape and the amazing colors of the *Quebrada*.

Land border crossings were always something of a crapshoot. Over the past year of traveling in Central and South America we'd been searched, interrogated, had items confiscated and burnt before our eyes, paid bribes, had our vehicles sprayed with insecticide, and had been welcomed with gracious smiles and best wishes. Just two months before, Mary and I, along with our new-found friend Ray Loud, had been denied entry into Paraguay by a small-minded customs officer who, after carefully looking us over and with a lot of huffing and puffing, told us Paraguay didn't allow entrance to foreigners with beards, backpacks, or short pants. He initiated new regulations right on the spot. According to his Paraguayan ethical standards, we'd committed the perfect triple crown of traveling decadence. We'd just walked across the bridge over the Rio Paraná that linked Foz do Iguazu in Brazil to Puerto Stroessner in Paraguay, so we probably did look a tad scruffy, but all our documents were valid and we were polite. We just ran into a cantankerous official validating his absolute control of the border. We pleaded and cajoled to no effect. Then Ray came up with a compromise.

"Let us," he said pointing at the businesses just a block from the customs shed, "go into Puerto Stroessner and we'll buy long pants, get suitcases, and I'll get a barber to shave my beard. Then we'll come back and get our documents stamped. We can't leave town without proper credentials, anyway." Incredulous as it sounds, the customs guy agreed and we all took off into town. Instead of finding a department store and a barber, we headed for the nearest bar and drank beer until we thought the official's shift was up. All three of us snuck back along the bridge shielded by truck traffic and confidently re-entered customs sporting shorts, backpacks, and beards. The shift had changed and a new rotation of officials welcomed us to Paraguay, stamped our passports, and sent us on our way. You just never knew what awaited you at border crossings.

La Quiaca and Villazon were twin outpost towns separated by an old stone bridge over the rivulet Rio de la Quiaca. You could spit across it without much effort.

Mar and I waited on the platform for the evening bus that would take us through Bolivian immigration and customs at the border to our destination of Potosi, a mining town high up in the mountains. Like most buses that crossed borders, ours was a smuggler's special. The annual wages earned by *campesinos* were so modest that even the centavos saved by buying household goods and clothing in Peru and smuggling them into Bolivia was worth the risk of confiscation. There was a certain element of risk for the locals bringing basic goods into Bolivia. It was less troublesome for the foreigners who were simply given more leeway. At the platform we were besieged by local women to help them get their contraband across the border. Mary's pack was stuffed with sweaters, undergarments, and detergents while mine now contained blankets, bars of hand soap, and three pairs of tiny running shoes. We declined a request to hide six bottles of champagne and so each was surreptitiously tucked away, along with a leather jacket, under the driver's seat. Nearly everyone on the bus had new shoes, wore multiple layers of new sweaters, sat on new blankets, and scuffed up the boxes of new purchases by jamming them under the seats or in the overhead racks.

At the Villazon customs shed we all traipsed off the bus, belongings in hand, and faced the first of several customs checks along the route. At each checkpoint belongings were confiscated, and the unlucky ones re-boarded a little lighter. But the women who gave us their goods planned well. At Villazon officials were amazed at the girth of Mary's new underwear but did nothing. Officials might have bought my story about the need for three extra blankets, but shook their heads at the need for twelve bars of soap and were utterly unconvinced by my purchases of three different sized running shoes, none of which fit me. They just shook their heads and let me pass with some remark about me being the most soap-conscious gringo they'd ever met. At each of the remaining checks along route, officials focused entirely on the locals and us gringos weren't even asked for identification. We had newfound celebrity status on board and by proclamation were proudly given the nickname of *Los Contrabandistas*.

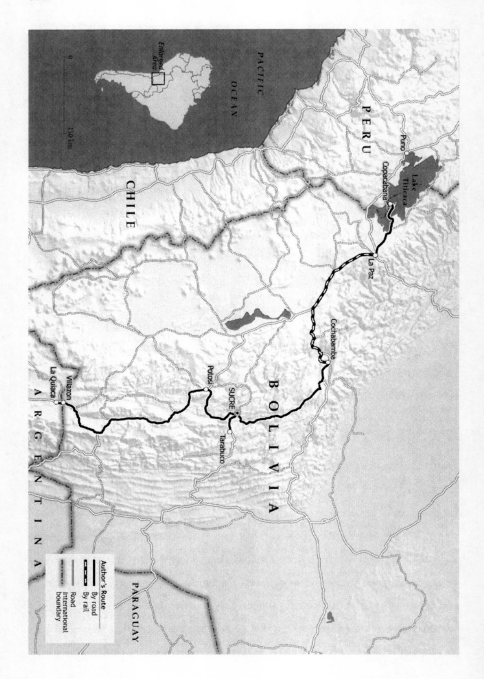

BOLIVIA

Monday, March 27, 1978: Villazon to Potosi, Bolivia

Villazon was an unattractive border trading town of dung-col-
ored adobe buildings with every business somehow connected
with the flow of illicit goods. Our bus of *contrabandistas* mostly
made it through each of the several government checkpoints out
along the highway. Toward nightfall customs men still boarded
and searched, peering with flashlights under the seats and into
the overhead racks, questioning the owners and, in some cases,
confiscating newly smuggled possessions amid loud protests. We
were on the Altiplano now, twelve thousand feet above sea level,
on that vast rolling plateau where the Andes were at their widest.
It stretched across the borders of four countries: Bolivia, Peru,
Argentina, and Chile. Even here, the distant mountains were
never really absent from the landscape, and occasionally spidery
spurs of rock stretched over the plains towards us. We motored
along the gravel highway, stopping at small towns and outposts,
discharging passengers and gathering more on our journey
northward. The cold, sunlit day had turned chillier as we pushed
along over rolling hills. The bus lights splashed along the gravel
ahead while we caught glimpses of the blurry silhouettes of cacti
and scrub passing by our window. Just beyond the town of Kucho
Ingenio, where the granite walls of the sixteen-thousand-foot

P'ukru Cordillera pressed down to the edges of town, we turned into the Andes and began to climb.

We were high up into the mountains before the driver found the contraband champagne. Back in La Quiaca, one of the passengers had stuffed six smuggled bottles under his seat thinking it hidden from the prying eyes of customs men. What she hadn't counted on was a thirsty chauffeur. We first noticed his champagne indulgences during a pee break on the narrow roadbed high over a deep gully. Under the illumination of the four-way flashers he tipped up the bottle, wiped his mouth with the back of his hand, and thinking no one had seen him, surreptitiously lowered the bottle back down beside his seat. The farther along we went, the drunker he became. The empty bottle flew out the window and he reached under his seat for another. Fortunately, the lady who secreted them there retrieved the remaining five. The driver who was feeling the effects of an entire bottle of bubbly began to talk aloud to himself, arguing and gesturing at some invisible adversary and weaving back and forth across the narrow road. He was navigating hairpin turns above high ravines that dropped off into the inky darkness, ignoring the pleas of fellow passengers to stop. The lady in the seat behind nudged me.

"*Vaya, vaya*," she grimaced, gesturing at the driver, "*toma el relevo de conductor. El es demasiado borracho!*" (Go, go, take over, the driver's too drunk). I appreciated her confidence in me, although her plea was probably more out of sheer desperation than any assurance that I could do better. I figured an experienced driver on a champagne bender still had better odds of staying on the road than some gringo ignorant of the machinations of a twelve-gear shift, and one totally unprepared for the road conditions ahead. Besides, I didn't want the blame for another slew of white crosses on the shoulder of some desolate mountain roadway, where future locals passing by would knowingly shake their heads and smirk at the story of some crazy gringo who, in the middle of the night, wrestled control from a veteran driver and sent the bus careening disastrously down into the ravine. Over the next hour or so we all sat alert, trying to keep the driver focused on the task at hand: keeping us alive. At five-thirty in the morning he pulled into some little outpost town not much bigger than the length of the bus. Passengers fanned out looking for coffee, which they miraculously found and force-fed it to the driver. Two-dozen passengers and I relieved ourselves, hidden behind whatever cover we could secure. I found myself whizzing next to a squatting *campesina* woman who gave me a toothy smile as I shook it off and zipped up my pants. Oh god—how the mighty had fallen. We were definitely back in the Andean culture again.

The sun was rising behind the shadowy eastern slopes of the Kimsa Waylla mountains, and down the valley, past the tin and silver mines of the Cerro Rico hills, Potosi spread out below us. Truckloads of miners, their faces wrapped in scarves to brace against the biting morning air, huddled together in open-bed trucks that lumbered up past us on their way to work.

Tuesday to Wednesday: Potosi

Local legend credited the discovery of silver in the Cerro Rico hills to an Aymara herder searching for an errant llama. In the bitterly cold Andean air he combed the foothills, pursuing his charge until finally exhausted he sheltered and started a fire for warmth. As the flames grew and the ground heated, a shiny liquid oozed past the shepherd's feet. The wealth and agony of Cerro Rico had begun.

Wealth and indigenous peoples didn't mix well in Spanish colonial times. It didn't take long for the discovery of the largest silver deposits of the known world to reach the Spanish. It was a godsend to the crown and a disaster for the entire Andean highlands. The wealth of the silver was unprecedented. Spanish galleons carried almost two billion ounces back to the court, which was enough, as one colonial viceroy said, to build a bridge of silver from the coast of Peru to the Royal Mint in Seville. But the discovery came with a terrible price for the thousands of Aymara Quechua Indians pressed into service. Deep in the mines the work was dangerous. So many died of accidents and lung disease that the Spanish imported slaves from Africa. To increase production they were forced into the mines on shifts lasting for months at a time, working, eating, and sleeping in the steamy darkness, never seeing the light of day. The *mitayos*, as they were called, didn't last long. Within the span of the two centuries over a million workers died from cave-ins and the appalling conditions in the mines, the smelters, and the mercury processing plants.

Like most silver booms, Cerro Rico's glory was not to last. Output declined in the mid-nineteenth century, and a drop in silver prices dealt a blow from which the area never fully recovered. Now in the late seventies, a worldwide demand for tin, zinc, and lead has resuscitated the mines of Cerro Rico, but the miners still work in conditions shamefully not far removed from colonial times.

MARY AND GEORGE AT THE CERRO RICO MINE IN THE HILLS ABOVE POTOSI

The Pailaviri Mine sat halfway up Cerro Rico, the bright green-and-blue control houses overlooking the city of Potosi. Below us the cathedral spires stood tall amid the rusty red of the tiled roofs that rolled among the hills. There were eighteen of us signed up on the company's log sheet for the mine tour. Later our guide informed us it wasn't only a log sheet; we had also signed a disclaimer for any mishaps or accidental death. Now, as we prepared to enter the mine we were dressed in black high wellingtons and rubber coats. We wore hard hats with miner's headlights powered by clunky battery packs clipped onto our web belts. We looked like a group of little munchkins as we entered the mine and headed over to the elevators, following the narrow track beside the metal railcars. The tour took us down five stories and into the steamy conditions where around 16,000 miners toiled much like their ancestors did, using picks, hammers, shovels, and brute strength. Then our guide asked us to turn off our headlamps and, in the utter darkness, he began to speak, interrupted by the occasional muffled thump of dynamite deep below us. He was once a miner, he told us, as was his dad before. He learned English so he could become a guide to earn a little more money, but perhaps more importantly, it got him out of working the mines. He had watched Cerro Rico sap his father's spirit and energy, watched as liquor became his father's crutch for coping, and watched him slowly die. His mother was a widow of the mines.

"Most of the ore is loaded on the small railcars, the iron ones we saw at the surface," he said, "but men and boys—the sons of the miners—stripped to their underwear and sweating it out for twenty-eight pesos a day, still haul sacks of ore up on their backs." The paradox was that it was the miners themselves who were in charge. They had wrestled control of the mines from private corporations and formed cooperatives owned and run by the local Aymara Indians. It was just that the mine managers sucked the wealth out more efficiently than the mineworkers.

We continued down another level and then walked along a long, lateral spur that took us deeper towards the center of Cerro Rico. As we worked our way along the narrow tunnel everyone felt it—the panic that crept up the spine, that claustrophobic sensation that once it grips you, it just won't let go. Of course we all smiled bravely, but after only an hour in the mines we all yearned for that light at the end of the tunnel, the one that led to sunshine and fresh-smelling air.

Potosi was a working man's town. Born of the silver boom, once the pearl in the Spanish crown and then left in ruins by the wars of independence, Potosi, the city that had paved its streets with silver, was now one of the poorest departments of Bolivia. Economically bereft, it was a city that really tried hard to keep its cultural relevance intact with the graceful colonial architecture, the balconies overhanging the narrow streets and its many churches, cathedrals, and *La Moneda*—the mint established two hundred years ago when silver was king.

Over the next day or so we wandered lazily through town, poking into shops, visiting churches and museums, enjoying the local street food, and just people-watching. Hats, especially those of the women, seemed to mark every social status and region. Here in Potosi the Aymara women wore black or gray high-crowned bowler hats festooned with ribbons. In the strong, cold wind they layered long homespun skirts and sweaters and tucked their babies on their backs inside brightly-colored shawls. We were greeted with smiles and the lingering looks that strangers always got.

Thursday: Sucre

The bus climbed out of Potosi on the same dusty road that travelers had used for the last four hundred years. We watched the city slowly disappear as we wound our way up the gentle hills and then down along the endless Altiplano. Possibly the best way to take in this magnificent view was in the back of the open-bed *campesino* trucks that trundled along, stopping for every local that flagged them down. We had traveled the open-air option many times before, the wind in our faces, jolting and bouncing as we hung on to the wooden side railings, the smell of diesel fumes wrapping around us. We mused about it while we sat in the relative comfort of our bus. Along our route we crossed bridges over drying riverbeds, passed plateaus and fertile valleys of cultivated fields, and herds of highland sheep and goats foraging on the thorny scrublands amid clusters of yellow gorse that pressed up into the mountains. It was harvest time. *Campesina* women stooped in fields of barley and quinoa, swinging sickles and leaving bundles of dried stocks behind them as they worked. Men were breaking new soil, leaving streaks of dark furrows as they tilled the ground with wooden ploughs pulled by oxen. Along the dirt road a horse-mounted *campesino* drove a small herd of shaggy alpaca, their heads bobbing in unison, urging his charges forward with the occasional snap of a long leather strap. Storm clouds were gathering in the distance as he urged the alpaca on to shelter.

CAMPESINO DRIVING HIS HERD OF ALPACA TOWARDS SHELTER

We stopped for lunch at Millares, a simple mountain village that spread one house deep along the roadway. Like all pueblo buildings and homes along the route, unpainted, earth-toned exterior plaster was cracked and crumbling, revealing patches of crude adobe brick. It was a simple mountain town with simple mountain food, but with generous mountain hospitality. A bright red metal Potosi beer sign was affixed to the outside of our restaurant. It depicted a young Andean boy, maybe six or seven years of age, dressed in patched pants and wearing a colorful *chullo* toque, standing beside a creek with a graceful arc of pee falling neatly into the center of the slowly flowing water. *Nunca beba agua!*, it proclaimed. *Beba Siempre Cerveza Potosi.* (Never Drink the Water! Always Drink Potosi Beer). It was impossible to argue with such compelling marketing.

The route took us northward along the narrow vales of the Rio Pilcomayo and into Sucre, the isolated colonial capital of Bolivia flanked by low mountains. Sucre was a beautiful, regal town of whitewashed buildings crowned with red-tiled roofs and punctuated with elegant churches. It was the heart of Bolivia, the country's white city in the highland valley and the center of cultural pride.

That night under the light of gas lamps around the Plaza de Armas we joined in the traditional *paseo*, a leisurely evening stroll. The single men walked in one direction, girls and escorts in the contrary direction, everyone circling, chatting, and flirting, enjoying the cool evening air. In the milieu we met Sarah, a Canadian girl from north of Toronto who was traveling alone overland across South America. The three of us swapped travel stories as we wound our way around the square. The girls had endless opportunities to practice their Spanish in short one-phrase bursts as we circumnavigated the endless loop of curious young men eager to dally with the pretty *gringas*.

Friday to Sunday, April 2, 1978: Tarabuco

We were wedged in, packed like sardines on a rickety bus headed overland to Tarabuco, a little mountain town two and a half hours out of Sucre. Sarah had slipped into the last free seat mid-bus. Mary squeezed into the middle of a gaggle of voluminous old women who overflowed the back bench seat. Ray stood in the aisle ahead of me, hunched over in a vain attempt to catch glimpses of the passing countryside. And I was shoehorned in, unable to even wiggle my toes and with someone's knees jammed into my back, sitting on one of the makeshift wooden benches that stretched across the aisle from seat to seat. They added a lot more capacity to an already overcrowded bus. The three-hour bus ride took an eternity.

Tarabuco was the center of the Yampara culture. Once an integral part of the Amaya, the Yampara were annexed by the Inca and subjugated by the Spanish. We still heard conversations in the old Incan Quechua language spoken as we sauntered around the central plaza.

We climbed up above the village, past the pastoral fields and into the rock-strewn grazing lands. We stopped and talked to a young shepherd boy and his sister who tended a small flock of sheep. While the sheep grazed nearby, he squatted almost hidden under a well-worn striped wool poncho, boiling water for tea over an open fire. His sister concentrated, spinning yarn on a wooden drop spindle. Undaunted, they chatted away with us, maybe even welcoming human company. Below us in the valley, the village of Tarabuco lay framed between fields of potatoes, corn, and barley and the ridges of distant mountains. There was a certain contentment to sitting there, undisturbed save for birdsongs and the bleating sheep, simply staring off into an endless blue sky and letting the mind roam free.

Tarabuco suffered from dissociative identity disorder, a kind of a split personality. On weekdays it was a quiet little backwater village, mostly deserted, the dirt streets empty except for a few locals chitchatting in the square. Dust picked up by the wind and bits of tapestries swaying in open doorways were the only excitement. On Friday and Saturday, Ray and Sarah, Mary and I were the four foreign curiosities in town—*los extranjeros*, easy pickings for storefront gossip—while we bided our time waiting for the Sunday market.

On Sunday, Tarabuco was mobbed. Yampara families streamed down from the outlying hills to trade in food, agricultural products, animals, clothing, and crafts, arriving by bus, trucks, and even on foot. By the first early light the market square was crowded, overflowing out into the side streets and into the plaza. Over the past two days we had admired the colorful dress of the men and women, but today it was a vibrant tapestry. Most Yampara boys and men wore knee-length traditional *pallados*—heavy-fringed wool ponchos of rich, cochineal-red that were banded with horizontal stripes of muted reds, blacks, and soft greens captured between narrow bands of brilliant yellow. Older men wore the ceremonial *pallados* of the deepest ebony, cut with bars of ochre and red. The boys donned the typical woolen *chullo* hats with earflaps, while the men and some of the older matriarchs wore the *montera*—a conquistador helmet-like hat formed with felt and edged with untanned cowhide, embroidered with bright wool flowers and then stitched with silver threads and sequins. Everyone wore thick-soled *ojatas*— the traditional leather sandals of the region. On Sunday it was a town rich in tradition, a day to wear their Sunday best, catch up on local gossip, talk about the price of root crops, and complain about the weather. It was also the day to sell and barter and gather supplies for the coming week. So while we tourists watched a colorful tapestry of tradition, the locals focused on routine life up here in the Andes.

A YAMPARA MAN WITH TRADITIONAL PALLADO *poncho*
AND MONTERA HAT IN TARABUCO

The four amigos decided to forego the regular bus service back to Sucre. We'd each witnessed firsthand how uncomfortable that journey could be, shoehorned into a crowded bus. Instead we chose the *campesino* way, the *camion*—a one-ton, open-bed truck fitted with chest-high, wood-slatted sides. We climbed in over the tailgate and secured a spot right behind the truck cab. Behind us, the truck was filling up, first to capacity and then to overflowing. No matter—we were a good head taller than the rest, and even though we'd have to stand for the next four hours, we'd also be treated to an incredible *al fresco* landscape all the way back to Sucre.

The truck roared its way out of Tarabuco onto the higher plateau of pale, grassy mountains. First gear, second gear: the ear-splitting engine growled, reverberating off the brown adobe through the narrow streets. Gathering speed, sliding through third and fourth gears, we left the town, climbing up on the highland and leaving plumes of unburnt diesel choking out behind us. However, it was soon apparent that regardless of vehicle type, the customary maniacal driving standards still prevailed. We were thrown back and forth around sharp turns, our driver determined to pass every other vehicle on the road, braking at the last minute to miss oncoming traffic or wandering animals, and generally more interested in a conversation with his companion in the cab than concentration on the road.

This is what travel should be like: Yampara locals heading home from the market dressed in their Sunday gear, braced against the wooden tie slats or squatting on the truck bed, their bundles tucked around them. It was a little microcosm of the market, of real Andean life with laughter, chatter, babies crying, mothers coaxing, people gesturing at passing landmarks in a language we could never understand and us nodding back, gracious locals offering us bits of pastries and other treats, and us smiling in recognition of their kindness. It was a diaspora of Andean life shared under a bracing blue sky and a passing panorama. We arrived back in Sucre with sighs of relief and a few new bruises.

Monday: Sucre

Proud, genteel, and isolated, Sucre was a city of whitewashed buildings, full of elegant churches, mansions, and museums. It was a charming place for exploration.

Alojamiento La Plata, our modest little hotel at the corner of Ravelo and Junín, was only a block away from the heart of the city, the central plaza of 25 de Mayo, and everything was in walking distance from there.

The Recoleta, the old monastery complex, stood on the foothills of the Churuquella and overlooked the city. A tile-topped arcade with dozens of white-arched columns sat at the edge of the plaza, framing the red-tiled roofs of the dazzling white homes below that crossed the valley up into the outlying hills. We had walked up Calle Dalence, struggling a little over the last few blocks as the roadway wound up to the church and monastery. We rested on the edges of the stone plaza, finding a moment's solace under the shade of a single rosewood tree with its view of La Recoleta, the old twin-towered colonial church with its brilliant white façade gleaming in the morning sunlight. With a simple turn of our heads we had the perfect panoramic view of the Recoleta, the small Iglesia de Santa Ana, and the remains of the convent. All the vistas from up here were beautiful, but perhaps our best view of the city was from the rooftop walkway above the monastery courtyard gardens, on the undulating, russet-colored brick roofline behind the bell towers. The expanse of earthy tiles set against the bight white belfry, the city sprawling out below, and the overarching blue sky formed a perfect canvas of colonial colors. A narrow passageway along a side street full of small shops off the plaza led us back down into the city center as that tantalizing view stretched out before us.

We wandered back to Plaza 25 de Mayo, the city's focal point and a wonderful place to watch the world go by—which is what we did, plunking down on the park benches right after sampling foods from the nearby street vendors. We could find anything on the streets: slices of watermelon sold from the back of a bicycle, sticks of bread stuffed with meats and onions sold from a glass-framed wooden case perched on an old Coke box, stew-like pots of chorizo cooking over tiny portable gas stoves, and of course pastries galore, pastries everywhere.

One of Sucre's slogans is *"Sucre, donde nacio Bolivia"* (Sucre, where Bolivia was born). Across the street from the plaza was the old Jesuit chapel, the Casa de la Libertad, where it all began. In 1809, right outside its grand archway, virtually where we sat eating lunch, the first shots of the Spanish Wars of Independence were fired. Sixteen bloody years later, it was inside this same building that Bolivia's independence was declared—the Republic of Bolivar. We did the tourist thing and roamed inside in silence. Bolivia's framed Declaration of Independence mounted beside a bronze bust of Bolivar himself demanded respect.

We all truly relaxed that afternoon, wandering through cathedrals, poking in stores, stopping occasionally for beers, and talking about past adventures. I confess, it was one of those afternoons that if we were at home, I'd probably be slumped on the couch waiting for Monday Night Football and listening to the nasally voice of Howard Cosell with his *"storied rivals, locking horns— lo, these many years as they prepare to do battle once again on Monday Night Football on ABC."* Instead, we just strolled aimlessly through the city, admiring the endless expanse of whitewashed buildings, cobbled streets, and red-tiled roofs.

Tuesday: Sucre to Cochabamba

Sometimes traveling by bus can be frustrating. I think it had something to do with my feeble abilities at the complexities of the Spanish language, the local dialect, and the sometimes unfathomable Latino mentality. It was dusk and the four amigos had just comfortably settled into (this was a first here in Bolivia) our assigned seats when Mary got a premonition—we were about to lose a backpack. I clambered up the roof ladder to check for our four backpacks only to find a tarp lashed over the rack. I yelled down at the driver, "*¿Cuántas mochilas que pusiste aquí arriba?*" I inquired.

"*Tres, quizá cuatro,*" he replied. "Three, maybe four, but don't worry, if we lose one the bus line will pay you two hundred bolivars." Words got a little stronger and the discussion heated in both directions until we were almost standing toe-to-toe, shouting in each other's faces. My modest vocabulary limited my insults, but he had complete command of the language, and judging by the amused bystanders who now surrounded us, he was making his position perfectly clear. Mustering as much dignity as was left to me, I climbed back on board and plopped down into my seat beside Mary. I know in her heart she wanted to comfort me, but instead she turned away, covering her mouth in a hopeless attempt to stifle her giggles.

East of the Altiplano, the Andes gradually marched down towards the eastern lowlands in a series of rugged, north–south mountain ranges, scarred with long narrow valleys formed by rivers draining to the east. The first two hours was across a bone-jarring, bus shaking, twisting road that threaded its way through the rough valleys and across rolling hills. Twilight brought a soft amber glow with long, lingering shadows in the gullies that slowly muted the pastoral colors around us. Around La Palma we wound our way down three thousand feet into the central Cochabamba Valley with its rich alluvial soils that followed a wide riverbed northward. Central valleys like this one were the most fertile and habitable areas of the country. Even at night the temperature had changed somewhere between the cold of the Altiplano and the tropical heat of the lowlands. We spent the night snuggled together, half asleep, half awake, passing through little towns and farming communities vaguely aware of passengers departing or vendors boarding with their wares. Somewhere, maybe out of the town of Mizique, the canyon walls closed in and we wound back up into the Andes, struggling over high passes with ghostly mists covering dark mountain ridges, then down once again into the dawn with a view of Cochabamba on a valley floor ringed by tall mountains. The altitude was about the same as Sucre but it felt more tropical, warmer, and the humidity sat heavier. Even the air smelled different. After a grinding eleven-hour bus ride we had arrived in Cochabamba. The driver threw down our four backpacks, looked at me with a smile and a questioning nod, and spread his arms as if to say, "I told you so." All four had arrived safely, just as he'd promised. Here's to the good ship *Humiliation* and all those that sail aboard her.

Wednesday: Cochabamba

Ray and Sarah moved on at sunrise this morning. There was an interesting dynamic between the pair of them. Both assertive, strong-willed, and independent, they seemed at times like the unlikeliest of travel companions. We'd watch them bickering like an old married couple, completely at ease, directing verbal body blows at each other with the assurance that whatever outrage they perpetrated would be forgiven in time. Together they planned to transit along the well-traveled Gringo Trail to Cuzco and on to Machu Picchu.

Mary and I were alone once again. There was always a certain pleasure when our traveling companions departed and we were alone in each other's company again. The conversations turned more intimate, the long silent lapses between them seemed more natural and comfortable. It was still early morning as Mary and I found our way over to the *La Cancha*, perhaps the largest open-air market in Bolivia. We arrived to find the weavers just beginning to set up their stalls of alpaca and llama goods so we drifted about through the alleyways amid the crowded spectacle of vendors, peddlers, beggars, hawkers, and wandering traders. The market was a teeming maze of stalls and rows that flowed off into infinity. The makeshift stands were run by *Cholas* girls and mestizo women who sold their goods under bleached cotton roofs hung between small wooden poles. They stood out amid the mass of haggling humanity, sporting their white top hats, wearing the traditional layered cotton skirts and aprons, and with money purses dangling from their petticoats. In the central market, rows of great soup kitchens sold *sajra hora* (mid-morning meals) and *almuezos*, the lunchtime special of the day. Every conceivable item was cooking in oil, reeking of delicious odors. Dirt paths led in all directions amid a labyrinth of vegetable, fruit, and meat stalls, and the more eclectic rows of barbershops, cobblers, hardware stores, and animals.

The market was a spending affair—some were afflicted more than others. We went with an open mind but got caught up in it just the same. After watching our budget carefully for the past few weeks, it was fun to go a little berserk. As our Dutch friends from the Amazon said, "Why not go nuts for a while?" Why not indeed?

Thursday: Cochabamba

We were lying in bed when Mary turned to me and quietly confided, "I've missed my period—I'm three weeks overdue. I think I'm pregnant. I think we're going to have a baby."

Time stopped. It just stopped, and was replaced with excitement, nervousness, and joy, emotions galvanizing and colliding in every direction. "We're going to have a baby." Those words changed the world. There were so many questions. How was she feeling? All that nausea I thought was from altitude, all those emotional bursts from sometimes trivial events, her easy fatigue up here on the highlands—all came into a clearer perspective. She wanted to wait to tell me until she felt more definite, but looking back it must have been a lonely vigil, that waiting with uncertainty. We just held each other very close. At that moment I never felt so much in love.

Mary was pretty certain, but we were novices on this baby thing. For the moment it was like living in a state of partial eclipse. We needed the affirmation of a doctor. We needed to find care for Mary. Not here in Cochabamba, but in the capital of La Paz.

Surely, in a city with a population of over seven hundred thousand we'd find a modern clinic and an English-speaking doctor.

The day had been a lazy one, just talking and wandering aimlessly through the city. We found ourselves out behind the bus station, climbing along the hill of San Sebastian to the bronzed monument of *La Coronilla*—the Heroines of the Crown. In the War of Independence a group of women who, unlike their men, refused to negotiate as the Spanish general burned and looted their homes, armed and barricaded themselves atop the hill of San Sebastian in the place known then as *La Coronilla*. The Spanish regulars charged the hill, cutting the women down with volleys of fire and bayonets. They held the ground for three hours, shouting their cries of "our home is sacred" until the last one fell. Those daring women lost the battle, but they won the memories.

It was quiet here now beneath the bronze. We sat there; Mary snuggled under my poncho lost in thought, gazing at the dusky city down below while I jotted notes in my journal. For a moment it felt like we could be anywhere, and maybe we were—if only in our imaginations. She turned and smiled at me. I put down my journal, moved closer, and together we wondered about our future.

Friday: Cochabamba to La Paz

Ferrobuses were like a Rube Goldberg project that had simply gotten a little out of hand: a combination of a vivid imagination and Andean practicality mixed with a wisp of comedic inspiration. We'd seen them in the distance, crossing the Bolivian high country. Early mining companies had lain thousands of miles of rail bed, and the tracks were as varying in gauges and widths as the needs of the companies that had put them there. With no standard track width, a universal Bolivian rail system was impractical. It was only a matter of time that Andean ingenuity solved the problem. The result was the ferrobus. The most astonishing ones were simply old, decrepit buses with the axles and wheels removed and then melded with a railway bogie and axle boxes that fit the track gauge on which they operated. In essence, it was a bus that ran on old railway tracks. Every ferrobus was an individual expression of the owner and route it ran. We saw ancient Bluebird school busses with luggage roof racks and cow catchers welded to the front bumpers, as well as a 1956 Dodge bus painted yellow, the interior decorated with strings of woven ribbons and religious icons while "La Bamba" boomed from the tape player. The remodeling and creative absurdities of some of these contraptions were endless and at the same time a refreshing approbation to the spirit of the Andes.

Our silver and blue ferrobus, the *Empresa Nacional de Ferrocarriles-Bolivia*, sat newly washed in the station yard near the central La Concha market. It was still early, a cool 53 °F when we boarded, our *mochilas* (backpacks) safely stored under a tattered canvas tarpaulin in the rooftop luggage carrier. This was a new service to La Paz and the dual-car ferrobus was impressive. Made by Ferrostaal in Germany, each coach car was emblazoned with stylized art deco wings and the FS logo of its manufacturer embossed above the thick metal cowcatcher. We sat up front on the simple bench seats close to the driver, watching out the panoramic bank of windows as he maneuvered through morning traffic, out of the city, and then along the dusty scrub plains of rolling hills. Like every travel day up here, the scenery changed from flat pampa to riding on the edges of deep gullies, to feeling confined as mountain spurs sloped down to the edges of the track. Every once in a while the conductor would leap off, clear a rock from the track, and jump back on. As we neared little villages, dogs appeared out of nowhere and raced us barking to the station stops. Up on the high ridges we could look down over the drying riverbeds, across the patchwork fields and the small farm villages. Distant hills topped with jagged red rock outcrops perched like rooster combs on the dry and patchy landscape. It was easy to believe, as many of the locals did, in the power of the spirits that live in those distant mountains. As we rounded a curve before the tiny mountain pueblo of Tolapalca we frightened a herd of burros grazing on tussock grass growing alongside the track. Confused, they scampered ahead, darting back and forth across the tracks, caught between the sharp, rocky hillsides and our oncoming train. One by one they found shelter in little gaps of widened ground.

OUR SILVER AND BLUE FERROBUS AT TOLOPALCA STATION IN ROUTE TO LA PAZ

From Oruyo we headed north, past a vast shallow lake that sheltered thousands of large red Bolivian flamingos. The noise of our train set the flocks to flight, flapping and skimming over the cold waters. The water turned to sprawling flats and the endless mud slowly changed to grazing land for sheep and llamas and finally to pastoral farmlands of grain crops.

Few cities have such a spectacular setting as La Paz. The city, just below the rim of the Altiplano, nestled in a steep canyon bowl, sheltering it from the cold winds. We saw it for the first time as our ferrobus crawled over the upper crest of the narrow canyon, that central cluster of church spires in a city dwarfed by the distant icebound peak of Illimani, the highest mountain in the Cordillera Real. Reaching out toward us even the harshest slopes of the valley hills were covered by the ramshackle homes of the city's poor. In La Paz, social classes were divided by altitude. The farther down the canyon valley we descended, the more oxygen, more temperate air, and more wealth we found.

There was a deepening economic crisis in Bolivia, strained by strong desires for democratization and an end to military rule, coupled with a widening ideological and class polarization. President Banzer had promised elections, but elections have always had a curious trigger effect in Latin America. People had heard these promises before and they simply didn't believe in the process. Here, the promise of elections almost always ended in fraud, re-elections, or simply postponements. Those bitter disappointments were a powerful catalyst to violence and revolution. This year, the call for national elections sent Bolivia into turmoil again. Last December, here in La Paz, miner's wives staged a hunger strike demanding the removal of troops from the mines and an amnesty to political prisoners. The strike had escalated and now union and student protests were turning violent.

Amongst that backdrop of stunning vistas and civil unrest our ferrobus suddenly braked, the iron wheels grinding metal on metal and screeching in protest along the tracks, finding friction and stopping beside an old washout. Moments earlier two men had pried boulders loose from the steep rock wall, jarring them onto the tracks in an attempt to derail our train. Our alert driver spotted them and saved us from a death-plunge down into the ravine. The conductor gave chase, capturing one who, amid curses and threats, was shoved roughly into the second car. Turns out he was just a boy really, maybe in his late teens, but he screamed his contempt at the rail line employees and wore his attempt to derail our ferrobus as a badge of courage.

La Paz was exhausting. Every step we took was either uphill or downhill. There was no level ground. Mary was dog-tired by the time we reached *Residencial Rosario*, our little oasis in the center of town.

Saturday: La Paz

The most unlikely gems of South American cities were often secreted down the back streets and narrow alleyways. *El Mercado de las Brujas* (the Witches' Market) was located just a stone's throw from the Church of San Francisco, one of the catholic anchors of La Paz. We twisted our way through the maze of tiny shops and vendors intent on their herbal medicines, witchcraft, folk remedies, and fortune-telling. These were serious businesses here, sacred traditions passed down through the ages. The irony wasn't lost on us as we wandered, poking into shops. The Holy See, the ecclesiastical jurisdiction of Rome, had once mandated the forced conversion of the Aymara peoples and the total eradication of their religious practices, and yet here, generations later and virtually in the shadow of the Church of San Francisco, in a demonstration of the stubborn persistence of their religion, they sold the trinkets, talismans, and totems meant to appease their ancient gods of the earth and moon.

Mary frowned at the disturbing boxes of gray-skinned llama fetuses with their sallow eyes and slack-mouthed grimaces. There were rows and rows of tiny llama corpses in varying stages of development, meant to be burned as offerings to the gods to bless a home or to be buried in the yard to improve the health of a sickly relative. Dried starfish were burnt for better health, special beads brought riches, and a carved dark amulet foretold good fortune. Put a cigarette in a dried frog's mouth and your household peace was guaranteed. At the back of one shop I spotted black candles formed into the shapes of skulls and coffins, and one in particular caught my attention.

"What's this black penis candle for?" I asked.

The old woman smiled, shook the penis high in the air, and replied, "*La venganza de la amante de su esposa*" (revenge on your wife's lover). There were cures and talismans for everything. Some of them might come in pretty handy.

Over lunch we joked about burning a llama fetus in some secret midnight ritual, imagining it might be an easier way to a good life than actually finding jobs when we got back home.

In the afternoon we caught a bus that took us up through the sprawling slums of unpainted houses but with dirt streets full of life, over the crest of the canyon bowl and then down into the canyon of the Rio Choqueyapu and the Valley of the Moon. Centuries of wind and weather had carved a canvas of stalagmites, a maze of clay canyons, and sandstone pinnacles. We cut through narrow trails that looped and wove us through a bizarre lunar landscape.

For all of its colonial architecture and amazing vistas, La Paz felt like a city. Maybe it was the business towers and high-rise apartment blocks, or the constant traffic, or the indifference of the people we met on the street, but the city lacked that sense of engagement. We thought it was just us, but other travelers we talked to had similar experiences. There was something missing— something lost in its rush to modernity.

Sunday, April 7, 1978: La Paz

If ever Mary and I needed a deterrent to doing drugs in Bolivia it was strengthened with a tour of the *Carcel de San Pedro, Panóptico,* the infamous prison just a short ten-minute walk from our hotel on Avenida Illampu. Our guidebook and fellow travelers suggested the eye-opening visit would be a glimpse of how penal systems worked in third world countries. *San Pedro* was built for society's worst—its murderers, rapists, and kidnappers. Just a few years ago Nixon had declared a war on drugs, characterizing drug abuse as America's *public enemy number one.*

"In order to defeat this enemy," he declared, "it is necessary to wage an all-out offensive." Nixon's strategy was to provide money and support military efforts to stop the drugs at their source. It sounded good. Money flowed southward to Mexico, Latin America, and into countries like Bolivia. Cocaine kitchens were routed out, supply chains disrupted, and thousands of suppliers and casual users were rounded up by the military and secret police and imprisoned. It did little to stem the flow of narcotics northward, but one of its unintended consequences was the hundreds of *Norte Americano* casual drug users caught up in the Bolivian justice system and added to the incarceration lists in the notorious prisons of Latin America.

Inside the fortified gateway arch of the prison's massive forty-foot walls, staff jotted down our passport information and inked our arms with indelible numbers so we could be easily identified and released at the end of our day. Noting I was Canadian they turned us over to Jacques, a French-Canadian prisoner from Montreal. Jacques earned money working at a prison juice stand but on Sunday he gave prison tours. He asked for money up front. So did the prison guard, who before we left the administration area, suggestively rubbed his thumb over his fingers, a universal gesture for "pay up." In *Carcel de San Pedro*, everybody got a little something from the visitors.

Once out in the prison yard there were no guards. The Green Penguins, as the prisoners called them, rarely ventured outside the secure office area. Even if they did, the locks on the cell doors were on the inside, not the outside. The inmate held the keys. If a guard wanted to see a prisoner, in one of the many amazing ironies of this prison, he had to knock on the prisoner's door and wait for the inmate to let *him* in. In the San Pedro prison the inmates ran the asylum. It was a society within itself, and like a normal society, it seemed the more money prisoners had the better off they were. Those with the financial resources, like jailed politicians and drug lords, lived in luxury cells with private bathrooms, kitchens, and even cable TV. The poorest lived in dirty, wretched hovels in filth and squalor, often doubled- or tripled-up in tiny, claustrophobic, windowless rooms. Crime may not always be punished, but poverty was.

Jacques took us through the eight living sections inside the prison walls. Each was a little self-contained community with two-story housing blocks surrounding a dirt quadrangle. Restaurants, bars, little market tiendas, medical clinics, and barbershops, all run by prisoners, were tucked behind open doorways or in darkened corners. In short, there was everything an inmate needed.

"At night," Jacques told us, "the rich neighborhoods seal off their section of the prison." The well-heeled incarcerated wanted separation and protection from the violence that nighttime brought in the poorer prison neighborhoods.

"I'm innocent, you know," Jacques told us. "I've been here for six months without even an acknowledgement of a trial, and the British embassy staff refuses to help me. Canadians are British subjects. It was printed right in my passport. But I'm a French Canadian and they want nothing to do with me. I only survive because I've found work in the *jugo* stand over there and take people like you on tours. I'll never get out." He visibly sagged as he told us he was resigned to be here for the next five years, maybe longer—if he did nothing.

He introduced us to his friend Louis, a melancholic thirty-one-year-old American who lived in the same section as Jacques. Their stories were similar; both pleaded innocence. Louis said he had been set up, his guilt nothing more than one of association. His hotel roommate and his roommate's Bolivian friends bought drugs from an undercover policeman—nothing much, a small amount of cocaine and a couple of pieces of hashish. But the two shared a hotel room, shared a nationality, and that was enough for the police and America's overzealous La Paz-based US Drug Enforcement Agency operative to arrest Louis. Police and the American DEA agent interrogated him. He was slapped, threatened, and forced to sign a confession in Spanish that he wasn't allowed to read, one that implicated him with people of whom he had no knowledge. That was almost two years ago.

Those in the US consulate that reached out to him, those that occasionally brought him books, newspapers, food, and clothing, had been threatened by the DEA, they told him, with recall or worse. Virtually all contact with the consulate had ceased. He was now alone.

Louis's stories of prison existence were chilling. "A prisoner," he said, "can buy a room or even build one if there's money." Money lubricated every facet of prison life. It bought food instead of gruel, bedding instead of cardboard, showers, medicine, books, and favors from the corrupt officials, and even drugs. "The prison food is called *rancho*," he spat. "It's cooked in a kitchen that resembles a dungeon, the walls and ceiling blackened with years of soot and grease." Food was cooked in oil drums over huge gas flames. Vegetables, the base for the stew, were dumped over the tables, and if they fell onto the pissed-soaked floors, no matter; it's only *rancho*. The vegetables were never washed and the cooks themselves washed rarely. There was a constant fear of disease like hepatitis, syphilis, and TB. The best alternative, he told us, was to pay up to two hundred US dollars to the prison mayor each month to eat in one of the five private restaurants run by his fellow inmates. The health standards were about the same, but the menu wasn't restricted to only gruel.

Jacques and Louis lived in Palmar, a kind of middle-class section of the prison. They were amongst the inmates who got money from the outside, from families or those that had jobs in the prison system and could pay for their privileges. The cocaine kitchens were in the worst of the prison neighborhoods, Guanay and Cancha, places where you didn't go at night. Stabbings were common as addled addicts fought over the dregs of the prison drug trade. Some of the best drugs in Bolivia came from kitchens of San Pedro. Louis told us five dollars would buy a gram of cocaine that was sniffed or shot up by inmates and even sometimes visitors like us. Plus, he said, there's grass, downers, uppers, liquor, peyote, and cigarettes. The prison officials knew of the cocaine kitchens—in fact, they encouraged them, as long as they got their cut of the profits.

Looking around he told us that only a small percentage of all the fifteen hundred prisoners there, including foreigners like him, had ever been found guilty of anything, let alone sentenced. Many hadn't even been formally arraigned. Using drugs in here was often an alternative to slowly going mad in this judicial twilight zone.

Louis' story touched us. We treated them both to a meal from a little *comedor* tucked into the corner of the green-walled prison housing block and, as we parted, I slipped Louis a little spending money. Maybe it would make his life easier—at least for a day.

We followed Jacques up to his tiny second-story room that he shared with a Bolivian prisoner. He confided to us then that he and his cellmate were going to try to escape. They were waiting for a cloudy, moonless night, when they would climb onto the railing, shinny up the corrugated roof, rope over the wall, and scamper off into the darkness.

"Don't tell anyone," he begged. There was a metal cage in the middle of the prison quadrangle we'd spotted early. It was where they put inmates who were caught trying to escape, Jacques told us. He'd seen fellow prisoners shivering unprotected from the freezing night air. His roommate lifted his shirt, making sure we saw the knife tucked in his waistband. It was his way of reinforcing Jacques' request for silence.

Monday: La Paz

We found a nearby medical clinic where a doctor spoke English. Well, perhaps "spoke" is a little too generous; "conversant" is probably a better term. We wanted some definitive medical verification that Mary really was pregnant. In the doctor's cluttered office Mary ticked off her symptoms; she was always tired and short of breath, her bladder had shrunk to the size of a thimble, she often found herself on an emotional roller coaster, and, most importantly, she had missed her period, now three weeks overdue. Taken separately, every one of those signs could be explained. We were traveling in the Andean mountains at elevations approaching fourteen thousand feet. Everyone felt out of breath, tired, and irritated. Any physical effort up here on the Altiplano was an exhausting chore. Here in La Paz no matter where we walked we were either struggling uphill or scrambling downhill. Who knew about the bladder? Each of us had worked through bouts of diarrhea and nausea. Sanitation and food preparation left a lot to be desired. So no single symptom could be conclusive. But the good doctor had seen these symptoms so many times before. In a display of professional courtesy she took Mary's blood pressure and used a tongue depressor to look down her throat.

"You're pregnant," she declared, "maybe six or seven weeks pregnant." We weren't sure of the medical procedures used for testing pregnancy, but we were pretty certain that a tongue depressor wasn't necessarily on the razor's edge of new technologies.

The doctor's affirmation aside, there was Mary's intuitive certainty that we were having a baby. It was a moment of spiritual renewal, of absolute joy. Each time we looked at one another it was different. Each time we held hands or hugged it felt different. Perhaps life's true journey really happened when you stopped chasing it. We were going to have a child.

That precious payload changed everything. Mary wanted to get home into a doctor's care, eating properly, resting, and gaining back her strength. "Let's go back to Lima," she said, "I'll get a direct flight back home and you come overland." She'd be with her family in Minnesota and I would be moving northward towards her. I'd see her in a month. I don't know why it resonated so reasonably, but it did. Hand in hand, we walked to the bus station and bought tickets on tomorrow's morning bus to Copacabana on Lake Titicaca, Bolivia's frontier with Peru.

That night we celebrated the day by capping off the evening in the crowded courtyard of Peña Naira, a folkloric restaurant across from the San Francisco church. There's something about the haunting simplicity of Andean melodies, with blended guitars, flutes, throaty zamponas, and drums that stir the soul. "El Gringo," the lead of a *campesino* group, sang songs and played traditional lilting tunes of the high mountains. Luis Rico, a young balladeer guitarist with a Stalin mustache, sang socialist, anti-government protest songs condemning the harsh treatment of his fellow Bolivians. The lyrics were lost in translation, but the power

of those songs was traced on the expressions of all those who surrounded us.

Tuesday: Copacabana

The bus climbed up onto the canyon rim. I glanced back over
Mary's shoulder as La Paz, ringed by snowcapped mountains, fell
behind us. We were back on the broad expanses of the Bolivian
Altiplano, on the first leg of the homeward journey.

Our last evening in La Paz had not been kind to us. Mary was
feeling the effects of altitude and pregnancy, unable to look at food
and barely able to keep anything down. I was feeling the effects of
a cheap, deep-fried meal of *lomo milanesa*—breaded pork I had discovered in a *campesino* kitchen of some back alley. Like Mary, I was
having problems looking at food today, although my symptoms
seemed to be confined to an entirely different bodily function.
The medication from the *farmacia* slowly worked its way through
my system. We were two queasy-looking gringos when we boarded
the bus this morning, but by the time we reached the village of
Haurina on the shores of Lake Titicaca, our spirits revived. We
wound along the shoreline while threads of the Cordilleras pushed
down close to the roadway, the deep blue lake never out of sight.
At the Straits of Tiquina passengers were offloaded while our bus
maneuvered onto an old, decrepit wooden barge powered by two
seventy-five horsepower outboard motors. Timbers creaked and
the barge sunk lower into the waters as the bus rolled on board.
Passengers boarded a second smaller boat that at least seemed like
it had a fighting chance of reaching the other shore.

Copacabana was set in one of the most picturesque valleys in South America. Surrounded by a patchwork of small farms and crowned with old volcanic hillsides surrounding the shores of the ink-black lake of Titicaca, the tall, white, Moorish spires of the Copacabana cathedral were accented by the deep blue Andean sky. It was a breathtaking view as our bus rounded the contours above and wound its way down into town.

THE VISTA FROM CERRO CALVARIO ABOVE COPACABANA

OVERLOOKING LAKE TITICACA

That afternoon, refreshed after a nap and shower, we made our way up a well-used pathway to Cerro Calvario, one of the lakeside headlands that anchored the city. We took our time resting by each of the Stations of the Cross. We sat there, arms linked, watching the sunset over Titicaca, the lengthening shadows falling across the distant hill of Cerro Kapia as we talked about our new future.

Wednesday: Copacabana to Puno Peru

In the rush to get an exit stamp in our passport from the Bolivian Immigration office in the square, we forgot to read the italicized fine print in our *South American Handbook*: "*Remember that if you wish to enter Peru from Bolivia you must have an onward ticket out of Peru.*" That oversight would prove a test to our ingenuity and strengthen our conviction that anything and everything can happen at border crossings.

A twenty-minute bus ride from Copacabana brought us to the frontier border town of Yunguyo and Peruvian immigration control. That's where the fun began.

Our bus driver, who had obviously done this countless times, separated his passengers into three groups: Bolivians, Peruvians, and everybody else who looked foreign. There were two doors in the soft, yellow-colored cinderblock shed. Foreigners got the door on the right and while we milled about, the *Aduana* inside yelled out, "Open your passports to the Bolivian exit stamp and be prepared to show me your exit tickets out of Peru." Those of our group who had actually purchased exit tickets out of the country lined up first. The rest of us, half a dozen unprepared travelers like Mary and I, kind of looked at each other, trying to figure out our next step. One of the travelers in front of us had purchased a TEPSA bus pass before he started traveling. TEPSA was a major Peruvian bus line, and he held an onward ticket from Tumbes in northern Peru to Quito, Ecuador. We convinced him to let us borrow it after he cleared immigration.

In fact, as soon as the *Aduana* examined his TEPSA ticket and stamped his passport, he simply handed it to the next person in line behind him. Same bus ticket, different person, same result.

Thump—the next passport was stamped and he in turn handed the ticket back up the line. The ruse worked like a charm until it was my turn. Actually, it was our turn, but Mary felt a little queasy and was sitting on the concrete barrier outside that separated the two countries. So I was standing alone with two passports in one hand and a single TEPSA bus pass in the other. Next! I handed him Mary's passport with the well-used bus ticket tucked inside.

"My wife," I said. "She's pregnant and not feeling well. She's right there." I pointed out the open doorway. He stamped the passport and set it aside, holding out his hand for mine. "Where's your exit ticket?" I desperately wanted to say "It's in my wife's passport, you idiot—it's the same ticket we've all been using," but that could have opened up a whole can of worms for Mary and everyone else. So I did the next best thing. I tucked a twenty-dollar bill into my passport and asked if he wouldn't mind keeping the money as a gesture of good will and proof I had sufficient funds to buy a ticket out of the country. He slapped my passport closed, gathered Mary's, and slid them both across the desk to me.

"Your wife can enter, you can't." No amount of pleading changed his mind. In fact, he locked the door and headed home for lunch. He'd be back he said, in an hour.

The driver was getting impatient. He had a busload of passengers cleared by immigration and one gringo who hadn't. Mary needed to get to Puno and rest, but I needed proof of passage out of Peru. Mary and I made a decision. She'd continue on with the bus. We'd meet in the main plaza in Puno today or tomorrow, or if not there, then later in the week at our little Hotel Familiar in Cuzco. Separating was risky, but Mary needed a place to rest and regain her energy. The bus pulled away with Mary waving at me through her open window. I watched her go and then turned back and sat down on the concrete porch of the immigration office while I tried to figure out my next step. The worst-case scenario was to take a day's trip back to La Paz, purchase a through ticket, and a day back to the border. There had to be a better way.

I'd been sitting there for almost an hour, and the immigration officer had already returned, un-padlocked the door, and disappeared inside when a collectivo with four passengers pulled in. They were Swiss and French travelers we had met at the hotel yesterday. Turns out they were headed for Puno as well. The driver had written them each an official onward ticket on his company stationery pad. For a little bribe and a full-fare collectivo ride to Puno, he wrote one out for me as well. According to my new official ticket, I had just paid 1,500 Peruvian soles—the princely equivalent of ten US dollars—for our driver to take me from the border, overland to Lima, and then up the coast to Bolivia—a 1,700-mile journey in a taxi. It didn't sound too implausible to me, but then again, I had a dog in this fight. I handed my ticket and passport back to the officer. He looked at the ticket, up at me, and then smiled, stamped my passport, and without even a hint of sarcasm welcomed me to Peru.

Mary's bus driver stopped for lunch not long after they left the border. Our collectivo made up the time and we eventually roared past Mary's bus midway to Puno. I leaned out the window waving. I was sure some of the passengers recognized me and passed the news to Mary.

Turned out it was just another uneventful travel day in South America.

AFTERWORD

Mary and I traveled overland from the Peruvian border through Cuzco, where we once again reconnected for a few days with Raymond and Sarah. We took a quick, two-hour flight to Lima where we sketched out our return to America and talked endlessly about our soon-to-be-born child and parenthood. On the evening of April 21, after tearful goodbyes at the airport, Mary boarded her Pan Am flight to San Antonio, connecting on to Saint Paul and home. Within a day Mary was home, excited to be surrounded by her family and friends, in the prenatal care of a modern medical system, and perhaps more importantly, just being stationary.

I moved northward overland, along the Peruvian coastal desert through Trujillo to Chiclayo and into Ecuador. I met up with Sarah again in Quito and together we explored the city and the nearby market towns of Otavalo, Ambato, Latacunga, and Saquisili, with a three-day side trip to Santo Domingo de los Colorados.

On May 9, I flew from Quito to Mexico City, caught the overnight train to Guadalajara, and after a string of long-distance buses that connected cities and sleepless nights, on the morning of May 16, 1978, I pulled into Freeport, Minnesota, and into the arms of Mary.

FRIENDS ALONG THE WAY

We met some remarkable people on our adventure. They passed in and out of our lives bringing us friendship, long conversations, and connections to home, and then like the landscapes we traveled through, they were gone. For the next thirty-eight years they were simply names lost within the pages of our journal notes that we never seemed to have time to look at. Over the years, time and distance separated us, but then came the remarkable ability to search for endless possibilities on the Internet. I spent hours of research time on Google following subtle leads, exploring dead ends, finding strings of information that led nowhere and everywhere. Slowly, over two years, I rediscovered them and reconnected. I uncovered Bill in America, then Frits and Wil in Holland, Raymond in England, Sarah in the near-north of Canada, and sadly, the final story of our prison acquaintance Louis.

Perhaps the greatest triumph was in finding our Amazon adventurer Shmulik. We only knew him by his nickname. We had no record of his real name. It seemed like an impossible task, like finding a specific man named "Tommy" in America. One afternoon as a friend and I dined in a downtown Toronto restaurant, two Jewish couples sat down beside us. We overheard them talking about an upcoming trip to Israel, so I leaned over and inquired if I could ask them something.

"Sure," they said, "as long as it doesn't involve religion or politics." I wanted to know how to put an ad in an Israeli newspaper and explained my story about our Amazon exploits and our companion Shmulik. Excitedly, one of the women said she had a blog that a lot of her Israeli friends read, and just maybe it might reach him, or at least jog someone's memory. Two weeks after she posted my story, a newspaper, the *Jerusalem Times*, emailed me asking if they could run the story nationally under the banner of *Shmulik, Where Are You?*. They just needed more details and some photos. The rewrite ran on May 23, 2013. Within five hours of publication I had an email from Shmulik with the subject line "Shmulik Found!!!!"

"Thank you for your article," he wrote. "Now I've got proof for my family that all my memories weren't just fairytales."

Mary and George Ayers

Mary and I returned to Canada and settled in Malton, Ontario. Our daughter Karolyn was born in November. I traveled extensively for work, leaving Mary with the yeoman's share of child rearing, which she did with love and devotion. I was transferred to Calgary and then to Vancouver. Mary joined me at every step, unselfishly putting her career on hold time and again. Traveling, job transfers, and personal associations strained our relationship until finally, after another move back to Toronto, it reached a tipping point. In 1986, Mary and I separated and divorced. Even in those dark times there was a true fondness and respect for each other.

After the separation, Mary focused on Karolyn and her career. With each passing year she developed new skills and took on more responsibilities. She spent the last ten years of her career at IBM, first in Toronto and then commuting to oil and gas projects in Calgary and St. John's, Newfoundland. She met Doug and together they embarked on a new and rewarding life. Mary and Doug still travel and have hiked extensively in Japan, Turkey, Republic of Georgia, Thailand, Slovenia, Croatia, and New Zealand.

During that same time I focused on my job at Konica Canada, and at an industry trade show bumped into Judy Zaczkowski, a former student of mine when I taught at the Saint Cloud campus in Minnesota. I had paid little attention to her back in those days, me a young professor too focused on simply staying one academic step ahead of the kids, but later in life, when we met again she asked, "Didn't you ever wonder why I sat in the front row of your classes and managed to visit your office so often?" She was a special person with a unique blend of beauty, intelligence, accomplishment, humanity, and purpose, and I fell in love with her. It was impossible not to. Over the next twenty years she showed me what true joy looked like.

In 1990, Judy, then a university professor, and I, a technical director, quit our jobs, married, and cofounded an environmental health and workplace safety company. Envision Compliance began with a prayer and two computers on our dining room table, but over the next decade the company grew. In 2008 we sold our majority shares and retired with dreams of moving downtown Toronto into the little townhouse we purchased. Sadly, Judy was diagnosed with colon cancer and passed away in September of 2009.

Several months after Judy's death, my daughter Karolyn and Mary introduced me to hiking. I loved the outdoors and the solitude of the trails and have walked the Camino de Santiago in Spain four times, hiked Ireland, the Avalon Peninsula in Newfoundland, and the Bruce Trail here in Ontario, but life is not the same without her.

Karolyn Marshall (Ayers)

Our daughter Karolyn was born November 29, 1978, almost seven months after our return. She grew from awkward childhood into a remarkable and beautiful woman. She inherited her mother's good looks and, unfortunately for her, my nose—and maybe a tiny bit of my obstinacy and sense of adventure. In August 2003 she married Curtis Marshall, a wonderful man and a homegrown farm boy at heart. Together they have two children, William and Louise Ann.

Bill Zolkowski

Mary and I first met Bill in the Amazon at the Shipibo settlement of Santa Clara on the shore of Lake Yarinacocha. Bill and his partner owned and operated an art import shop called Baobab Folk Art and Design in downtown Ann Arbor. The name Baobab, from the African tree symbolizing strength and wisdom, was emblematic of his business trading in ceramics, art, and mysterious artifacts from around the world.

In the early eighties he closed the business and settled into a career of teaching, eventually taking on the role of principal at Thurston High School. In 2009 he moved to Plymouth Canton Educational Park, Michigan's third largest school district, to a three-school high school campus with more than six thousand kids. On his first day, one school board member quipped, "Good luck getting your arms around this one." Bill did, managing the school until he retired in 2013.

Now Bill has another love. Bill's Beer Garden is a small, successful, open-air craft beer emporium that he opened in 2013, just a stone's throw from his original shop in Ann Arbor.

Frits van Moorselaar and Wil Snel

Frits and Wil had traveled through Africa a few years earlier and wanted to come to South America as soon as Wil finished her studies. Wil's sister lived in Sao Paulo, Brazil, and when her second child was born they decided to visit. After visiting, with no clear plans other than vacationing with the family in Recife in mid-November, they traveled to Salar de Uyuni, Bolivia's great salt flats. From there they traveled overland to La Paz, Lake Titicaca, Cuzco, and Machu Picchu, over the Andes to the Nazca Lines and north to Lima. They crossed the Andes once more, to the snowcapped peak of Mismi, the headwaters of the Amazon. We first spotted Frits (twenty-nine years old) and Wil (twenty-seven) on the banks of the Ucayali River in the Peruvian outpost town of Pucallpa. They were searching for a way downriver. We traveled together to Manaus, sharing adventures on one of the greatest rivers in the world. Frits and Wil left us at Manaus, flying south to Recife. They had New Year's Eve on Copacabana Beach in Rio de Janeiro, celebrating Yemanjá, The Goddess of the Sea, and launching thousands of miniature boats with lit candles, offerings, and mirrors into the waters of the South Atlantic.

Shmuel (Shmulik) Meiri

Shmuel started his South American voyage from Luxemburg via Barbados, Venezuela to Bogotá, Colombia. We met Shmuel onboard the Amazon riverboat the *Lord Kelvin* at Benjamin Constant, Brazil, and traveled together with amazing adventures to Manaus, Obidos, Santarem, Macapá, and finally Belém.

After our long Amazon River venture he traveled southward, meeting other traveling companions. For the next few months he journeyed through Brazil along the coast, through Natal, Joao Pessoa, Olinda, Recife, and Salvador Bahia (where we met up once more), inland into central Brazil until finally, traveling solo, he reached Porto Alegre and an emotional return to his teenaged family home. In Argentina, after a brutal police raid on his room left him overnight in jail, he headed to Bolivia where he explored the tributaries of the Amazon with Herbert, a Swiss companion, until his friend collapsed with hepatitis. He put his friend on a flight back home then traveled overland to Lima and northward along the Peruvian coast to Ecuador and into Colombia, completing a circle back to the start of his journey.

In 1982 he was a reservist in the Lebanon war. Shortly after, he met and married Naomi. In 1987, following Naomi's research in art history, they spent seven months in Northern Italy, looking for long-forgotten twelfth-century murals.

Their son Amos was born in 1990 after a troubled pregnancy, and was diagnosed at the age of four months as suffering from a rare genetic syndrome called Cornelia de Lange Syndrome (CDLS). Shmulik wrote that he is a great kid, a real fighter who copes well with his disabilities. Their daughter Tamar was born in 1997 and she is a really bright, athletic, and sweet girl.

In spite of the great difficulties of raising a family with a child with special needs, both managed to pursue academic careers and completed PhDs, Naomi in Art History at Tel Aviv University and Shmuel in Museum Studies at the University of Leicester, England. Since obtaining their advanced degrees, they've continued their research while teaching in various academic institutions in Israel.

Shmulik and the family travel practically every free summer. Wanderlust is still in the blood.

Raymond Loud

We spotted Raymond Loud relaxing in the deep pool under the twin waterfalls of *Dos Hermanos* in Iguazu National Park, Argentina. When he heard Mary was American, he told us that his grandfather was a piano maker in the 1830s out of New York and Philadelphia. Together we crossed into Paraguay at Puerto Stroessner, tricking the customs agent into allowing us in under the guise of Ray shaving his beard and all of us buying long pants and suitcases. Beards, short pants, and backpacks weren't part of the agent's interpretation of customs law. We met up again in Buenos Aires, later in Santiago, and then he traveled north with us across

Argentina and up across the Altiplano into Cochabamba, Bolivia. He and Sarah headed into Peru to visit Cuzco and Machu Picchu.

Ray is currently Managing Director at Buckingham Fine Art Publishers at Milton Keynes, just an hour or so north of London.

Sarah Munro

We first met Sarah in the crowded Plaza de Armas of Cochabamba, Bolivia. Sarah had started her journey from Guatemala. She flew to the coral islands of San Andres and then on to Cartagena, Colombia. She traveled the country, exploring the small towns, ending in Cumbal in the southern mountains near the Ecuadorian border. She bused overland again to the Colombian coastal town of Tumaco, just north of Ecuador. The only nervous travel experience she remembered was being frightened by a big black spider crawling across the bus station floor. As she edged her way past, it suddenly sprang about four inches in the air, not retreating but rather striking a defensive posture. Sarah traveled south in a small dugout boat from the mangrove swamps of Tumaco, Colombia, and out across open ocean waters to Esmeraldas, Ecuador. From there she trekked overland through Peru and Bolivia, then northward through Lake Titicaca, Cuzco, and Machu Picchu.

When she returned to Canada in the summer of 1978 she taught in northern Quebec for six years, first on the Mistassini reserve on the edges of Lac St. Jean and later 150 miles north in Chibougamau, an isolated mining town in central Quebec. Moving to Montreal she completed a Fine Arts Degree at Concordia University. After graduation she moved to Haliburton, Ontario, where she taught elementary school for eighteen years.

In 2005, Sarah retired back to her hometown of Whitney, Ontario, where she lives in her family's homestead house.

Louis Hepburn

We met Louis (thirty-one years old) during a visit to the San Pedro (Panóptico) prison in La Paz, Bolivia, where he had been confined for almost two years. Unclassified US Department of State documents indicate he was arrested on July 18, 1976, charged with possession of small amounts of cocaine and two pieces of hashish. He had a hearing on January 24, 1977, and was last seen by an embassy official in April. Louis wrote a number of letters pleading for help. I obtained a copy of one letter, written to the Committee of Concerned Parents, a prisoner exchange advocacy group. In late autumn of 1978, a few months after we met Louis, under a newly evoked reciprocal agreement with the Bolivian government he was transferred from Panóptico to the Bynum North Carolina detention center to serve out the remainder of his sentence. But prison life in Bolivia had taken its toll, and he returned to America paranoid and harboring an irrational fear and distrust of everyone around him. According to his brother Andrew, after parole from detention, he had a ghostly, troubled look that he masked by a deceptive cheerfulness. His brother Sam hired him at his bakery, but Louis' demeanor frightened off some of Sam's best customers, a group of local nuns. Sam explained that he never knew nuns could run so fast dressed in habits. Louis married, but the relationship faltered, ending in divorce a few years later. He held down a number of jobs including caring for the elderly. In a way, that work was an extension of his prison experience, where his gentleness and medical support for other inmates earned him the nickname of Doctor Lou. Louis died of heart failure on November 9, 2005. He was fifty-eight years old.

ACKNOWLEDGEMENTS

I am indebted to the following people for their contributions to this book:

To my former partner and current dear friend Mary Ayers, for providing her diaries and letters, and for sharing her memories on the events and activities that took place during our travels.

To my hiking companion and friend Helen McDiarmid, for transcribing the handwritten scribble from my journals into an electronic format. Without her work the words would have remained in the journals.

To our traveling companions of many years ago, Bill Zolkowski, Frits van Moorselaar, Wil Snel, Shmuel (Shmulik) Meiri, Raymond Loud, and Sarah Munro. You all enriched our stories and added to the adventure.

To Andrew and Thomas Hepburn, brothers of Louis, a young prisoner we met in Bolivia, for providing details of his life story.

To Doug Frizzle, editor of *Never a Dull Moment: The Autobiography of A. Hyatt Verrill*, for his permission to use some of Hyatt's descriptions of the market at Huancayo.

To Kathy Doore, author of *The Mysterious Stone Monuments of Markawasi Peru*, for her review and comments of my descriptions of the Nazca Lines and my meeting with Maria Reiche.

To Lisa Shero, a fellow writer, for her encouragement when I had difficulty putting words to paper.

To the editorial and support staff at FriesenPress, for their critique, comments, and assistance in turning a dusty manuscript into a credible book.

To all my friends and family, who smiled and put up with endless quotes from the book. Thank you all for your support.

SELECTED BIBLIOGRAPHY

Aguirre, Carmen. *Something Fierce: Memoirs of a Revolutionary Daughter*. Vancouver: D&M Publishers Inc., 2011.

Ayers, George L. *Chasing the Dream*. San Francisco: Blurb, 2012

Deuel, Leo. *Conquistadors Without Swords: Archeologists in the Americas*. New York: St. Martin's Press, 1967.

Doore, Kathy. *Markawasi: Peru's Inexplicable Stone Forest*. Independent Publishers Group (IPG), 2006.

Eakin, Lucille, Erwin Lauriault, and Harry Boonstra. *People of the Ucayali: The Shipibo and Conibo of Peru*. Dallas, TX: International Museum of Cultures, 1986.

Grann, David. *Lost City of Z: A Tale of Deadly Obsession in the Amazon*. New York: Doubleday, 2009.

Hardoy, Jorge E. *Pre-Columbian Cities*. New York: Walker & Co., 1973.

Jacobs, Michael. *Andes*. London: Granta Publications, 2010.

Jara, Joan. *An Unfinished Song: The Life of Victor Jara*. New York: Ticknor and Fields, 1984.

Morales, Waltraud Queiser. "Bolivia moves toward democracy." *Current History* 78 (February 1980): 76-79, 86-88.

Morris, Craig, and Adriana von Hagen. *The Incas: Lords of the Four Quarters*. London: Thames and Hudson, 2011.

Neruda, Pablo. *Alturas de Machu Picchu: The Heights of Machu Picchu*. Translated by Nathaniel Tarn. 22nd ed. Noonday Press Farrar, 1995.

Our Disappeared—Nuestros Desaparecidos. Directed by Juan Mandelbaum. United States: Geovision, Inc., 2008. DVD, 99 min.

Reiche, Maria. *Mystery of the Desert*. Stuttgart: Heinrich Fink GmbH, 1976.

Schreider, Helen, and Frank Schreider. *Exploring the Amazon*. Washington, DC: National Geographic Society, 1970.

Verrill, Alpheus Hyatt. *Never a Dull Moment: The Autobiography of A. Hyatt Verrill*. Edited by Doug Frizzle. Stillwater Lake, NS: Doug Frizzle Publisher, 2008.

von Hagen, Victor Wolfgang. *The Ancient Sun Kingdoms of the Americas: Aztec, Maya,* Inca. Cleveland and New York: The World Publishing Company, 1961.

Wallace, Alfred Russel. *A Narrative of Travels on the Amazon and Rio Negro.* New York: Dover Publications, 1972.

Watson, Fiona, Stephen Corry, and Caroline Pearce, eds. *Disinherited: Indians of Brazil.* London: Survival International, 2000.

Wright, Ronald. *Stolen Continents: Conquest and Resistance in the Americas.* 10th ed. Toronto: Penguin Canada, 2003.

ABOUT THE AUTHOR

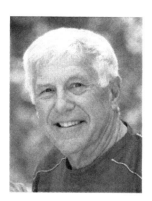

George L. Ayers is an author and lifelong adventurer. George was born in Trail, British Columbia, spent his formative years on the Canadian prairies and grew up in small town Ontario. In the sixties the family moved to Australia, sailing around the globe on the great passenger ships of the day. Those early ocean voyages filled him with an indelible sense of exploration and curiosity that never faded. Since then, he has continued to travel extensively, backpacking across Central and South America and hiking the trail systems of Europe, Asia, and North America. In 2012 he published Chasing the Dream, which documents his experiences with Mary as they explored Canada and worked their ways south to Mexico and Central America. Buzzards and Bananas is his second book in an ongoing travelogue series. He currently resides in Brampton, Ontario, where he spends his time hiking and scribbling in his journal. Befittingly, he is an avid member of the South American Explorers club.

CPSIA information can be obtained at www.ICGtesting.com
Printed in the USA
LVOW07s1056250116

471422LV00006B/364/P

9 781460 279120